战时讲演与随笔集

（1914—1917）：

儒家视域下之世界大战

林文庆◎著

林　曦　冯宝仪◎译
宫旭东◎校译

厦门大学出版社
XIAMEN UNIVERSITY PRESS
国家一级出版社
全国百佳图书出版单位

图书在版编目(CIP)数据

战时讲演与随笔集:1914—1917:儒家视域下之世界大战/林文庆著;林曦,冯宝仪译.—厦门:厦门大学出版社,2019.5
ISBN 978-7-5615-7345-7

Ⅰ.①战… Ⅱ.①林… ②林… ③冯… Ⅲ.①儒学-文集 Ⅳ.①B222.05-53

中国版本图书馆 CIP 数据核字(2019)第 091048 号

出 版 人	郑文礼
责任编辑	章木良
装帧设计	李夏凌
技术编辑	朱 楷

出版发行　厦门大学出版社

社　　　址	厦门市软件园二期望海路 39 号
邮政编码	361008
总 编 办	0592-2182177　0592-2181406(传真)
营销中心	0592-2184458　0592-2181365
网　　　址	http://www.xmupress.com
邮　　　箱	xmup@xmupress.com
印　　　刷	厦门集大印刷厂

开本	720 mm×1 000 mm　1/16
印张	16.75
插页	1
字数	212 千字
版次	2019 年 5 月第 1 版
印次	2019 年 5 月第 1 次印刷
定价	58.00 元

本书如有印装质量问题请直接寄承印厂调换

厦门大学出版社
微信二维码

厦门大学出版社
微博二维码

献
辞

力 行 近 乎 仁

莫 叹 世 无 圣 贤 久 矣

谨 以 此 书

献 给

今 之 克 己 力 行 者

序

今之人以为说教者，当年豪杰以身践之。子曰：力行近乎仁。则林文庆先生固为力行者，目之为近世圣贤不为过也。

捧读林先生大作，深夜唱颂，不能自已。中以一句最为压卷："Patriotism is meaningless without self-sacrifice."（"若无自我牺牲，爱国毫无意义。"）林氏生平之风采，正可为斯语之煌煌写照。

吾居香江已逾十年，不意又遇二友，亦可称今之力行者也。一为宫兄旭东先生，一为冯姊宝仪小姐。吾识冯姊于先，职场相交以来，久而弥敬。姊为资深律师，当时叱咤风云之楷模，固不待言。而专业勤勉之精神，颇愧男子。逐日朝九晚五（凌晨五时）之作息，多年如一日，非常人之资所能及也，所成就亦非常人可以想见也。宫兄乃于古旧书店中得识，缘耶？命也！于今思之每不禁额手称庆。兄交游甚广，世务极重，而爱书之性未少改。每于深宵辄有所得，文思勃发不可遏抑。与予探讨对联诗句之工稳，是予至乐也。

三人意气相投，兄姊以真情待予，切磋琢磨之幸，不让于上下古今之人。而其又奖掖后进，不遗余力。证吾之婚姻，助吾之初心。一言即合，慷慨解囊，赞助本书出版，故信古道热肠，于兹未绝也。

原书乃厦门大学前校长林文庆博士之英文著作，偶然自英国

1

旧书店得之。该书由新加坡海峡不列颠出版社于 1917 年出版，现已极为罕见。林氏一生潜心研探华夏文明，痛感欧战摧残，人心浮动。遂将其系列讲座内容集结成书，欲以东方哲理挽救时弊。其主题为儒家观点对世局之考察，包含对大战成因之剖析、各国关系之反思以及未来和平之建议等内容。以今日眼光视之，犹颇具参考意义。视书中戳记与藏书票，知原为英国高院法官内维尔拉斯基所藏，后于 1936 年赠予其家乡之曼彻斯特图书馆，并于 1940 年重装，现一并付印于后。

林曦

2019 年 3 月于香江

致　念

亦师亦友

已故 李希蒙德·威廉·赫利特 文学硕士

多年之莱佛士书院校长及教育局局长

感佩阁下

高自标持

弁言

　　此等讲演及发言，乃于其他冗务之间隙，应不同社团之请而备。若干文章为讲演后忆而记之，故不敢期报告所言与当前所载确乎一致。兼无闲暇重写，疏舛难免。该等讲稿及出版之主旨，乃为人类普遍文明之联结，并为人类生于乱世所有嘈杂、纷争与兴替中之"永恒真理"引致注意。"和平主义"于多处功成，表明良好政治理论之需，与人生及其鹄的之现代观点一致。英译东方之旧说，或可坚守某些老生常谈之真义，不因其过于熟悉而忽略。

　　末章内正义及自由之原则，为协约国和平条款之基础，施于大英帝国，为各民族之参照，其共同忠于祖国与国王而团结一致。将来须就帝国内民族问题，发见一满意之解决方案。唯仅以真诚运用英国民主准则以应各个社群所需，并以当地条件及实际环境做必要调适，方能觅得。相互间须做让步及牺牲。唯若吾等于大英帝国内，未能实现民族独立与个人自由之理想，即帝国与伟大民主之邦最英勇子民所如此慷慨献身者，则大战之磨难将为抛诸脑后。

引
介

　　林文庆博士具二重风骨。余罕遇与其同等博学、谦恭、大度之欧罗巴人，亦未见纯亚细亚人中有如此集众长于一身之完美典型。其另一特质亦常暖吾向其之心。其以身为亚细亚人为豪，正如吾以身为欧罗巴人为傲。而其为彼民族自尊之理据所做深挚研究，远超吾所能贡献于已者。无人可夸大其研释古代经典以效劳中国人之价值。最伟大之工作，乃说明遍世大哲至睿之思如何紧密相连。任何从事此项工作之人，乃学历于东西，心智为之广博。过往九年来，余曾数度与林文庆博士共论文哲话题，并常讶于古老东方经典内所钩取思想之珠玑，投射一丝崭新慧光于貌似现代之论题。此为欧人之美好体验，其自认聪明，以为智识之圆日升于西方，缓缓东移。斯实升自东方，并熠熠煊赫于正午，时西方正处暗黑之中。阴幕或垂，唯暂朦胧。东方有新天拂晓，将重显其一切过往与本真。

　　吾承惠允，于此讲演与随笔内，拟订些许引介文字。林文庆博士已生动阐明世界大战之实况。更尤以其引述伟大中国经典，对成千上万受教育之华人具强烈之吸引，彼等为吾等众多忠诚子民，以及其他于英国法律与正义庇护下生活富足之移民。其所贡献之服务，实非欧人所能。因罕有欧人具其学识，更无人知其如何陈述事例，俾使之全面符合亚洲人之心意。就东西读者而言，宣称优秀遗产乃对个人、小国及普世人类职责与正义之根本原则，

1

斯为协约国之基础，乃可资饱飨之启示。德国对该等原则之粗野背离，使一切现存文明中最古老之中华民族最适于与较年轻之西方民主邦国同道，为正义而战，反对强权。

经本书所载讲演及其作为海峡殖民地立法会议员之发言，林文庆博士已使华人忠诚情感更趋深广，而吾等有据为证，即自1914年以来本地发行甚多战争基金，各界华人群起慷慨响应。

林文庆博士以其郁烈特质与热忱，作为受认可之领袖，抬升伟大社群之政治与社会基调。其于一切公众问题为进步之使徒，唯以政要之谨慎调和其改革之热情。本系列末篇随笔所探讨"民族与帝国"之理念，吾极欲向生活于大不列颠治世所有民族深思熟虑之人士推荐。今日吾辈子弟为自由献身，明日吾等须以行动展现充分之理解，并非孤立偏狭之民族情感，而乃信守吾等庞衮帝国未来赖以稳定与内部和谐之原则。困难必不可免，姑克之以成吾辈之荣耀。偏见难除，唯所存于个人者，尤强于国家。斯以整体之智，当逾其个体最智者。笔者与吾辈自身不同，就所设想之目的而言，其更高明于我。若吾等预备欢迎与笔者一流人物合作，则解决肤色问题之任务，可获珍援。

世界大战已证明大英帝国非倚武力以维持内部稳定。其以忠诚之丝绳牵合，而非以臣服之铁镣铐拢。而吾辈之职，乃增此忠诚。就尊吾旗帜各民族公民义务与责任，勇于略为先行，而不敢稍后于彼之完满。

A.W. 斯蒂尔

新加坡，1918 年 2 月

目录

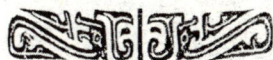

战时讲演与随笔集
（1914—1917）

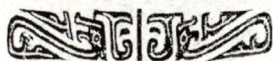

一

儒家视域下之世界大战

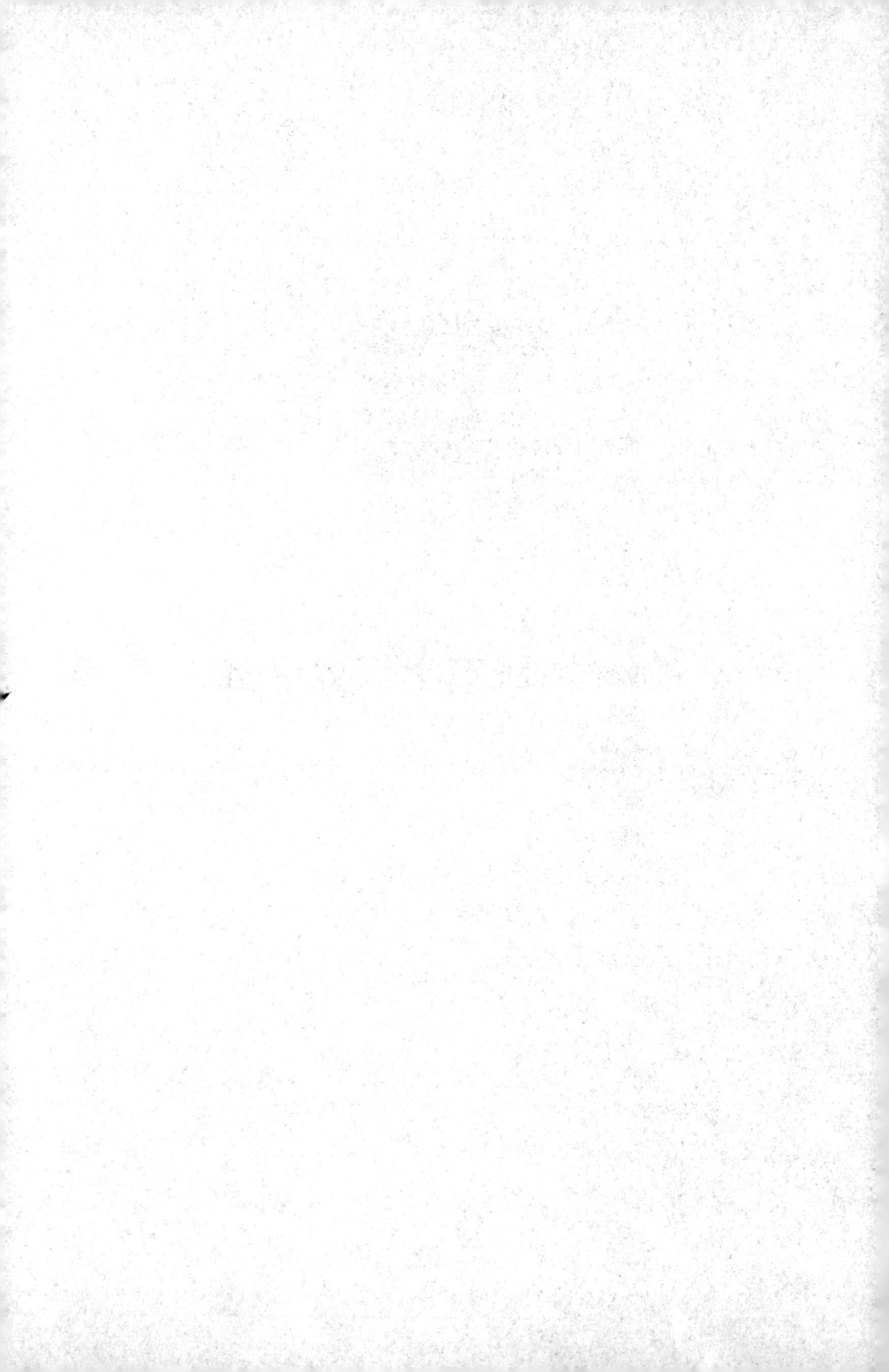

　　欲得清晰陈述儒家观念，须先阐明儒教之真面目，及其对待大战之根本态度，方可检视儒家就此多国战争之展望。

一般原则

　　中国经典虽已移译为所有欧洲文字，唯不妨言，儒家一般教义仅为哲学界内少数学人所知。多数受教育者了解若干不证自明之孔夫子思想，而除些许司空见惯者外，外界对儒家之观照，不在其作为宗教及伦理、哲学、政治系统之本质，乃就其所谓缺陷每多有不友善之批评。中国经典与《圣经》相似，不宜为外人之教材。因其大批资料呈扑朔迷离之态，从中无可抽绎教义之任何统一体系，颇如《圣经》经文。

儒教之为宗教

　　欧人之批评，常欲证儒家仅为一种哲学，而非一门宗教。此观点流传自 18 世纪天主教之讨论，时耶稣会士曾成功获中国朝廷之好感，并几于包罗万象之教会内实现儒教之消解。绝无必要检视此声名狼藉之争议。中国史于此甚明。中国传统联结儒家教诲与最古老之国民宗教——某种经充分发展之自然崇拜，唯承认上帝为宇宙灵魂主宰之观念，实难与旧约中古希伯来人所持看法相区别。中国古人信天命统摄现世俗务。唯此理非神启之果，毋宁是接踵贤哲格致之力。

有神论

经典内甚少论神。神祇无须赘言。信仰素未讨论。天道之治从未成疑。无神之论不可思议！与信仰法力无边、大慈大悲之天神相连者，为人性皆善之说。人类种族之进化不言而喻，带动社会进步及智识启蒙，并确保正义稳妥支配人类事务。利他乃真理之标准，亦为人类异于野兽之别。对神明之定信助长无上乐观，并已引领每一儒者哲人沉浸于未来太平盛世景象，如以色列人与基督教徒视弥赛亚之降临。该等基本理念皆在儒家之先，已于周朝（公元前1122—前255年）开国王室订立政教礼法之思索中钩元提要。

备战之必要

有史以来，中国人便憎战争之恶，并视之为天灾，以惩邦国及其罪孽。按此观点，战争为上天所为。唯演绎中国史志所训，并不认同天意眷顾大军之俗调。因中国人坚信并断言至少就长远而言，正义必胜。因对前朝治下暴政与压迫之伟大反抗，周室成立。社会重建时，军备之需占显要地位。封建制随五等爵并按与国君对应地位成比例之军备加以推行。共产社会成功实现，而每户须应国家军队征召以偿土地之分配。国家以各公社耕作公田之税收维系。① 孔子赞赏此宗法制度之效率，且社会得益。唯惜于公元

---

① 原文疑缺句号。——译者注

前551年孔子生前许久，互相残杀之战争及蛮夷侵犯，使政府建制及封建贵族之相对地位变化甚大。

孔子年代乃中国奥古斯都时代开始瓦解之标志。可称中国文明自周代开国之君设立政教制度时起步。周公于其名作《周礼》描述文武各司各部之细节，强调人民有责为国之荣誉与安全而战。据载，孔子谴责以不教民战，由此赋其施行军训之重权，可紧急征召人民抵抗侵略、保卫国家。

《竹书纪年》载帝尧设立首支常备军。其治始于公元前2145年，据云当时已驱遣野兽参战。

《史记》^①内有段落提及军备，并对周室或有之军事成就表示乐观。注者论其确指军备之重要，乃和平之最佳保障。于同一部典籍内，为人民有权反抗暴政辩护。而此群众之一致意见，乃人民之心声，作为上天之心意。庙堂之恶，降灾于国。而上天悲悯其所爱之民，遣复仇使者惩罚作恶之人。遍览旧时典籍，笃信上天将降罪治主，因彼行事使信任其统领之子民艰难悲苦。切实巩固周朝之武王，自称"受命于天"。

孔子之观点

就孔子观点特加详察，吾等为其显著现代精神之气息所惊。问其为政之要（《论语》第十二之七）^②，答曰存于三者。一、确保人民足食，乃政府之首务。二、军备充足。三、政府须得公众信任。其续强调一事，即无末者则政府不立。其亦认为如国有善人之治，期以七年，则民可即戎以护国矣。基奇纳伯爵已向世人显

---

① 原文为 The Cannon of History，由描述内容而言，似为 The Canon of History，即《史记》。——译者注

② 原文为："子贡问政。子曰：足食，足兵，民信之矣。子贡曰：必不得已而去，于斯三者何先？曰：去兵。子贡曰：必不得已而去，于斯二者何先？曰：去食。自古皆有死，民无信不立。"——译者注

示于十八月内其所能为。孔子着重军训，唯其于军务则不建言。斯以柏拉图《理想国》内苏格拉底之逻辑为据，即其非受训及职业之军士，而无实际经验。唯其坚称以不教民战，应属干罪，因其乃"率民而弃之"。

按儒家之伦理要则，善与智时遇考验，唯常负坚忍，并以胆魄明其对义行之深信。如今日欧洲通盘专制与扰乱之时代，依孔子之见，有原则之人士宁死不辱，或宁伤身致死，亦不愿舍理义以存。（《论语》第十五之八）[1] 由此忆其名言，曰不克为仁则怯，因而亦须诲曰为仁之职不可须臾逃也。

于《论语》（第十四之十三）[2] 内，孔子告知吾等何为其所思之当世完人，即斯人直面得益念头之时，置公义于私利之先；而处危境之时，则愿杀身成仁，且无论许久而不忘其诺。该等片言只语之观念，述于两千载以上，足以自证儒者如何定然痛谴并憎恶德国对待比利时，及于当前大战苦难中与其同列邦国之态度。

孔子非不抵抗教条之信徒。其对作恶者之态度，更似罗马之斯多葛主义者。其认同痛击与惩罚，唯其恒常申求正义。虽不懈于颂祷和平，其所诲正如人类史所训，昏君须受严惩，而各国有责依文明之益行事，使作恶者悔改归正。

孟子

孟子宜称为儒家之圣保罗，乃伟大之民主领袖，其乃圣人孙儿之弟子。感于时世之法纪荡然与混乱骚攘，其痛诉黩武、遍谴独裁。其曰仁者举世无敌。其伤于封建时代皆无义战，因彼观念全为向对手攫取某些物质或其他利益。孟子毫不隐晦、全力抨击

---

[1] 原文为："子曰：志士仁人，无求生以害仁，有杀身以成仁。"——译者注

[2] 原文为："子曰：今之成人者，何必然？见利思义，见危授命，久要不忘平生之言，亦可以为成人矣。"——译者注

侵略战争。现代欧洲政治家与外交官所文饰为"军事探险"者，孟子举发为劫杀。其提醒吾等，孔子曾斥一弟子助暴君致富强，并辩称勠力屠杀以据赃物及领土者，乃死有余辜之罪人。

鼓动军国主义并结攻防同盟者，孟子称之为"民贼"（《孟子》第六章第二节之九）。[1] 因其蛊惑国君以物资、财富、贸易及军力为成功政府之主要目标，全然忘怀人类之正义仁爱为治民之真实正道。其言辞绝似大战前欧洲状态之预言。当年孟子与暴君探讨政治之时，指其大谬，言语并无矫作。

于文明之现状下，战争乃必须之恶。孔孟乐见其履世界道德警察之职。孟子直言征伐叛国乱邦之纠正措施，显合人类整体利益。

君子之风与仁爱

孔子主张，人须于各可能情形下甚至战时践行仁爱。其个人生活秉持如是原则，故其钓而不纲，虽钟情狩猎，仅射飞鸟，而不射宿鸟。孔子之虑在于，无论处境如何，君子不应忘其风骨。而吾等可从中国史推断，最伟大之战士因其对敌之宏量与义行而闻名。

战争何时为合理

儒家对战争之一般看法，可由论家司马穰苴[2] 总结："古者以仁为本，以义治之之谓正。正不获意则权。权出于战……是故杀人安人，杀之可也。攻其国，爱其民，攻之可也。以战止战，虽战可也。故仁见亲，义见说，智见恃，勇见身，信见信。内得爱焉，所以守也。外得威焉，所以战也。战道：不违时，不历民病……

---

① 原文为："今之所谓良臣，古之所谓民贼也。君不乡道，不志于仁，而求富之，是富桀也……而求为之强战，是辅桀也。"——译者注

② 原文为《司马法》，乃司马穰苴著作之名。——译者注

故国虽大，好战必亡。天下虽安，忘战必危。"

源自封建时代实践之原则，可施力惩罚虐民之君。斯为孔子政治最瞩目特征之一。政府须维护庶民之安乐，而非为独夫食客之利。国君为人民之领袖，并依天职而衷心履职。若于之有忽，则经自然因素之途受诸多间接惩罚，如旱涝饥疫等。各国固视战争为灾临君民有罪之邦。由中国圣教可知，一切国君皆须或应以维持世间善政为务，而任一政府有责惩罚虐民之君，及背信弃义违仁之主。由此，儒家政治区分侵略战争与宣告惩罚败德君民目的之军事征伐，例如英国征伐锡袍王。儒家谴责以军事为扩张手段，并力斥一切对各国社会生活之专横干涉。

太平盛世之梦

与此主题紧密关联之另一儒家大本，乃人类同一之认知。文化之目的，乃于文明范畴中容纳全人类，并确保全人类得一切善政之庇佑。儒家于其伦理、政治及宗教三层分野之中，尽力使个人于家庭各得其所：教育家人以知其于国家之身份，以引领各邦国君明其所负教化与仁慈之责。欲播此高贵理念，和平必不可少。人非为一己而生。其为民族之一分子，并须生而有益全族。儒家之太平盛世，名为大同（Great Communion）。据《礼记》所载，其乃举世和平，于中法理均为仁爱所替。至此战争艺术必可驯以正义之益。

唯孔教典籍之一《大学》预示，文明传播之后，当有方国。中国古史可资累牍，表明经诡诈与结盟手段所安排之权力平衡为一场空。该等人为安排之失败所引致之冲突，常较一般战争为重，因其释出长久敌意。古今联盟告负，因其大体默认武力为最终凭借，罔顾公义之吁请，而以向更强者展现物力优势为要旨。古时出于对时政之不满，令人惊异之处与吾等时日于实质方面并无不同，公元前 546 年，古代中国之政治家共同举行弭兵之会。会后，正如今日之海牙会议，无人愿启裁军之事。孔教素来关切实务，已未再试图采信如斯理想安排，唯诲曰各邦应有高效及随时就绪之军备，而国君愿为崇高文明进程与人类进步使用武力。利用人类潜能之理想，为和平之益，改铸剑① 为犁，固为儒家理想主义者与犹太人、基督徒所共有。孔庙之圣约翰颜回，言其渴事之君，乃化民望为社会生活与农事之艺术，由此尚武精神与矜能伐功之冲动可逊位于人类整体进步之努力。大君独夫募役建造长城，最终胜利后将其大批军器熔铸为各式钟鼎及造像。

正义之战

简而言之，战争自属大恶，唯对野蛮暴力之驯默温顺为恶更甚。军备为防卫之根本手段，兵役乃一不可或缺之责。为家园、国君及国家赴死乃仁人之极责。唯邦国亦应以惩恶之普遍文明理由使用军力。任何政府皆无权镇压其臣民。邻国有权以仁爱正义之缘由进行干涉，唯不可为自我扩张觅此托词。

于此简述一般原则，由之吾等于今可知儒家如何看待德国强加于世人之大战。

---

① 原文为 turnings words，疑误，应为 turning swords。——译者注

战时讲演与随笔集
（1914—1917）

二

何为文明

接续考虑之主题乃何为儒家之文化与文明观，将以批判德国之方法为据。

吾等已见儒家人类社会之观念纯属入世，并不求神授以加强其伦理准则。唯儒家思想有两大预设，一是人类民族之同一，二是正义法则普遍有效。其以利他为基，构建伦理、哲学及政治之完整体系。全天下以上天之旨意治之，而各国君主须以提升人类整体福利作为各族群各自努力之终极目标。国际交往之规则，应建于与圣哲理想协调一致之道德观念，而一国对另一国之肆意侵略，正属盗匪之罪行。

故文明为一集体，包容所有国家，并需每一个体之精诚奉献。唯为实现此人类社会道德秩序之观念，须以普及伦理教育为根本。为预备此最令人期许之境地，儒家思想谆谆教导孝悌、爱国与忠、诚、勇、仁。

与基督教精神相似，儒家思想最高教导为爱所有人。唯其有别焉：基督教义未对利他与不抵抗设限，而儒家思想与之相反，坚持人人有拒恶惩奸之权责。任何人间威权不得借宗教为遮掩，行其邪恶暴虐之事。国王，或总统，或教士行为不端则应受惩罚，而正义须得伸张。此儒家教诲不折中之态度，已于历史进程中造出许多殉道者。乱世之人固然称颂罪过，美化其主之恶行，儒家思想仍致力置武力于理性与善意之下，人文精神终须成功居上。

文明实为人类有史以来诸多力量对各民族彼此作用之融合结

果。其流未断，唯其力向由社会生活变革之要素所决定。其多重转化可比万花筒中所呈图像无尽之转换，形式虽似无穷，吾等知其元素不离其宗。因莎士比亚洞悉人性，举世崇之，尤以德国为最。纵然其痛恨一切英国事物，亦无人打算攻讦此人性不朽之诗人。儒家思想与基督教精神具此真义之发轫。德人于18世纪已制定文明律法。从康德哲学范畴演进至黑格尔唯心论，将国家与防卫战争神化为道德工具。此二宗师为卡莱尔、拉斯金及霍尔丹所激赏，举世沉迷于其玄奥哲学命题之深广，忘却康德及其弟子实立于中国、印度、罗马与希腊哲人之伟大基础，以及卢梭与法国百科全书派成员慧思之上。其实，虽康德颂扬战争之道义价值（《审美判断力批判》，英译本，1911年版，第112页），其《永久和平论》正可视为最纯粹儒家之专论。旧时德国哲学令人尊崇之处，乃强调对宇宙道德秩序之认同，并使人类行为须与利他[1]理念一致。惜德国之科学教化，已使其思想家倾向明显源于自然调研之观念。叔本华与尼采两副疯狂而天赋美妙头脑之空谈，无疑导致现代德国深化军国主义之要素，并已提供素材经伯恩哈迪、冯·德·戈尔茨及他人发挥甚大效用。德皇正可称为现代军国主义、强权伦理与大条顿王国之父。在德皇威廉为有志于教学者所筹备之讲演与文章内，其已保留就"身体、智识及宗教训练与纪律相协调"所持高远理想之明示，为鲜明展现"祖国伟大成就"而教授历史。高中及大学鼓励决斗，使年轻德国学子走向世界时获所需坚忍之水准。[2] 学校即招募为日耳曼精神献身者之场所。

德皇坦承"经美化形象"，其母"所思所虑皆为艺术"，已致其"以人类美好和睦之意识所当发见者，严格限定人民生活，并增其美、进其艺"。其亦宣称德人独持伟大理念，以"劳作阶级能以美为乐，并发展梳理其日常所思"。至此，对军国主义目标

---

① 原文为 ultruism，疑误，应为 altruism。——译者注

② 原文于此句后仅存下引号，故未能确定所引范围。——译者注

之争议无多。

　　唯当德皇及其外交官向英国保证帝国政府之和平意愿时，另一股力量于德国稳步生发。伯恩哈迪计划以统治世界为泛日尔曼同盟之终局，英国视其为狂热沙文主义不负责任之呓语。唯战争爆发后，世人方知日耳曼民族已窃奉冯·崔茨克之伪哲学为军国主义之分部，并已采信其崇拜武力之宗教。崔茨克偷师马基雅维利专制国家之概念，为高度独裁做出辩解。其认同强权国家，对腓特烈·威廉四世之军国主义，以及最无理之侵略赋予道德裁断。和平宣传不特愚蠢，而且不义。恐惧成为完美德国军国主义强加于劣等后进民族之手段。德国文明之布道者如是说："若史家试图以欧洲相同标准，衡量于非洲及东方之欧人政治，则愚也。未能于兹鼓动恐惧者，则败也。"（《论政治》）[①] 由此德人显然不为其士卒残暴过激行为所动，因其所教视"恐惧"为战时妥当之事。据伯恩哈迪之见，德国唯存二途：统治世界或毁灭（《世界权力之衰落》）。

　　自儒家观点言之，邦国并无权置身于人类律法或道德准则之上，正如个人不得宣称其独立于全体同胞之外。国家为文明社会秩序之一环，须顺适各国之领土，且遵从文明之伦理观念与道德约束。无人可为一己而生。儒家告诫人为家庭、国家、民族以及人类之整体利益而生。各国同样不得漠对邻国命运，并为人类与文化利益负惩恶扬善之道义责任。故儒家秉持自由原则，不许任何形式之种族排斥；而其力图改善次等民族之境况，且设置条件通过进步与启蒙使各国和睦平等相处。斯为儒家之理想。其亦为一切伟大世界宗教即伊斯兰教与基督教之理想。唯儒家推定该理想终将自然而然实现，并仅能经所有民族为人类利益之奋斗，坚决协力而达致。

---

　　① 原书待考。此外，原文此处缺一上引号。唯原书体例不一，亦有书名未加引号者。——译者注

　　故与伯恩哈迪及其学说相悖，弱小国家确有生存发展权。强国应加以协助引领，而非对其洗劫，令之为奴。于儒家眼中，造成毁家灭国为罪之甚。维护国家独立完整之原则，乃儒家政治第一义。虽军国主义所引致后果之史实具在，儒家仍信于斯理，因其笃信存乎道力以塑人类命运，物物终将各得其正。于瞬息变迁之人事关系以外，存乎正义律法，人类之精神据此由吾等现有智识每常难明之理引导。故见飞机之运作，抵抗重力吸引，因而似有人类行为违背社会与文明律法，加以详察则可见其与真理全然相谐。于是儒家坚信正义必胜，泰然审视各国兴衰起落之潮流，知晓人生并不总为全然空虚，而风暴之后吾等可期灿烂前程。据儒家观点，文明乃缓慢而确然实现人类社会中正义、仁爱及真理之崇高理想，乃人间天国之完成。

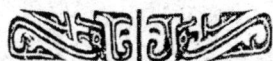

战时讲演与随笔集
（1914—1917）

三

控诉

　　吾等于今可见对德国及其民众所做之控告，以及大敌德皇威廉自家臣民对协约国之反诉。

　　诉词为德国已干犯系列行径，有悖于理智、法律、正义、道德、宗教、人性之要求，及其自身认可代表之庄严承诺。以简明方式陈述该等控诉之时，吾等可知德国为其行径所列之动机，而该等借口自成对其控诉之一部。

　　1.全德国无理密谋灭亡法英，并决心尽早予以摧毁时，施行各手段向其意欲加害者做出保证。

对谎言与伪善之控诉

　　2.其经谍报系统，滥用善意，随意剥夺已赋予民众之利益及其他权利。

背信弃义之控诉

　　3.设定其意志及私利为唯一是非准则，并损害世界。

利己主义与蓄意造成伤害之控诉

　　4.德国唆使奥地利向塞尔维亚发出一项最后通牒，后者作为独立国家，若不屈尊损誉，则无可能接受。

煽动不法行为之控诉

　　5.德国对大战爆发负有责任，因于奥地利罔顾俄国警告，动员军队准备侵略塞尔维亚时，其向俄国发出立即遣散军队之要求。

引发战争之控诉

6. 德国杜撰法国侵犯比利时领土，以掩其自身侵略比利时之背信弃义。

欺诈与背信弃义之控诉

7. 德国试图以物质利益之妥协行贿大不列颠，以纵容其劫掠、有预谋之罪恶及丑行。

怯于道义与非法得益之控诉

8. 德国罔顾列强警告及比利时之抗议，违背各国法律及其自身书面之庄严保证，强行遣师入境，侵犯比利时之中立。

暴力罪行与引致伤害之控诉

9. 德军于鲁汶劫掠，及对妇女耆幼施以战争之行径，违背海牙公约及文明国家之惯例。

野蛮与毁坏之控诉

10. 德国海军批准攻击商船之海盗行径，未予警示，无视老幼男女，造成无辜非战斗人员死亡。

不人道、海盗行径与集体屠戮之控诉

11. 德国政府同意炮击不设防之城镇，虐待战俘，并有意忽略维滕贝格营之病患。

违法残暴与滥杀之控诉

12. 德国政府即德皇及其军事统帅，对和平无望、干犯罪恶行径负有责任。而德国教授唆使纵容，并为其君主之罪行与蠢事开脱。除十余位人士以外，德国乃将可恶罪行及可怖愤怒加诸人类与文明之帮凶。

辩护

吾等以全副耐心与一切尽可能之公正，听取德国之辩护，并为即使承载一丝可能印象或一缕残存真相之任何事物，给予妥当裁量与善意推断。

1. 针对第一项指控，德人申辩法人决意为1870年之战争复仇。俄国为野蛮之邦，其泛斯拉夫倾向置德国扩张于险境之源。英国海军驭伏波涛，唯英人堕落，即使店东 ① 亦不足为。按鼓吹者海克尔、崔茨克及克劳塞维茨 ② 自达尔文发轫之研究演绎所得进化圣法，德国已成最强、最智、最尊之种族，如正义之最高形式为力量。德国正遵循天道，得其所哉，并从苦海中夺取尼普顿之权杖。

2. 针对背信弃义与经谍报系统滥用善意之指控，德国再次以受制于斗争生存法则为借口，并认为国家之需求至高无上。结果可证方法之适当。虚情假意与背信弃义乃战争之美德。唯有成功与胜利为要。协约国可依样随意行事！

3. 德人炫耀其力量，蔑视并挑战世界，以战斗之苦难验证问题。

4. 德皇声称为和平缔造者，并谴责英国宣战，因德皇不遵其粗野蛮横之命，停止因应奥国准备而采取之必要防御措施。

5. 成群结队之德国知名教授于《德国之真理》内，抗议俄国负有战争责任，宣称包括其在内之全体德人欲求和平。俄国已准备侵略战争并向其进攻。

6. 柏林政府断言法人绝无可能悖此行事。无论比利时援法，抑或法人进入比利时，而其军队已属入寇比利时。无论如何，德国愿赔偿比利时之损失。

---

① 拿破仑嘲英人之语。——译者注

② 原文为 Clauewitz，疑误，应为 Clausewitz。——译者注

7. 贝特曼·霍尔维格博士不解大不列颠"对待片纸之尊严"。德人声称感到委屈，即英人欲置道德考量于与具长头颅指数之条顿种族之亲缘问题之上。

8. 德人先承认武力侵犯比利时之中立属于过失行为，并承诺适时补偿。唯其随后申辩法人侵入比利时领土，并声称已发见英比协议拟经比利时入侵德国。

9. 所有著名德人均已公告其信念，以恐惧为战争中进攻之一部。德皇欲其兵士学习匈奴，不发慈悲，并不留俘虏。军头、教授及政客相信残酷强硬战争之血腥与恐怖，可粉碎一切对抗德国之诱因。主帅冯·迪富特有言："若依吾等理解之无情发动战争并登峰造极者，吾等是且必须是野蛮之人。"

10. 德人回应，英国封锁造成德国婴幼饿殍。

11. 就不人道及草率屠戮之指控，回应一切战争行为本质上均属公平。一切对敌之恐吓及伤害，均有助军队，并有益国家，此外更无紧要事。

12. 德人仅于战争及成功中荣耀，唯其急于将引发战争之责置于他人之肩。各协约强国已出版官方文件以应对其借口。

战时讲演与随笔集
（1914—1917）

四

裁断

全情陈述之后，可稍稍简要提出儒家陪审团之裁断。首先，勿误以中国人之观点必为儒家，如以德人之立场必属基督教。儒者态度须以妥善建于公认经典及孔教信条之准则为基。全用儒家伦理为式之遣词造句表述判断，乃为适当。

1. 万事其来有自。因其果，论其树。所有仇视及战备之源，乃生活之物质观念。孟子曾云，若以获益为政治与个人生活之成功标准，竞争无可避免，而更狡黠之徒将利用实诚之人。一切视尘世利益为文明主要目的之好战者，皆有罪孽。唯德人最应谴责，以其使之成最高自然生存目的。

2. 力量并非一切。暴不胜勇。残酷与怨恨对溺于其中者无益。智仁之举，以难测之途，克服蛮力及兽性。史上迫害每归失败。德人陷于妄想，并为人类带来无数苦难。其为曾经繁盛之地带来彻底毁灭，将恶有恶报。其已诉诸暴力，而因其不义、依赖武力、蔑视仁义，上天将摧毁之。

3. 军国主义与暴政意图延续暴力之治，及生存斗争所必要之动物性生活条件。其违背理性之律令，而斯乃成就文明各要素之风度、慈善、仁爱、正义及利他。正如人类已征服野兽及蛮族，故文明必优于武力统治。一切武力打造之帝国迟早崩溃。蒙古侵入中原，终完败于一穷困潦倒、目不识丁之沙弥。有一难民

25

如尤利西斯流离于陌生异国，身无一卒，不名一钱，却终结清帝国。袁世凯总统行使之大权，为1915年底离开新加坡，手无寸铁、孤身入滇之勇士所破。亚历山大、始皇帝、恺撒、阿提拉、成吉思汗与拿破仑之命运，证明以武力大规模征服之徒劳无功。该等暴君所犯罪孽均为记载，永受声讨。德皇威廉并无[1]拿破仑之天赋，却试图模仿之，并待其母系亲属之最良善者以卑鄙之忘恩负义。其依赖军力击败文明。其听凭自身欲望，并拒绝其父辈珍视之崇高原则，招致家庭、民族及帝国永世之耻及彻底毁灭。天人诅咒降诸其身、其幕僚及其军队。高深莫测之上天所持精神力量，将鼓舞更强之队伍征服群氓，而真理及正义必胜，见证基督教、佛教与儒教之胜利。

4. 对比利时之背约乃对文明与人性之犯罪。于正义之上奠基制度及律法之全体中立国家，应挺身而出，并尽全力以惩罚国际罪行。协约国代表宇宙之精神力量，及作为上天之工具以解决人类之祸害，并将嗜血贪婪之德人引向正义。

5. 由于德军所施一切虐待、屠戮、恶举及暴行，德皇及其官员应受今后一切仁人最严厉之谴责。协约国将要求对一切损失之物质进行赔偿。上天亦必以其道惩之。所造成他人悔恨、羞愧、堕落及耻辱之痛苦，将同样降诸其身。上天不可轻慢。人类出于厌恶将于各可敬之社会驱逐德人，直至其及时悔改，补偿因条顿民族野心对世界所施之大谬。

6.[2] 德人之行证其有罪，而依道德与宗教之需，凡有原则之人士，应尽一切可能襄助协约国，使祸首罪有应得。全体人类之道德谴责乃一烙印，对德国之损害更甚于百战失利。

7. 大战前协约国未悉心呼应正义之需。德皇促兵仿效匈奴人入侵中国时，基督教之强国未作抗议，而今遭天谴，欧洲也遇

---

① 原文为 withont，疑误，应为 without。——译者注

② 原文此处无序号"6"，疑缺。——译者注

到如此光景。

8. 仅有严守公义原则，方能保永久和平。各国应先考虑人性之主张，并需撇开相关商业利益或领土并吞之小节。冲突源于对显要地位之争夺，而争夺地位之战斗已将诸多神圣事物践踏于尘土之中。正义、自由、法律、国家解放及少数弱小战败而不设防者之权利等问题，仅能由理解自然环境之需，且为至高文明理念所激励之人士予以解决。义请惩罚，唯爱求仁。

该等简述为儒家对此史上最宏伟战争所呈多重问题之看法。战永为恶，唯或得善果，因自然界阳光普照，而人类仅能从认识事物反面为学，乃吾等生存之别致反讽。若无黑暗，光不可见。若无限制，万物归空。若无极恶，至善不察。以此恼人悖论加诸吾等智识，目的为何？其属宗教及哲学所解决之题。唯吾等颇可依此自儒家立场确定，人之定命乃超升至精神更高之处，抛弃为生存之凶残争斗与为世俗占有之无益竞争，并于明亮正义之国度，达致灵魂之完美平和。

战时讲演与随笔集
（1914—1917）

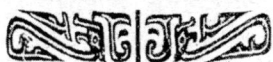

五

世界之和平

民族之文史常映显于其言辞。故英文"peace（和平）"使吾等思及诺曼人所设之封建制度，而此英法文字皆可于拉丁文"pax（和平）"寻其字根，而"pax"相应源自意为同意或遵守之另外一词。罗马人之和平，乃战争及神圣协议之结果。若有违背，则必将即刻唤起罗马之全力动员。

古条顿民族中，和平观念以意味休憩或自由之词表述，唯亦无疑反映无处不在之罗马人无情战争。对该等蛮族而言，和平意味免于罗马人侵犯之自由，以及免于南方侵略者所强加束缚纠葛之自在生活。

中国词语之和平，似拉丁文"quies（安静）"，意为宁静或休憩，唯与拉丁文"pax"对等之恰当词语为双音节词"太平"。吾等固然皆知其为霹雳州繁荣矿镇之名，亦能忆及戈登于中国大规模内战时所助力镇压者，名为太平起义。唯或未周知太平意为举世和平，而创此短命天朝者号称上帝之使，为受难之世带来和平。

无论如何，太平一词实际意味之"平等"，乃取自儒家经典。而吾等发现太平意味中庸之平衡，各国依此延续喜乐富裕之生活，其时公义将引导人人之行止。而当社会秩序与人类律法不再必需，人将克服自私，举世联合以提升人类福祉，深化智识与文明。斯为儒者与基督徒之属同待太平盛世之拂晓：

至战鼓不再擂动，战旗收卷

31

于人类之议会，世界之邦联。①

即便如此，寻常词语之意蕴亦得文史着力阐明。

何为自然所教

当吾等考察周遭之世界，以发现何种现象引致和平之概念时，吾等发见黯淡人性之外，自然甚少或全无表露和平，反似无休战争之角斗场。吾等徒劳于有机世界遍寻和平，于没有生命自身之情况下，保留有这可怕的疑虑。于无生命之事物中，唯仅存表面一片宁静，甚至地球及宇宙物理化学之力存于其中，争夺最终主导。而表面之静止仅为爆裂之先声，俗语云暴风雨前之平静。

今日公认动植物中斗争存焉。冲突愈加激烈，生命有机体进化愈高。归功于达尔文与华莱士之耐心观察，发见适者生存之伟大生物法则，解释每一个体及每一种族似为争夺霸权而冲突之明显乱象。因此"劣者淘汰"之结论似由科学数据证明。俘获萧伯纳想象力之尼采哲学，建于对此自然法则之误会与曲解之上。超人学说距真理何等遥远，于吾等发见适者生存解释无防卫能力鸽子之存在，以及人有不便阑尾之时，实能一目了然。另外，贯穿地质时代最为狂暴、最为嗜血及最为有力之兽类已告消逝。而于暴力之无穷混乱中，不具禽兽爪牙之人类崛起，唯拥有智识、理性及利他之气度，而外表无防卫之血肉之躯已统治野兽，并已克胜龙族及世间一切残害生命之兽类。

唯人可以和平

进化之研究虽揭示自然永恒争斗之态，亦阐示理性与仁爱之发

---

① 英国诗人丁尼生于1835年所作诗歌《洛克斯利大厅》（"Locksley Hall"）之两句。音节数相同，押韵，译文如是。——译者注

展，并证明除破坏之外，尚有他力存在。如俄国亲王、社会主义者彼得·克鲁泡特金已充分演示进化科学，展现互助运作与社会合作并不少于为生存之激烈争斗。唯人类仍受周遭险境之灭绝威胁。其自身须防范自然之暴力、野兽之攻击及其同胞之阴谋。因获取食物之难，蛮族甚至不能避免来自同族者之威胁，其有时杀尽年老族人。据格林所云，古代德人处死其老病者，甚或活埋之；而今日世界骇于条顿人粗野残暴之返祖现象。而如已故亨利·卓蒙德教授诗意所述："进化并非物质之发展，乃精神之升华，其中并无限制，即最富人性、最合理性及最具神性。"

于漫漫岁月进程中，仁爱与理智缓得其方，克服战争之严酷现实。并非由相斗而同归于尽，人类做出妥协，并议定和平，使臣服者生活宁静，条件乃以个人服务，[①] 以金钱或其他贡品，及以领土与其他权利之让步，满足征服者之意愿或需求。

史载强力与正义间无尽之争斗。和平之议定仅为进一步战争之准备，及佛教、儒教与基督教以仁爱与人性为共同基础黏合人类之可悲失败。独裁不能灭绝人类自由燃烧之余烬，其一有机会即会迸发火焰，直至和平保障自由而非奴役，确保人类精神于更为适意之范畴发展。各帝国、王国与共和国之史志确载，无论如何渴求永久和平，唯当良善政府以正义律法运作，使人民得享自由与满足，方存可能。

君子之风或武士道

与时推移，剑化为强力防御武器。纵览封建时代，武士虽对其佣仆粗暴无情，唯对同侪与妇女具高贵品性之修养。故君子之风成荣誉与宗教之保障。自古以来，中国武士为圣人之教所励，与其行为不端或受辱蒙羞，不若以死为贵；而斯为每一儒者卫弱

---

① 原文此处疑缺一逗号。——译者注

惩恶之本职。京都教授新渡户认为，日本武士及剑客受武士道影响，实行儒家伦理，挥剑以捍卫正义与和平之益。

人之善意

儒家思想进而告诉吾等，世上将无和平，直至每一男女受教并体认何为人生：对他人所负之责何等神圣，及民族命运何等光荣。个体须意识利他之主张。其须化爱为生命之力，亦须终其一生展现珍视父母之爱，作为恒例以拓善意之有益影响至众人。唯有依此，则家庭满意和睦，国家平静有序，世界和平喜乐。贪婪与自我须予根除，并置正义与仁爱于其位，而后诚意将力促人类之转进，使和平理想不再虚幻，而为文明之真力。

开明人士逐渐觅得方法互助协作，并解决导致冲突及异议之因素。查尔斯·达尔文于《人类之由来》指出，人之"社会属性"与其"对自然武器之需"大体抵消。因工业开发之文明深化劳资之间对利益之竞争，已使工业安全之维持成为必要。于英国，由讨论结果之共识而树立信心，谈判之目的乃防止罢工与停工条件之友善讨论过早破裂。另外，工人组织倾向超越政治限制之领域并国际化。其目标在于普世之劳动联盟，而其极端团体如工团主义者与无政府社会主义者，宣称战争乃彻底反对一切已建立之制度甚至理性自身！

所有自由国家各阶级内存在不可调和之差异与激烈之反对，德人于1914年对此甚明。其冀于英法相残得益。心存不满之工人阶级对工业之怨恨，可叹可悲至何地步，吾等可自其对有效施行战争所设严重障碍而得判断。唯即使于德国自身及于美国，阶级野心与无情商业引致之力即将于合适心理时机撕碎社会。世界文明实有败坏，因于高调陈词掩饰之下，个人无情利用同胞，个体与阶级为权财之倾轧，绝不少于国际军备竞赛之败德。

列强参与此军事与海军竞赛之唯一可能结局，乃打压文明之可怖战争。唯战争自证恐怖，要皆来自德国领袖之愚癫。未来之阶级战争，劳资于其中争夺主导，可能更为无限凄惨骇人。因心存不满者与邪恶学说久抑之怒，可即刻否定道德之实际约束与宗教之神圣诫令。……更大规模戕害同胞之阶级战争，如同令人毛骨悚然之幽灵，于当前末日云烟之后浮显。除非国家与教会以不祥之兆为警，西方将无和平，而致力和平正义者之辛劳，将虚掷于西西弗斯式任务，全无胜算。

战争之缘由

唯亦有充分之希望，即大战可令众人深刻认识若干有益真理，并可引领各国人民深思持续和平之实益，斯非建于征服者对受征服者之些许暂时利益之上，而建于公义永久功德之上。战争为力量冲突之果，并依于各项缘由，可对其加以研析，其精确等同于台风成因与预估威力之描述。自古以来，伟大军事领袖之野心随胜而癫，并经其奴仆之谄媚，更为激气使力，成世界和平之绝大威胁。马其顿之亚历山大、汉尼拔①、尤利乌斯·恺撒、拿破仑、始皇帝及诸多他人使用武力，以实现其虚浮之野心。

各国苦于野蛮侵略，或许无国甚于堪怜之比利时及不幸之中国。条顿民族已成欧洲之祸根，并对人类及文明造成无可估量之损失。自安顿于大不列颠诸岛之海盗，哥特人、汪达尔人、法兰克人、伦巴第人，直至德人实施对比利时、法国及波兰当前之入侵，条顿种族显出同等野蛮及傲慢之精神。唯于任何地方，条顿人不能长久维持原有性格，而一旦忘怀战争之可怖，德人便模仿受害者之气质与风尚。随后和平期间，条顿人于其攻克之地为其劫掠

---

① 原文缺逗号，疑误。——译者注

与虐待之民族吸纳，以为惩罚。直至吾等时日，条顿人之非日耳曼化稳步进行。德国侵略引发之战争最终对其祖国之元气造成更大损失。此乃命运之嘲讽，德人确已知悉，唯其特为迟钝，未能发见此非民族化之真实缘由，并施其呆板智识之全力，筹划于摧毁英法之后，以泛日耳曼同盟统治世界。

再者，诸多战争由宗教狂热引发。诸如萨拉森人与土耳其人之入侵，以及中世纪基督教世界对穆斯林之十字军东征。种族憎恶强化心理与社会之对抗，如所见于汉人与鞑靼、凯尔特人与撒克逊人、条顿人与斯拉夫人之间者，将长存为战争之诱因。

普鲁士之罪恶

于好战国家眼中，政治考量亦使马基雅维利式原则为合理实践，以弱邻为壑，罔顾正义，并蔑视庄严之协议。于此方面，整部世界史内，自腓特烈大盗（或称大帝）时代至今，并无一国之罪恶甚于霍亨索伦之普鲁士。威廉二世较其任何无赖先辈若非更劣，亦属同恶。尽管其就爱国做出粗俗声明，事实显露其真正人品实为现代伪君子。

而又有经贸利益相关纠纷引发之战争。近数世纪之欧战、亚洲之破坏、非洲之瓜分、欧国之殖民扩张、日本发动之现代战争，尽属此类。古时由经济压力与竞争引发最有趣与最可怖之战争，乃罗马与迦太基间之宏伟战争，于罗马力竭与迦太基邦灭亡后，方告结束。

临末，吾等勿忘为正义与自由之故而进行之正义战争，为摧毁暴政，为反击侵略，或为保卫弱者及无辜。美国内战将永远助长合众国之荣光，因其为宗教与人性之最高利益而战。今吾等所对之大战，就协约国而言，乃维护国家理想与自由之宗教战争。

大不列颠不止于是，其亦可充分宣称为捍卫文明与维护协约尊严、为保卫虽小国而乃英勇盟友之正义事业而战。

一服万灵药

此乃战争缘由之简述。自古以来，人类不欲面对战争之恐怖，诗人唱颂和平之佑，先知伸出橄榄枝，并谈及战争终止与各国不再哭泣之幸福时光。

为抑制竞赛之狂暴精神，已有诸多补救措施之建议。唯至今并无明效。战争如瘟疫须予承受，直至人类自其精神之蛰伏苏醒，并着手人间天国之传承！

公元前546年中国首次弭兵大会

热衷争论之古希腊城邦，由若干史上最智慧与最伟大之人引导，奋力防止战争，通过提交世俗争议如宗教歧见与外交差异，由近邻同盟裁断。彼由各城邦代表组成，并经召集城邦对违反者宣告圣战以执行其决定。唯惜如圣战之需所明示，无论希腊人之智慧抑或近邻同盟之威权，均不能为希腊城邦带来和平。

而史上以和平会议之方式实现裁军之最早尝试，可远溯至公元前546年中国之诸侯国宋国，在今之河南省。对现代欧洲政客而言，颇为稀奇与羞赧者，乃沉思古代中国政治家切实预见当今所有国家产生裁军问题之看法。

当时，中国分裂为诸多争斗之国。无休之战争乃时代之诅咒。人民倦于战斗。沃土常化为狼藉，最美之城市已成荒芜。贪婪、野心及自利指使扩张之密谋，战士之军事热情助其造极于封建荣誉准则，即任何有关贵族尊荣之事体，均颇存歇斯底里之神经过敏。就战争之挥霍与险恶，提出警示之时机似已成熟。

向戌为一宋国官员。其劝说国君召集主要国家之会议，以讨论裁军问题。该问题于理论上看似甚为简易，昨日欧洲之政客要员，正如古代中国之前人，为一美丽诱人之妄想而徒劳。会议实已召开。该运动之创建者一度动念，自以其为人类最伟大之造福者，并宣称其计划将可防生命财产之毁灭，而后要求宋国国君应厚赏其为国之伟大贡献。若吾等自宋国国君屈服和平主义者敦促之举判断，其意志颇为薄弱。唯就所建议分封土地之问题向司城讨教，彼反对将赏赐与荣誉赐予天下和平之空想者。司城子罕有勇，批评国君认可妄人所献之计。按其观点，应声讨所鼓吹愚险之说，因裁军将置和平于危境，亦将诱惑矜矫不法之徒妄求权力。向戌终承认其为荣耀之可能性所误导，未考虑最终结果。故首次大会归于惨败。签署各方皆无行动，而各国均待他国启动此权宜险策。

为和平奋斗之成就，无过于沙皇尼古拉二世。其努力促进海牙公约并已取得可观之硕果。自 1908 年以来，战事不断发生，而虽有安德鲁·卡内基捐赠之宏伟和平宫，史上最大规模战争仍几于其门打响。且德人之野蛮将世界掷回数世纪之前，并使战争变得如此丑陋，战士如同来自黑暗时代之人。

就战争与荣誉之文明规范，于今无须列举所有研究细节。各国代表按军事实力划分其等级，为世界之教化做出庄严规范。呜呼，海牙公约当前仅为“一纸具文”，而宋国司城之正确，在其谴责以裁军作为不警惕者之钓饵，并为不择手段之徒如今日德国无可避免之诱惑。

基督教不抵抗之教义

不抵抗与不作为，有伟大而奥妙之教义。隐士老子云：“女慎……淖约柔乎刚强，廉刿雕琢，其热焦火，其寒凝冰……绝圣

弃智，而天下大治。"（《庄子》第十一）

佛陀与耶稣之教诲可以圣马太之言总结："有人打你的右脸，连左脸也转过来由他打。""① 你们的仇敌，要爱他；咒诅你们的，要为他祝福；恨你们的，要待他好；凌辱你们的，要为他祷告。"

该等深刻真理使吾等微薄信念脑眩眼盲，使吾等行事全然伪善，"所见和所赞同者更佳，而所求者却更差"②。吾等虽不能确识人性无底之渊之完整谜团，唯对灯塔之光绝不阖眼，无论其看似如何遥远。

一项实际补救措施

唯以吾视之，儒家思想建议有一实际方法，以应对干犯有大恶之敌。

子曰："以直报怨。"

故自儒家立场而言，和平应基于正义，而正义之惩罚须施予行恶并引致他人苦痛之人。

儒家思想亦坚持军备与军训应为日常教育之部分。日本武士道仅为军人使用之儒家伦理规范，即全体人民皆宜为国而战，一切国家应预备自卫及以正义之名征讨。

与任何恶行及不公妥协而修补之和平，乃有罪于文明。无论代价为何，文明人士须抵抗邪恶势力占据高位。可杀不可辱。如是信念为儒家思想实在而重要之教诲。

最终持续之和平当为每一战争之目的。远至公元前597年，或劝楚庄王立碑纪念所获胜利时，其以如是名言责其官员："夫文，止戈为武。夫武，禁暴，戢兵，保大，定功，安民，和众，丰财者也。"（《左传》）

---

① 原文缺上引号，疑误。——译者注
② 出处待考。——译者注

运用

运用适才阐述之原则于欧洲大战，吾等须下定论，直至击败德国及其仆从国，或其愿认错，并无条件向各协约强国投降之前，无论如何不得考虑任何和平建议。

如美国作家普赖斯·科利尔曾言，按美国之观点，任何牺牲、任何战争皆优于普鲁士式塑造民族之支配。其须依此受罚，即不得利用随后之和平为更大战争做筹备。

必须给予受难者公道与赔偿。

未来

协约国已自行结盟捍卫全体国家之自由与正义。其应保有自愿之姿，为国际警察之中坚，以维护国际律法。

由此恐怖邪恶中可期之幸，乃新时代之破晓。吾等希冀，此时代将有于国际成长之理性，及对真理与正义更多之关注，并对人类种族实质团结之更佳理解。唯此，世界或有和平之福。

> 是的，和平！何须战争——
>
> 是的，平静！风暴已过——
>
> 因完成劳动之目标，
>
> 而终究下锚停泊。①
>
> 和平——唯何人可主张？
>
> 诚实者于其道程，
>
> 保持着战斗之行列，

———

① 原文于此处有下引号，疑误，应于诗末。——译者注

所说之事皆实诚：

归属于上天之和平，

并将归属于大地；

宫殿之回声在反响

欢歌与笑语相随。

《圣·伯纳之韵律》①

J. M. 尼尔

战时讲演与随笔集
（1914—1917）

六之一

艺术对文明之影响

　　人类生活中，最具特色之非凡人性，无过于天然爱恋一切感官所能体会之美与艺术。如哲人所料，自然之秩序、系统与美丽似神思之反映，唯无疑于人类意识内，总有对壮美之微妙与莫测之感知。人脑中有关涉和与美概念之功能。其亦创造理念，转入诗歌、雕塑、绘画、音乐与建筑形式。罗素·华莱士博士发见，审美能力作为进化结果，其起源难以解释。此脑中模糊区域之美妙功能，起源定难追踪。实务乃确认人类能够欣赏形、色及音之美。若掌握一门智慧语言乃区分人类与其他一切动物之标准，美感则赋其通神之声明。剥离美、和、甘之世界将为可悲之混沌，绝不适合人类心智之发展。外部世界实为振奋人类心灵之永恒源泉。而艺术为壮美之事体，由智巧之人所造。如诗与乐，其为内心至深处关于何为真人精神之迸发，或曰可唤起美感最微妙之情绪。人将乐于应对美之刺激，乃自然最绝妙事体之一，并为科学、政治及宗教深远影响后果之一项事实。

　　天才之创造，人称艺术工作，或多或少为作者理想之忠实化身。以愉悦与节律形式之书面表达，幻化壮美之思时，即为诗歌。音乐则更妙，以其无穷音声之和谐变化，及其音色与其他声响元素之组合，产生使人兴奋之影响。音乐述说之天国语言，为精神所理解。故名副其实之宗教，无不借诗乐之助而得发展。各国之庄严国歌成为人类实质一统最有力之证明。于各式各样语言、风俗与习惯中，就精神事体而言，今日人类家庭之团结较过往更为突出。若诗乐强力作用于宗教本能，正式宗教将相应对诗乐施以更大影响。欧洲最宏伟之乐曲致献予上帝。于每一文明国家，其艺术不为宗教舛见所扼杀，则宗教仪式无不配有歌乐。如汝等定然所知，古代中国悉心教授并规范歌乐，由专门国家机构予以密切监管。孔子认为此二者之培养乃个人至要职责之一。即使今日，寺庙之祭拜以音乐伴奏，尤于天坛与孔庙。

悦耳诗乐之影响以外，吾等具其他美术之分支，以其形色之美受赏。吾等切勿缓行建筑、陶瓷、雕塑及制模之主张。其于提升人类之幸福，并助人识其以各种感官实现更高之使命，皆起重要作用。纵贯一切时空，宗教已施全力影响其所造之物；并就所造物而言，已助推宗教之益。

因贵会尤嗜画艺，吾等可予专门留意。而汝等虽为贵会命以甚谦之名，诸君中已有人尝试油画，并于极困难之主题完成颇值称道之工作。

汝等自当欲吾以中国艺术之主题为限，因汝等定知吾于欧洲艺术之伟大主题，较汝等任何一人而言为无知者。若有人参观欧洲伟大画廊，并有观览欧洲大师作品之极佳机会，离开时当有痛苦之迷糊印象，因过度之眩光实蒙蔽景致。唯最瞩目之物仍将凸显，并不为最乏味者所掩。到处可见画艺与宗教至亲密之联系。如吾等所愿，远溯文明至埃及令人生畏之庙宇及其俄西里斯与其他神祇之怪异象征，或亚述与巴比伦崇拜之圣地，吾等可发现人类已运用形形色色之图画表达，以向他人传递不可言说之理念。孔子生前之时代，君王与贵族之宗庙以壁画或浮雕饰墙，展现古代传说或重大历史事件，时时透露些许道德或宗教训诫之观点。降至汉代，似延续该做法，因于清初，发现并保存重要庙宇之浮雕。该等图像已经出版，而巴黎沙畹教授已为之出版一部重要及有价值之专著。该等图像显示古代中国人与埃及人、亚述人存在某些关联，因所绘之景于轮廓颇具启发，使人熟知其与埃及艺术相关。

此外，神木之形令吾等思及亚述纹章，及旧约伊甸园之圣树。而战车内之武士，填补画面空隙之鸟兽，及飞人形象之画面，皆甚动人。相似浮雕或绘画于埃及与亚述之废墟中发见。

中国画艺甚为早熟。中国画艺之原则为南齐朝① 谢赫于 4 世纪末所定，流传至今，并为众所公认。较中世纪欧洲画家而言，其与现代欧洲艺术更为接近。

智识界之宗教哲学，显然造就中国艺术所认定之形式。缺乏若干对民族生活情智要素之认知，无人能解为何中国画艺与欧洲区别甚广甚久。自希腊时代以来，欧洲有一渴望，欲超拔人于自然以外，并继之以宗教及艺术。造物主已成艺术、诗歌及哲学之主题。人之堕落与神话构成长期搅动欧人想象之最严肃问题。随后于欧洲艺术，人之形象凸显，粗暴解剖之形象、人之工作、历史事件、受难及人类攀升至精神高处，悉数组成绘画、雕塑及诗歌之反复主题。

唯于中国,《易经》之影响，已赋予宗教与哲学一种特别倾向，趋于超验与动态之理想。恒视全宇宙为一统一生命体，而人生仅如宇宙中无穷无尽涟漪之一丝微澜。按此世界观，哲人欲缩小而非夸张人之重要性。当世生活律动之成分，视为心智之组成。而谢赫合理要求一切艺术工作应表明其所称言之节律与生活。形式之原型须遵从初始，其他规范为首要原则之必要推论，即图画须为自然之真，色彩亦须协调。画家之天资与天赋决定其构成，并予其必要之完结。欧洲艺术批评家近年已给予中国人精制高标准应得之赞许，并已公正思量，就风景画之门类而言，中国一流作品仍属不可逾越。

中国画艺常显见画家对自然生活印象之理想。中国艺术家努力表达思想，而非描摹入微，故有时其无须明暗配合之力助，以

---

① 原文为 Southern Sui Dynasty，疑误。——译者注

寥寥数笔醒目而重要之线条，为自然之真实呈现，有效唤起记忆之微振，如留声机碟中槽线所能重现之以太声波。艺术家偏好之主题内，可见宗教变化之影响。于唐宋伟大时期内，几乎每一画家或艺术家亦为当时最知名之思想家。书法与绘画则为君子所需成就者。故吾等无须疑惑，伟大画家如唐代顾恺之与宋代李龙眠，可体现儒家学说之哲学与宗教观点。其时风景画如此壮观别致，因其尝试实现伟大发明摄影所最终成就者。中国艺术家常酷好自然之运动。海之运动不止，风吹、雨打、雾飘、雪落，竹柳无穷之叶摆颤不休，野兽活动、群马跳跃或鱼游于水，皆表明自然为生命体之密切主题。中国画艺乃人类天才于亚洲之最高成就，并为东方周遭各国建诸其上之标准。

宗教使人之灵魂与宇宙精神节律协调活动。于忘形与献身精神中，人之心智超越肉身所限，并窥得一缕永恒。于信念与虔诚激励之下，精神图像精准化为肌肉之动作，相应体现为线条，而彼等相应重组初时构图之空灵震颤。于此密径，经人之精神，意念中之图像可传至他人。起初之冲动，乃神智中图像之创作定式，可见于旧石器时代野人之原始雕塑或蚀刻。猛犸与其他动物之绝妙形象已揭示一股表现之新力，其于未来时代为人类幸福与满足贡献良多。中国考古学尚未诞生，唯吾等可期硕果将近。其后将可发现史迹证实中国传统之主张，人民于暗黑至光明之途，缓缓求索其路。前行途中，未有助力甚于书法及其姊妹艺术绘画者。如埃及象形文字与"汉字"所充分证明，绘画实为书写之先导。

中国人对书写致以最大敬意，并自古以来珍视艺术作品。其尊崇画家与书家，并敬重英雄、圣贤与神仙之画像。斯似为信仰自然乃一大有机整体之颇当结果。其确为原始泛灵论之回想，于中国蓬勃发展数千年。

中国人保有最原始之人性观，信仰不朽与死后灵魂仍在。于此信念影响之下，过量思索见于传记、诗歌及遗迹。为记载英雄或钟爱者之事迹，艺术家受召以图画保存心存感念之后人欲纪念之场景。该做法颇为普遍，吾等可言其为文明人士之特征。对此习惯，吾等感激古代伟大艺术作品，古欧洲之庙宇，现代美国纪念馆，中国、印度、柬埔寨与爪哇之浮雕，遑论古墨西哥与秘鲁之伟大遗迹。唯惜中国于汉代相残战争之可怖屠杀后，宗教与文明开始衰落，虽于唐暂时振兴，中国文明已然停滞。

外国宗教之进入与国家信仰之阻滞相合。景教与佛教觅得无数信徒。其虽促进艺术，唯从未创造与更原始中国哲学之同等影响。佛教乃介绍印度艺术品位之途径。人物群集，佛陀、菩萨之衣着，及佛塔显示印度传教者之影响。唯印度之影响并未提升本土艺术，整体而言为有害，因印人对华而不实色彩之喜爱，及沙门礼节所需约定俗成之形式，已对本土品味不断产生恶劣影响。

伴随真正中国宗教与文明之衰退，佛教兴盛一时，而画家及雕塑家已于其影响之下创作颇丰，吾等所称艺术工作之进行多与佛教相关。有趣者为，欧洲艺术作品由罗马天主使团支持之下介绍入华。大量青少年经欧洲艺术家训练绘画、制模及雕刻。该等少年多属孤儿。其复制耶稣受难、圣母与婴儿，以及其他罗马天主教会特有装饰作品之经典图像。"圣图"经教会代理发售，往往仅能削弱艺术感悟与艺术精神。

于佛教影响之下，伟大画家起而摹绘佛陀生活之场景与圣贤肖像。阿弥陀佛之形象为中日艺术家选择之最著名题材。最为流行之神祇或为观音：印度之阿缚卢枳帝伊湿伐罗①，其于中国传统为慈悲之女神，亦正似圣母之常型。

旅行之哲人与佛教权威相争于创造式想象之工作，并相信任何神秘之断言。其全盘吸取佛教仪式，并已充分丰富大地上下之国度。故现代道教亦促进艺术创作，其中万寿山、②老子之形象、

---

① 原文为 Avolokeshtara，疑误，应为 Avalokiteshvara。——译者注

② 原文缺逗号，疑误。——译者注

道家教主骑虎之肖像，及各式各样组合之魔怪，最为人知。

英雄崇拜之盛行，与古代自然及先人崇拜存留之结果，乃有一整班艺术家尽其全力于肖像画。守护家庭神祇之画像到处皆可购得。战神关帝之尊贵画像此前极受喜爱，因清政府选此三国时期名将为护国神。马尼拉华人依据该城传统，笃信其 18 世纪受西班牙人迫害时，关帝于此残酷腐败之城现身，予以保护。

人民大众所赏之全部重要艺术作品，实具信仰及宗教之特质。

既有伟大宗教复兴，亦有物质主义与重商主义之激荡，艺术、观念及作品将有相应剧变。且欧洲理念之影响正为人所感知，而透视学已为所有严肃中国艺术家研究。

艺术是否为文化之必需？其教化与鼓励是否为民主政府之职？答案乃强烈之肯定。如音乐、诗歌及一般审美追求，美术至为民主，因其为超群之人性。中国画艺已特为尝试各项不同工作，并已将最为资产阶级之体裁提升至最为经典历史主题之水平。中国人将发现，普遍传播一种音乐与美术之智识品味，有助其建立真正民主之持久基础。

至此吾须收束。而完结之前，吾谨表一冀望，此冗长散漫之言辞，或可唤醒汝等对中国艺术创作之兴趣。而汝等探寻典型与灵感时，可如先人一般，从真实慧见之源泉寻求指引。汝等虽属业余，应知一切名副其实之艺术家，因热爱自然、真理及美好而工作；故若认为汝等因非专业艺术家，无须艺术基本运用之灵感与勤勉，则汝等不如费时从事户外运动，而有利健康，胜于制作无价值之复制品以"消磨时光"。

战时讲演与随笔集
（1914—1917）

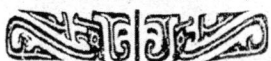

六之二

国家停滞及其救治

一、一般观察

无论转向何处，吾等皆遇无休止之动作，并不存在彻底之停顿。故参考吾等所知之任何事物而言，停滞仅为速度之相对缓慢。此为自然之基本事实，其触及事物之本根，并有助解释渗透一切世事之宇宙进程特质。

参照此普遍运动，另一至要之事实为其速率从未一致。无论于何处观察，其总呈现周期，随决定动作每阶段形式与时长之变化，与各形各色影响而有所不同。

研究文明之变迁，朝代之兴衰，宗教体系内外之人类思想学说，充分表明若吾等愿将人类成就调减为数值形式，波动可以大略形式呈现。吾等整体运用人类社会一般术语诸如进步、停滞及衰退。而一般该等借用词汇并不令人满意，因其易令人误解。

人类并非以直线匀速而以周期波动向前进化之事实，最终显示无论第一运动存在与否，驱动吾等生命之力，以明显方式大致对应弥漫宇宙之力。

追踪该等力量之源乃哲学领域，释其运作并测其命运。而若可能，假定其特别之征。史学仅处理现象，并纯由经验数据中演绎具实用性之教训。

运动定律为普世之运用。停滞意味动作之延缓。速度之损失是否因外部阻碍与摩擦，或若干耗损内能之固有缺陷？纯以物理及自然现象视之，人类社会之停滞源于多种力量之相互作用，而须真切理解社会与国家停滞之确实性质，以明了特定情形下衰退之最佳解药。

分析影响人类演化进程之全部组成因素，显示须区分纯粹物理宇宙之力与更具奥妙品性之他力，斯未有更为确切之名称，或可称之为精神。于众力之漩涡中，人类自我之活动凸显，作为强力冲动而塑造人类命运，并对宇宙运动之性质做新阐述，揭示纷乱中之定然秩序，并指出同振之和谐，彼促进宇宙一统之感官，与人类所感知宏大自然运作之目的。

不可能精准陈述人类进化中该等宇宙力量之物理、精神与人类因素所发挥之作用。认知其存在确为人类行动力学更深智识之踏脚石。事实与人类经验说明，决定论之学说并非全无真理，唯其亦证明存有空间供自由之行使，与世间人类精神之活动。而如中国古典所示，人见自身处于物质宇宙与上天之间，历矛盾冲动之迷局，而上下求索其解脱。直至最终其发现一种和谐，处无尽运动与物质动力相互作用之间，斯乃自我及创造精神活力之自觉。

存在悖论之发现，不须使吾等悲观，亦不须因人类史发生之停滞而致绝望。人类史恒常持续成长，虽个体可能老去，或部落与种族可能消逝于记忆，人类家族仍将于相当规模之文明中崛起。停滞阶段仅为连续波动之次要压抑 [1]，其将愈进化愈高级，至人类想象突破智力与理性之局限，及神圣直觉为人类之典范奠基为止。

---

[1] 原文为 depressinos，疑误，应为 depressions。——译者注

二、停滞之特征

1. 无进步

纵贯历史，进步之阻碍为自然停滞最明显之症状。其可于人类文化任何阶段发生。某些种族长期维持静止，虽一度呈现显著之活动，唯复返昏沉状态。中国人已作为社群生存至少四千年，穿越兴衰之交替循环，唯此民族永向更高理想进发。

约至千年以上，德人仍为野人。而整体上，斯拉夫人于较晚之时转为开化与先进。现代之野人当会保持静止许久。虽毛利人等多展现制作石骨武器之技巧，其较旧石器时代之人改造不同寻常之箭头，杀死引人注目之猛犸与其他已灭绝生物，看似并不优越。

原始人似间或于其手艺取得进步，每一步为重大发见之先驱，使人得以克服环境之影响。于是石器时代必持续许久。随之为取火之发见，按中国编年史所载，为一圣人发明以两枚木片之摩擦取火。希腊人则有普罗米修斯之传说。火对人类文明所施影响甚大，便易知先民何以高度重视其发见。而用火引致制陶与铜铁之使用，其为人类逐步发展之标志。

狗、猫、羊、牛、猪之驯化与家禽之供应，颇改原始人之习惯。农业随之为村庄之定居生活备妥条件。历史确认考古之发见，并显示牧民如阿拉伯人与蒙古人如何仍为游牧，而所有埃及、卡尔迪亚及中国之农民许久以前已依附于土地。

吾等于今已见大地诸国如何保持数百年之静止，直至突然之间，蒸汽用为马力予文明以新促进，而一世纪内世界工业已彻底革命。煤炭时代各方面胜于人类史上任何纪元。可能较未来逊色，其时人类获得更多放射事体之知识，并能以明白有效之方式使用电、光、镭或其替代物。

颇多人民仍满足于已知许久之事，其将维持静止，并无实现进步之可能。一项新理念启动一整串新观点与新设想，以及原理与方法可能之组合与运用。故当未受束缚之时，发见接续而来，至科学成文明不可或缺之女仆。

2. 无知与迷信

停滞之最重大后果，乃见于普遍之无知与迷信。故印度、中国、波斯、爱尔兰、俄罗斯与土耳其之蒙昧土人，可能全然不知 20 世纪以来世界发生之一切事件。其仍持当前二三百年以上之信念，故称之为迷信。

教育或受忽略，或整体缺陷，令人不满。故印度、中国与旧日本之人民，几世纪来切盼良好之教育。唯其虽有精神训练，仍不能取得任何进步，因其所获知识颇受舛误与谎言之玷污，及方法存在缺陷并缺乏实验系统控制之设计，对自然一切之探寻成无用功。旧文学充斥意见与推测，唯无新意可陈。科哲教条之唯一结果，乃建立无可逾越之障碍，以迂腐诡辩与欺骗之蛛网阻滞真正科学之发展。中世纪时期，欧洲颇受该种有识无知与虚假科哲体系所致之害，正如培根反复所作之精细辩论所证明者，其常使明白道理致于更恶劣之混淆。于此情况之下，损失颇多努力。唯当往日欧洲宗教篡夺并滥用国家功能，不特于精神事务，且于一切所思所行之领域，欲建纯正之一统。最恶劣结局不可避免，直至 19 世纪之拂晓，邪恶教会人士仍以陈旧之先验观，回避科学危及其不解问题之脚步，并反对归纳研究具深远意义之结论。故每一教会次第一致反对每一科学发见，而此等科学发见推翻教会学说所采信之虚假自然教条。自伽利略至达尔文，欧洲科学与宗教之争已成无休止之决斗，从未停战。唯幸最终科学与理性完胜，而调和信仰与所立之真理。

未受启蒙之一切人民，仅能由科学赐予鲜活知识，其骇人之蒙昧与相随之迷信，可经 16 世纪欧洲文化状态与今相较而验定。明治时代以前之日本亦为良证，而于此刻，中国之转变快速推进，令人诧异。

迷信发挥有害影响。其于人性深处植根。人类心智期稳厌惑，而迷信提供完备之运作理论。故有神话、史诗、传说、鬼怪故事，讲述虚构人物所致奇迹，深受先民喜爱，并使得遍世少年兴趣盎然。各已知现象已得解释，而科学破晓之前，迷信提供手段，满足好奇与求知而无须配以证据与证明。其给予似是而非之解释，恰合流行之观念。灵魂可行神迹易为接受，唯自然抽象之定律不易理解。故儿童与心智未全之人民，举例而言，理解灵魂使风吹动毫无困难，唯不能体认起风之科学说明。所有国家熟知造物之故事，唯要求一普通校长解释今日科学之宇宙起源，将为对教师能力之一项严重考验。若教师成功，学生将可觅得全然逾越其思维深度之经验。唯国家觉醒之先兆，总为不再迷信与真正宗教之改革所表明。

3. 思想之贫乏

前述境况之最重要结果，乃思想之荒芜。不论何时何地，人民陷于停滞状态，思考不再为其人生之重要目的，除非涉及日常事务与工作。

有关人类堕落与社会停滞之怪事，乃受影响之人民对其命运确然无知。其通常甚感满意。对其而言，并无未解之题，诸物各得其所，而人人知晓一切事物。故无好奇以学，亦无好胜以行。较此无望之精神态度，世间并无他物更致瘫痪。绝大部分极落后之半野蛮人民维持此状态。

中印有甚多东方迷信，以说明于其周遭发生之各种事物。其虽对任何新发见易表欣赏，唯立即依旧时神话进行解释。其似无惊讶之能！故其不劳烦自身做任何探询。由神话与类比演绎，诸事易于解释。如中国人满足于称任何复杂动力为电力。于中世纪，奇迹为任何不可理喻事物之佳解。

4. 懈怠与漠然

于停滞之人群中生活，乃无穷常规之枯燥乏味。受教育者深埋于往日陈卷。蒙昧之人绝望劳作。通常独裁与压迫使举国愚氓，并鼓励人民不理会推动世界之力量。

人民顺从其命运，仅有考虑生活之时间。其于亚洲多数地方，任何时候皆漠不关心，进步之影响于当地尚未觅得出路，可见人类为至薄之薪如机器般劳作。除食与眠外，并无时间可行他事。一切所需别务于工作暂停时完成。苦工、苦工、无尽之苦工，夜以继日，直至大脑疲累。人类精神为肉体所枷，而男女仅为机器。劳作之分工，过度之竞争，新职之事务，及普遍之贫穷，皆促使人类可怖堕落至麻木不仁之状态。

随和之马来人仍于其乡村享受生活，其中停滞亦为绝对支配。吾等于兹可见另一形式之懈怠。其由安逸之满足而生，乃缺乏刺激而无从发展之结果。

生活中财富与成功对个人与国家同样危险。其若非造成自大与淡漠，则为国家衰退之多重缘由。罕有人能静承巨富，有成守财奴者，有挥霍无度者，而他人陷入冷漠状态，满足于享受生活中一切美好事物。对其而言，无须工作、思考或努力，而通常结果乃思维最终不能续作。除非此趋势已由适当教育纠正，经验表明如年轻国家海峡殖民地之富家儿童，总屈从于过剩财富之麻木不仁。不断运动乃生活与活力之条件。聚财将使轻松过活而无须劳作之人怠惰。

饭来张口使思维失去一切刺激。习惯即刻成形。静止之思维意味空虚与懈怠。当维持空虚成为习惯，将不易振作。故欲使此社群成人生发兴趣最为困难，其任自身人生随波逐流，更无努力，仅事平淡业务运作所需。此"今日事已足"何止为邪恶。丑陋之怒视，欲消解一切他人，乃该种生活之结果。除培养自私乐趣外，社群迟钝无感。感官与欲求之享乐构成唯一幸福。一切其他考量不得其所。由于自我之鸡毛蒜皮及其卑下趣味，于熊熊燃烧之自我外天地间并无要事。宇宙为一死寂之暗夜。

5. 柔弱

痛恨费力之活动，导致对休息之喜爱。惯于休息，造成对努力之反感。为名誉或他物奋斗至死，则较任何代价之和平似为不智。须对理想做新评估。

停滞如某种嗜睡症，对群众具镇定安眠之功效，导致其不愿付出更大努力。无物扰动情绪。诸事由得失之冷血计算而推演。其为极端唯物主义。

大恶搅乱和平。极不幸者，乃对个人之伤害。愿存平静。为和平，一切牺牲皆可付出！

该等人民自不好战。以不能自卫，其不得已臣服于所有屈辱。今爪哇人处此不幸状况。中国人与印度人直至晚近并未更佳。

其自各种苦难退缩，并尝试以任何代价逃避。其忍耐慢性压迫与奴役。其已丧失每一自然生命之火，并甚至已忘却自卫之先天本能。故印度人甚至惧于回敬以最野蛮之攻击，除非其有机会于暗中刺杀。

亚洲人多受不抵抗与利他学说之影响。正如基督教据说已使野蛮条顿人更为温和并失其野性。佛教同样须为全体人民之柔弱负责，彼于佛陀大爱之控制下，热爱侵略者与无底线之人，对敌友一视同仁，而无论何等残酷不公，行无限制之不抵抗。

佛教弟子与基督徒固实温顺于不义与迫害，此因其确信敌人将受之惩罚，较其自身所能施者为多。唯然，自然偏好斗争之原则。未能为其权利备战者，必屈服于入侵、压迫与奴役。无论何者引致停滞状态，柔弱为其恒定特征。罗马征服之后，斯于希腊人中显见。其乃诸多民族积弱之由。

6. 道德之堕落

作为先决条件长期运作之必然结果，道德普遍堕落。道德品性松弛。于控制反社会倾向及加强公义需求之一切努力中，懈怠盛行，可见国家之柔弱。

妥协得以容忍。接受权宜以作奸恶之借口。社会生活与国家淡漠同一水准。

处此社会之人不做牺牲。其注视骇人听闻之邪恶、卑劣与不义，颇为无感。仅留意保有其世俗财产之完整，将纵容权势之恶，并将屈从于极耻之辱。其人不期望自由，实不能领会其益处。

三、国家停滞之缘由

就综合造成国家衰退之诸多缘由，仅可能做甚简之揭示。

1. 衰竭。经无数原因如战争、瘟疫、专制、恶政等，国家以死亡或移民而失其刚毅之气。国家衰竭与贫穷密不可分。最劣形式之停滞通常乃其结局。

2. 孤立。地理位置时而揭示国家进步之乏。以其明显，无须详述。

3. 傲慢。据察，自远古以来长期和平与繁荣均随之以堕落与衰退。人民或因自给自足，或如德人之例，过度自大而开始忽略维持其声望所需。其呶呶不休，而借一恰当俗语，乃"贪多嚼不烂"。一方面，其将自内腐坏；另一方面，其将受外力所扰。

4. 言语障碍。一门困难与异乎寻常之语言，无疑为进步之大碍，除非人民创设学问与科学之新中心。

中国人、俄国人、日本人及印度人于追随西方文明之伟大进展时，颇为不利。而于西方，观念交流乃为简捷，东方人民发见移译科技语为白话，几成不可逾越之障碍。俄国人迫于科学探索自如使用法语及德语，直至其于自身中建立科学。日本人所为亦复如是。中国人与印度人迅速采纳英文为第二标准语言，以此克服障碍。唯至科学依文化之本土元素教化时，方有一切伟大民族之真正进步。

5. 内部纷争。持续内斗之影响，固为衰竭。故此缘由，适足可附于此标题之下。唯历史表明，国内纷争如何常致国家进步瘫痪与外国入侵，有充分理由认为人民领袖之分裂为停滞之潜在原因。一瞥可见，国家危机之时，仅因内战颇有可能至于险境，如大英帝国面对大战之当前景况。虽大英帝国或称正处健壮有力之顶峰，唯国内争端之爆发何等致命。希腊人相残之战争摧毁希腊城邦。中原内战一再为外敌之征服铺路。

最有益之教训或为条顿人民之历史所献。其长期互斗，并成为杀戮自身部族之佣兵。几至拿破仑战争时代，不计俄罗斯与土耳其，德国乃欧洲最落后之国。一旦达致一统，尤于1871年后，日耳曼城邦各自及全体实现世界所曾见之最大进步。

6. 教育之缺陷与适当科教之缺乏。纵贯每一时代，教育之缺陷固为停滞之因。欧洲中世纪呈现最瞩目之图景。于陈腐封建制度上，并经最困难与最强势之语言工具，日本之疾速崛起全数归功于现代科学之引介。德国今日于和平与战时每一方面处难以克抑之地位，皆因国家教育与科学组织作为国家强大之手段所致。

7. 宗教之影响。宗教于人类发展担纲不寻常之功用。呜呼，唯于其衰退之时，亦造成进步之妨碍。世界史乃此宏大主题之痛苦注释。就人类进步而言，宗教甚为必要。

61

8.民族之因素。社会风俗与民族习惯或颇为思维与理念之成见，若无非常之动荡，进步则无可能。法国革命乃为欧洲民主辟路之雷鸣。

印度、中国等古老国家，种姓、传统及固定观念使庞大社群墨守成规，罔顾欧洲之伟大进步及优越，陈于有眼能视者之前！

若仅以语言之麻烦相较，该等民族因素更为重要。因其渗入思绪与情感最幽隐之处。

9.恶性之循环。构成国家衰退趋势之实在境况，能加剧一切情势，促进停滞之心理、伦理及政治特征。下降过程一旦启动，则飞速推进。因大众无知、无力及无财，患上丑陋社会及不洁之恶，摧残国家命脉。当全民进一步为暴政及外国枷锁所压迫，其或处于最卑微之境地。

10.放荡。一切国家堕落时代显然忽视道德束缚。此见于古巴比伦及古罗马。同样发见亦适用于现代国家及人民。

经历道德堕落之社会，其人民并非更为邪恶，唯其漠视伦理之需，并炫示其薄弱之处。此松弛产生助长荒淫无度及纵欲狂欢之氛围，损耗任何国家之气力。漠对其邻之意见，可致其轻视正派，不存任何形式之任何约束。人类常陷入自大之淤沼，并溺于懒惰无能之泥潭，木然以对一切激发精神之冲动，唯耽于麻醉种族尊贵感性之乐趣。

世上任何民族于任何时期最伟大之进步，无疑总由至高道德愿力所励之人民完成，并由高尚宗教动机维持。反之，忽视道德乃灾毁之必然先声。就此问题，认同一切宗教，并于此牢固基础上，人类所有冲突信念应以宣传为天国之基。

正义擢升国家乃老生常谈，彼每为单纯物质成就所蛊惑，尤与成功征战之荣耀及胜利结合时。此为德国之情形。虽比利时人暂时见逐于其家园，吾等无须犹豫，可信侵略者之恶行将迟早报于其身。世上存有道德良知。终有一日，悔恨甚至将使条顿人放弃暴力。任何情况下，愤怒民族之正义尊严将为上帝不可战胜之武器，实现公义之律法，以防蛮力奴役温顺者。故如旧日狂妄野心逾越自身，而曾经自豪与威武之条顿人，将为其恶行引致之力所粉碎，并确将于大战后为停滞后果所困，因一切物质、道德及心理缘故已得引证，除非其 [①] 领袖摒弃驱其永劫不复之恶念。

四、补救

全部疑难在于文明动力之问题。今欲用此譬于其解决方案，吾等可称宗教、哲学及科学须发见能施何种反作用力，并使多种多样之激励影响甚大，以行使于最有益人类之合力方向。

主要困难在于人非纯粹机器。各人于遗传、传统及环境所加之惯性下劳作。人心为纠葛所限，充斥致命之危险，更甚于战场。

对恶行、毒害及痛苦之宽容，乃上天之慈礼，否则此世将倍惨于地狱。不幸此特质，其习性如此速成，常对任何补救之施行予以实际之抵抗。

有人深陷蒙昧，且受道德冷漠之麻醉，仅能由持续努力振作之，经教育及宗教方式，灌输新精神予青年。数百年之功，非数月或甚至数年所能抵消。"罗马实非于一日建成。"

于数百年停滞中唤起一民族，并欲治愈于社会人心自身所产生之一切恶果，非仅由一场革命所能达成，无论其如何恐怖及如何血腥。此类激荡，仅耕作之人所从事森林清理可资比对。伐倒树木，整座废林须纵之以火，尽管如此，种植工作几未开始。一场革命所得，无可再多。自巴士底狱风暴至今之法国史证乎此，而中国革命颇足怪也，将于吾等眼前，重复无情命运之相同讽刺及相同悲剧。

每一宗教及哲学系统已宣告救赎之道。唯似人民保持顽固，

---

① 原文为 thir，疑误，应为 their。——译者注

并不易打动。

吾等实须应对青年。须清扫一切成障碍之丛木或森林。须于不毛之地培育一新文化。该法则显然适用于精神与物质世界。

无论何人，欲植何物，而忘剔除杂草与不受欢迎之林木残枝，结果多为无可弥补之损失，因最终将无可栽种，唯存次等之丛林。

故教育须彻底。其执行须始终如一，坚持到底。过往一切事物不得妨其发展。此于日本已达不可思议之程度。

个人采信何种宗教并无关系。于各虔诚奉行之宗教影响下，人类已得进步。唯惜当宗教仅为遮掩，而无实质之时，无论何种宗教，停滞无可避免。愿布道者不负教诲及理想，将获诚实者之尊崇，并定将行善于社群。

需觉醒者，须预备治疗。

创新精神乃为大要。正是其提供凝聚力并确保功成。政府须引导此新力量并通过教育予以精心培养。人民之品性须如是，与常变相谐，为改动之环境所需；或换言之，人民愿改变其习俗并使自身适应生活之新环境。故吾等见中日间之矛盾，二有力民族对西方文明影响之反应不同。于中国，不至史无前例之事件、生发国民新精神与新气质以振奋国家，则人民仍如狮身人面之像，欧美于神智各方面之冲击，如波浪自海岸顽石无功而返。

国家如同个人，须有生活之目标。其珍视若干理想，不惜任何代价，以此立志。有时其为军事统帅所驱遣，如马其顿之亚历山大，及拿破仑大帝。如出一辙，人民说服自身，于极度虚荣有所成就。英雄崇拜乃人类心理之一项强力要素，因而每次进步以主导者命名。故革新者与领导人须转化迟钝者，而为反抗一切恶劣影响，其仅能期以殉道为报。直至利他主义养成愿为改良同胞而献身者，国家停滞将有望让位于进步与行动。

该等一般原则若用于具体案例，则更为易晓。

无人能否认，不特吾等一社群存停滞与退化之症状。岂不见人民随人生漂泊，未有希冀，并无志向？宗教之影响或属欠缺，或仅皮相！教育仅助使笼罩之黑暗更为明显。缺乏活力。精神如未死去，亦属麻痹。大众之理想为何？

此麻痹状况是否全因情势？

唯该等社群须对青年进行良好教育。教育须使其成男子汉，而非仅为书呆子。心、智及手①，汝等可称三 H，须受训至心灵与正确者、美丽者、纯粹者、高尚者相谐。

科学须提供自然之真实观点，并于其真实角度中，表明一切事物之关系。

而青年将怀生活之趣，并将以尽力推进人类利益为最高职责。清醒之乐观者将驱散蒙昧之黑暗，对未来之信念将促进满足。虔诚与爱国将驱动青年于职责之路前行，以自我牺牲为其追求之最高荣耀。宗教将成真实纽带，超拔人民升至天国。心智将保持警惕。奋斗不休，以求改良、进步与发展。

若人民真切觉醒，将随之以青年道德之复生与智力之敏锐。全社群将为公众福利而行动，而学校将增进知识并吸引世界各地之人民。

沉睡之社群，需以何物醒之？一曰宗教，二曰知识，三曰活力或毅力。其序须为得宜，且无之则不能得全体人类之普遍进步。

尽管表面体现财富与物质财产之光彩，英属马来亚人民中正生发一种停滞，如强力之石笋。人种于此混合，无论种族如何，急欲致富享乐，唯于此地营利者，当中甚少为其幸福而思虑劳作之人。进步潜移默化之影响，须予接纳。政府可经学校及他法行之。不管如何，斯土每一爱国子弟，固有义务贡献其力，无论何其微薄，扰动死水以赋其生命。先驱之子弟较其祖上种族之优良②品质，是否同样优秀甚或更佳？其熟悉基础英文，与吾等制度之智

---

① "三 H"指 heart、head、hand。——译者注

② 原文为 stirling，疑误，应为 sterling。——译者注

所能赋予者相同。唯其他更为重要之品质何如？耐心、品性、技巧、毅力、节俭、恒心等。呜呼哀哉，须坦承各方面应较其父辈优秀之人，因更佳社会地位与家庭财富增长，绝大多数情况下罕能与其先人相侔。其更为富裕，所受教育更佳：其讲究饮食，并为一切赏心乐事之出色鉴赏者。唯其丧失征服丛林及取胜武力世界之坚毅精神。其已于通行之文明中，巨饮喀耳刻①之药水。其为繁荣年代物质财富倾泻而下之结晶，将增强大众之顽固，终将阻隔真正进步及真实快乐之途。

各民族之后裔共处一船。其已呼吸相同臭气，并饮下相同魔酒。除非空气净化及施用解药，则将不得解脱。而英国、荷兰、葡萄牙、中国、阿拉伯、马来、印度或犹太之儿童，仅能于较友好之地，获暂时庇护与避难所而逃离魔法！知文明背后之力摇摆不定，吾等自应采取该等必要之预防措施，以备国家或其他情形或然之需。于物质甚为繁荣之时代，教师与哲人须警诫群众，安逸与财富所予人萎靡之影响。而于萧条、衰退或停滞时期，人民须持续为原始直觉与理智之恒久吸引而奋起。政府应以人人受训为发展中国家公民之方式，组织并管控国家之教育；并将于家庭与学校，唤起充分及强烈之责任感与求知欲。

愿吾等境内，义务养育后代之父母，确保其青年围绕于所有该等影响，斯乃树立高贵品格之助，维系自由职责与忠诚之精神，及生发勇武之冲动，以维护正义，并不特为其自身，更为世界而奋斗。吾谨重申，宗教、教育与公众精神为创造文明之力。大战使现代文明受严酷考验。甚至于马来亚之边僻，吾等当感此绝大冲突之回荡。而若该等肉身之苦难与精神之癫痫，不能全数唤起吾辈履其顺天应人之职，则吾等道义与精神必死。

---

① 喀耳刻，Circean，《奥德赛》中之魅惑妖女。——译者注

战时讲演与随笔集
（1914—1917）

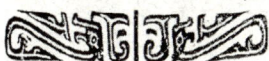

七

自我牺牲

对国王爱德华七世医学院学生讲演之主要内容

先生们：

当受邀对贵社团讲演时，吾觉份内有责贡献于汝等之系列活动。唯吾颇知，就不特自身有趣亦有益于此恐怖时代之主题，吾几无时间与贵社团做充分之讨论。吾之选题，于此世界史之关键时刻尤为重要，唯对预备从事医疗职业之人，就医学伦理所谈论甚多却常受误解之话题而言，其亦可作为一项基本介绍。于医疗职业所认同之伦理准则中，确无纳入特别之行为规范。医学之基础乃恕道，任何其他道德准则亦复如是。依医疗职业最高理想而生，医疗人员须对自我牺牲之含义有清晰概念，并须抱决心，不豫不怨以履其全职。唯自我牺牲不特对医学生为一则有益问题，其于文明社会实不可少。士兵之生命，简直乃此美德之颂赞。因士兵为国家利益而献身。故勿以自我牺牲仅适于讲坛布告之道德主题。人生处处突发问题，其须于人我之间裁定。此为利益冲突之缩影。自我，抑或他人？突然，汝等将虑及有机自然之伟大法则：为生存而斗争。自然所教吾等何事？马尔萨斯许久之前建言，食物问题将为生物中瞩目竞争之关键。达尔文之进化研究表明，最激烈之争斗并非徒然，无数个体牺牲，唯最终民族、部落或种族存活。故借此意涵之曲解，超人哲学崛起。真正之德人，丢弃文明之陈腐道德准则，恕道、贞洁与慈悲之律法，以及对自我牺牲之坚持。超人于与道德懦夫及身体颓废者之竞争中存活。怜悯、仁慈及宽容乃堕落之属性。唯即使于德人冷酷纪律之准则中，要求人民自我牺牲以致胜。试想自 1914 年以来，大众遍掷其身于凡尔登固若金汤之要塞，及守卫者所作之牺牲，而汝等将知吾所提请思索之主题，具重要及引人之兴味。

于战争疮痍之凡尔登，汝等可研究自我牺牲哲学及伦理之全盘问题。吾等于彼有整幅自然图景。陷于狂暴之大批德人，以其全副摧毁之力，代表经动物学家悉心研究之动物世界，向吾等展现所有当前进化之观念及其推论：适者生存之学说。唯于要塞内，精神作用之运行，强于铁腕之暴力。其内，法人为国家、为文明及为人类牺牲自身。其外，德人实于炮口寻觅野心之妄想。故凡尔登可代表世界大战之缩微。毕竟新旧之间与动物及精神之间两股力量冲突之自身结果，将支配人类之生存，直至世界末日。于此世界史之图景中，宇宙进化论者注视于纷乱中走出之世界。随后而来者，乃生命形式无尽循环之系列景象，及灭绝不适者之可怖屠杀。最终人类登上舞台，而其渐废暴力规则，并以理性、同情及仁爱进行改造。帮助其族之虚弱病患，仁慈待敌。其经相同之社会冲动建立家庭、城市及邦国。至人类登场之前，适者与强者击败弱者，并无情掠夺其食物。于人类社会，一股新力自为显现。利他之理想渐成思维之推进力，而人类乐于为家庭和谐或社会进步之目的，牺牲自身之时间与欲望，乃甚早所见进步之首要品质。观察者径由人类至动物世界之全体动物对无助后代之母性本能，以及蚂蚁、蜜蜂、群居哺乳动物之社会习性，确可追踪此利他冲动。

故亦可表明，抑制个人之口胃或欲望，或前述代表另一事体之力，作为进化之果，已于斯世成长。于人类中，伦理训练与普

70

遍教育决定自我牺牲以何种方式践行。父母对其孩童之爱乃本能，并为自我牺牲最常见之缘由。以重要性言之，异性之爱与其并列，且与父母之爱存有某种晦涩关联，因性爱之全部现象，唯与种族繁衍及保存相关。若父母不愿为其孩童牺牲，人类家庭不能生存。且不常以此为美德，因其诚为一项纯粹之职责，唯大体于所有基本细节，其实乃自我牺牲。父母之影响与示范将决定孩童之性格。兄弟姐妹将能无私相处否？于家庭中，正是爱为最有希望起作用者；若于幼儿时未能实现，于商业社会便毫无可能。故儒者之家庭并肩而立，因人人受教为公益牺牲自我。当一人应先照顾自身利益之观念盛行时，甚无可能维持团结。而欲维持人类社会之团结，颇需某种程度之自我牺牲。自然直觉乃自我主张。每一未受训之儿童，如野兽或匈奴人，乃恃强凌弱者。此攻击性须由精神力量所驯。由理性、同情及仁爱引导，揭示真实品性。当前战争使人人深思国王与国家；而对国家之爱或爱国精神，仅为家庭兄弟般情谊之延展形式。若无自我牺牲，爱国毫无意义。人类知识发展伴随利他冲动之延展，即对自我之抑制。若家庭责任化为公民道德，后者扩充为爱国奋斗，则依次可进为对人类利益之热诚。

于人类精神攀升之每步，需增强自我牺牲。起初，汝等为父母及亲友牺牲自我。其有助汝等理解为何于必要情况下，为邻人而克己。随之而来为整个国家之主张。最终冲动不可抵抗，而爱众生与万物之天命得以实现。于该等考量中，吾等未思索自我牺牲可获之回报，因通常根本不做计算。当有人估算某种自我牺牲行为所付出，并合计将获之回报，则恐无所事事，或几无所成。人类之绝大多数记忆短暂，甚少回报人之善行，直至其葬身百年以后。唯欲解放自身之精神本能无可抑制。不公不义激奋人类精神跃升，并鼓舞英雄保卫无助之人与弱者。故此欧洲大战乃自由精神奋斗之结果。大不列颠与协约国代表精神力量，并因此已为可怜之比利时与塞尔维亚做出牺牲。若大不列颠漠然侧立，德人将摧毁其敌，而世界进步将受极大阻碍，未来英人是否境遇更佳？自我牺牲之话题，须持续引起青年注意。吾等东方盟友之岛屿帝国，乃世上最具爱国情操之国家。武士道风行，以儒家思想形式施于中世纪日本之封建所需。于其教诲之下，青年常受教深思仁爱、正义及荣誉之需，并于严肃家庭集会时实践，演练切腹之可怖行为。此事于今已属过往，唯其记忆于现代日本生活中熊熊燃烧，并一直鞭策民族迈向英勇刚强与自我牺牲之最高境界。故其于此骚乱与焦虑之恐怖时代，似将极利吾等。吾辈全体逐日尽力实践些微牺牲，直至克己之力变强，而个人预备为国家或人类之益献身。

结束之前，吾谨说明欲成为一名好医师，自我牺牲精神何等重要。除医界之外，并无其他职业要求专家承受生命危险而无特殊酬金，亦无须随时应召照料病患，未经事先安排，不计成本。或于一日辛劳后，汝正安坐，拟进晚餐。忽铃声大作，而召汝至六英里外之病患处。汝或已安排携家人赴剧院。该医师微微一笑并匆匆结束晚餐，可能并未食尽，便赶赴远方之病人，任家人自寻其路。瘟疫、霍乱及伤寒肆虐时，医生承受感染之极大风险，而不能预备冒险并做牺牲者，不会以医为业。针对感染，固应采取一切预防，唯医者仍须预备其生活每日之某种自我牺牲。病人须汝等放弃自身时间、愉悦、闲暇、睡眠及餐饭，而若汝等无耐性持续做不断牺牲，将或失去病人。故从医者须习自我牺牲之伦理，并付诸实践。此外，亦须应对其他从医者。某些愚蠢病人或荐于汝，而离开其原先之医生。汝若知实情，将明智拒受其空洞之恭维，并劝其跟随自身之医师。尤对青年而言，自身炫技之诱惑实属巨大。唯对惯做牺牲之人，不于邻人缺席时占其便宜，将仅为简单职责。如此应对汝等之业界同仁，汝等亦将预备为同志之利益与职业之荣光而做牺牲。

于今之时，不欲做某种程度之自我牺牲者，吾等以何称之？

唯醉鬼、财奴、孤僻者、卖国贼及懒骨头耳。

　　总而言之，吾等发见宗教、文化及自由之爱等所教诲，于人类道德提升之每一步，皆需自我牺牲。

战时讲演与随笔集
（1914—1917）

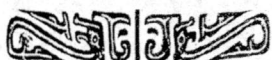

八

为何中国须对德宣战？

一封致黎元洪总统之公开信

中华民国支持和平与民主，希望加强与各国之友好关系。其自由与文明之理念乃建于既定社会道德真理之上，并经过往数千年历史之检验。其已建立，以维持民族之权利，机会均等与自由发展之宗教不受压迫及暴政之束缚。其维护正义范畴内人类正义与自由之神圣权利。其宣称道德律法之普遍，并声称将一切政治外交行动建基于恕道准则之上。其认同全能治者统领一切人类行为，故而赐予全体人类宗教自由。

于该等宣告与声明中，中华民国之目标，实与大不列颠、法国、美国及其盟国，所承担与德国及其同伙作战之希望与理念极为相似。大不列颠与法国代表世界民主政权，德奥则为力量与独裁之霸权而战。强权间之角力，实为民主自由与军国专制之争。弱小国家自由发展与独立政治存在之权利，将为协约国之胜利所保障；而德国之胜利，意味镇压所有受征服民族，以适德意志帝国一统之军事需要。若由德人过往于其殖民地所作所为，尤以其对有色及落后民族之举动以判断德意志帝国之精神，吾等或有把握认为德人之胜利将使所有非欧洲民族与部族，置于其严酷军事统治之下蒙受奴役。赫雷罗人与东非凄惨穆斯林之命运，当为亚洲人之警诫，彼或已听信德国鼓吹者之诡计。

中国人民有圣人尧舜至孔孟之言，指导其于此世界大战中本国所应持之态度。子曰："见义不为，无勇也。"中国伦理认同文明与人类社会之结合，而中国史亦有无数民族之例证为鉴，其因正义与自由之名发动战争，以维护弱小受欺民族之正当防卫。大英帝国与美国寻求参战不为私利。其为道德与精神考量所驱，为人类做出必要牺牲。中华民族面对同样考量之诉求。按中华民国之道德与政治理念，并无邦国可独存其身或置身事外，须与邻国合作以维护文明及人类进步。文明自身正受德人军国主义威胁。世上非法行为肆虐，德国领导之同盟国，漠视一切法律与惯例，擅自将其残忍霸道强加于一切国家，罔顾男子、妇女或儿童之生命财产。由殷切所需之吁求，并据动物生存之法则，德人凭借其军事机器及战备，宣称其为超人。其鲁莽罔顾一切君子协定，对老弱病伤之暴虐中并无同情与内疚。其对妇女之端庄亦未表任何尊重。强悍之德国民族及其违法盟友，一举堕入中古野蛮之深渊，而其已以超逾上古之野蛮肆意残毁，并不具借口或理由，如哥特人、汪达尔人、匈奴人、突厥人或蒙古人等野蛮部族为其凶猛过激行为所能申述之辩护。无望使德国政府恢复理性，其残暴攻击中立国，已迫使美国与其断绝外交关系，并最终向背信之条顿人宣战。中华民国亦受美国崇高范例之鼓舞，立即与该国断绝外交关系，彼已于世上文明人士中脸面无存。若外交之政治与道德因素全无问题，赋权总统批准国民期望，与德国断交，则中华民国不复有其他理由不得宣战，并予西方民主政权一切援助，此或存于中华之力量中。西方之争斗必持久而苦痛。其非以领土之胜果而定。其将仅因某一方或双方极度疲乏而终结。故于人性、正义与自由之甚大利害中，中华民国与文明人士共度患难极为重要，其牺牲一切物质利益，代表弱小国家以使文明遍布寰球。中华民国已做最佳外交行动，国家百年来力图截断与阴诡匈奴人之一切外交联系。今政府别无选择，唯有推进已发起运动之自然结局。

中国其弱之甚乎？由数千年来一流思想家之教诲，中华民国诚然熟知人民之实力不特依赖军备，更要者在人民之团结与爱国。因中华民国已舍弃过往之传统，并已于最古老专制之基础上建立民主政府，国中上下四方之民，热切期待重大决断，以知总统是否将决意与世上民主政权共进，并为自由与正义之缘由做出可能必要之牺牲。犹豫不决对国族之害将莫大焉。中华民国不得孤立于世界民主政权之外。其利益、理想、抱负与美国、法国、英国相同。其须合群，否则必于相残之纷争与外国难题及阴谋中消亡。专制政权蛰伏之要素仍在闷燃，并将随时迸发火焰。人民大众之教育与识见仍极落后。迷信仍为此国之极大诅咒。以一贯之故，民国政府须立即宣称深恶痛绝于德国罪行，并须与西方伟大民主国家之政府共度患难。

处此当前地位，颇为模棱两可之取态极具风险。断绝外交关系有何益处？德国政府对待中华政府之行径，乃愚弄与藐视。民国总统欲拯国家尊严，唯一途径乃要求参议院准许宣战。中华人民能予甚多襄助，以使德人尽快屈膝。有数百万人体格健康，可于任何战场战斗。数月内可训练百万人。且唯中国能立即协助派遣工匠与农工，无疑可解决如英国之食物问题。五万农工之于法国，同等人数之于英国，以及于一切行业成千上万其他劳工，将即刻解放英法相应数量之人手。中国有极多工匠，其为一切健全之人士，并无需过多训练，便可从事兵工厂之所有工作。

故就人力而言，中华民国能给予重大协助，若能迅捷及明智提供，将于更多而非单一方面发生效用。甚至于资金事宜，中华民国可于美国、日本及英国大行举债，以妥善落实对盟国之协助。今中国虽为贫国，唯潜有非常之财。而当妥善发展时，单凭殷切需要开发之工矿及农业资源，其必跻身于当世一流国家中。故当举世掷入大熔炉时，若国家欲维护其于未来伟大国家行列之地位，参战乃为必需。战后举世商业将为变更，因德人对欧洲文明国家之所作所为，须对德人于世界市场做出区别。后续将有贸易战争，将有社会阻隔。无论外交人员言行如何，战后及至少于吾辈世代，德人将为弃儿或贱民。中华民国须置身于伟大民主国家之列，因其作为独立民主政权生存之唯一机会，将完全倚赖法人及其盟国之胜利。

甚至本应知之更多者，尚且大声质问中国参战可能之获益。自经济与外交观点而言，易述中国可多方受益。唯物质利益之问题全非紧要。中国须独据正义决断。诚以儒家之明白准则，及如闻战争警钟之孟子言辞，亚洲民主第一国为道德理想之完满，须准备履行儒家自我牺牲与自我奉献之理想。中国圣人岂不曰"志士仁人，无求生以害仁，有杀身以成仁"？鉴于德国政府对人类之大恶，就其不特对交战国，亦对中立国于陆海同时所犯之可怖罪行，中华民国须应国民之抗议做出确定之声明。中华民国应决定就此道德事体全力参战。中国对德宣战妥否？能得何益或须做何牺牲，纯属次要，并不得遮盖所作抗议之真实目的。于道德缘由内，无益之动机须置于一旁，并须全盘驳回。为文明之故，中国须挺身预备承受至苦。斯为中国古宗教之诲示。此乃伟大盟国之信念，以巨大力量，自专制与暴政之梦魇中解救世界。此诚为向世界表明之机会，即中国未蒙恰当之理解，而其人民于一切重要事务总受道德考量所励。亦甚适当者，中国人应协力推翻德皇之黩武政治，因其残忍及肆意漠视人类情感与人类权利，北方之中国人已有痛苦经历。

子岂不云："四海之内，皆兄弟也。……有教无类。……道之以德，齐之以礼。"恶人须受惩罚。德人及其援军为人类之敌，须恢复理智。而中国为世上最古老之文明，须全力对大不列颠、法国、俄国及美国施以任何可能之影响。若中国政要考虑此绝大之国际问题时，能摒弃一切物质与经济事宜，固为最佳。唯易揭示者，完全为正义与自由缘故采取立场之明智决定，不特甚为正确，自各观点而言亦属有益。应无犹豫。人类本性之自然提升，上天声音之回响，召唤中华伟大民主政权向残酷、无信及狡诈之德人宣战，彼已践踏一切法律与条约，并已漠视两千年来宗教、伦理与人性于人类社会所建树之一切良善。中国人已于相当程度承受如同德人对无害及不幸之比利时人所造成之一切恐怖与屈辱，彼等已英勇守卫其家园，几无胜算。中华民国作为自由独立之国家，具诸项义务以挺身协助比利时人及其盟国，以使和平于公义之稳固基础上迅速恢复。

［补记：自上文付印后，中国亦已经历另一场革命，受德人所鼓动恢复帝国之尝试，已适时扼杀于萌芽。而新共和政府已向奥匈帝国及德国宣战。］

战时讲演与随笔集
（1914—1917）

九

海峡华人之前景

于马六甲华人文化协会之讲演

主席与诸位先生：

令秘书精力充沛，置其锐目于吾身多时。故今晚吾终为其坚请之牺牲者。近来吾须参与诸多事务，故对诸君为此讲演不惮一切烦劳所做之安排，实无言说可以为报。

吾望其将成引发汝等全体兴趣之一则话题，唯吾发觉对彼之处理，较乍看之下更为棘手。唯以汝等迁就，吾将冒险向诸君陈说未来吾等具前途社群之展望，并简介作为生命体而运作之吾等社会，以何方向为吾等利益施以影响。望汝等能宽宥直言不讳，及就前方可能风险之任何警诫。

社会工作

自社会立场而言，吾等认同维持健康乃一大困扰之问题。而除非身体健康，占有过多财产仅为悲惨与苦恼之源。作为社群，吾等须唤起社会意识此邪恶趋势之存在，彼不特破坏当世且亦来世之健康。鸦片或酒精之麻醉为恒久之难题。问题在乎堕落与恶疾伴生之邪，如瘟疫蔓延，于危害健康与精神方面之效果同等致命。民族之体格正在恶化。吾辈面对影响婚姻之复杂问题。吾辈

85

须解决脆弱而重要之问题，斯有关吾等妇女同胞自由及教育。吾辈亦不得忘怀更高生活审美之价值与影响。艺术、音乐及体育于未来须受充分注意。

宗教问题

亦有宗教问题。有嘲笑迷信之趋势，正如半受教育之罗马人所常为。唯吾等多数人所受不完善之英文教育，乃极不可靠之引导。甚多智慧存于老旧做派，而于吾等实能提供更佳替代之前，令人民相信精神之不朽与长存更为稳妥。该信仰为全部孝道教义之基础。而若干欧洲最佳之头脑，如斯特德先生、奥利弗·洛奇爵士、威廉·克鲁克斯爵士、萨利比医生与莫里斯·梅特林克先生①，以及其他精神世界之奥妙见解，以不同凡响之方式，终似实证所谓东方之迷信。

职是之故，吾信仰儒教。其教诲于一切事物之适度与敬畏，并谆谆劝导以利他为正义、公道及人性之基，不应于此过渡期忘之。其教导吾等顺天应人及吾辈自身之职。其指出完人之伟大理想供万众跟随，亦提供合理与实用之伦理统系。

教育

唯于诸事之先，儒家思想注重个人之妥善教育。其敦促吾等须分辨纯然指令与教育。以事实"填充"青年之头脑，绝非教育。真正之教育须触动全人。良知良能须予激活，而浑身上下须予转化。

唯独文化于今并不足够。于某些有益艺术须做充分训练，并须使吾等之青年知悉老规矩已不"够好"，而现代之需引致研究精密科学，及事物与机械过程一手知识之延展。

于此激烈商业竞争之日，吾等皆正成为物质主义者，并常遗

---

① 原文为 Dr. Saleeby M. Maeterlinck，疑为 C. W. Saleeby 与 Maurice Maeterlinck。如是，则缺一逗号。——译者注

忘古中国之教育观点仍然有效，即教育之主要价值乃获克己之艺术。吾等动辄需索甚多指令，或事实之纯粹知识，而忽略教育之真正品质。多年来，专家每言须学德国，以此运作吾等之教育。吾等已见于比利时、法国及波兰毁坏地区中，单向物质教育之苦果。世界震惊于其庞然自大与不合理性，且不言德国之野蛮。一切均来自伦理与教育之分离，及自私运用科学方法以做野蛮征服计划。自颇为不同之立场，吾等须以疑虑视未来世代相似教育路线之成效。应以何理想置于吾等孩童之前？以何方法供其估量事物与人类行为之根本价值？

现存之恶

唯教育如药物，当应吾等之需而开立。于量充足，并于类妥当。如中国谚语所云"搔不着痒处"，则近于无用。适当之教育须杜绝一切不可取之事，并植入使生命振奋及高尚之物。

蒙昧或以不实之冀望及瞬息之福分鼓动吾等。唯实永无明智之人能建空中楼阁。若现存之恶不得补救，而吾等闭眼不见，可能暂未受损，唯将如德人所为，仅享乐于愚者之天堂，而幻灭迅即将至。故无论如何，须引入健全而平实之教育，俾全体海峡华人男女伸手可及。

常闻父母及丈夫向政府疯狂吁请，助其制止妇女赌博。吾等听闻赌博猖獗。人人诚须知晓，若不诉诸极严苛之措施，并无政府能绝对制止一切赌博。因赌徒常能回本，赌博之要害不甚为金钱之损失，而在于养成"消磨"时间之恶习，及生发一种精神态度，对道德与文明之最高利益颇为致命。如同一切恶习，赌博奴役其迷恋者，导致自私、"伶俐"及狡诈。故精神习惯可颠覆人类所有一流文化。

显然海峡华人自身，不能维持如中国人通常所为之协调及合作。或常为"主厨"过多，因其领袖有冲突之理念，并以疑妒看待他人。

有经验者言吾等缺乏公众精神。斯为一项公允之观察，而吾等须承认其乃社会环境遗传之特征，甚至今日领袖以之洗劫人民，如于中国。唯每一海峡生人认知自由公民之职乃视海峡利益如己身，正其时也。而其若求享和平与自由之权利，则要调试自身，乐于承担市民之责任与负荷。

吾等之失败，何等程度归因于热带环境，不易裁断。吾等目睹周遭马来人民处朴实之喜乐。吾等是否继承马来先辈某种物事，反对艰巨持续之努力工作？此与作为一民族之中国人，有绝大区别。如孟德尔所表明之遗传法则，揭示个体之返祖重现，肖似一位或其他先人。斯为每一海峡家庭所面对之现象。吾等不得闭目不见其存在。吾等须信任一有效训练体系，其中教师个人之注意可给予特殊高等学校之每一儿童个人，以救正儿童个性之异常情形。普通学校对该等儿童无效，甚或有害。该等男童逃学，反叛一切威权，并颇安于复归马来环境与习俗。其为自然之孩童，不喜文明及规例之束缚。其并无野心。其为挥霍之人，并如麻雀，不愿工作，亦无烦忧。对其而言，现有之物已十分充足。于旧式严厉儒教家训之下，吾以为社会趋向更受习俗力量之顺利压制，而儿童经频繁之重复，取信于旧风俗之神圣，并尽力维护上古共产主义所残存者。唯于当前条件下，该等人士表露典型并受个人主义鼓动之烦躁不安，而个人主义已满渗现代欧洲之思想与制度。

作为社会单元之生活完全缺失。社群仅间歇以行。于社团内，吾等实见若干为社会目的而组织之尝试；唯吾等须承认，许多社团之影响，整体而言并非有益。海峡英籍华人公会努力负责，将极有助于整体社群之进步。

就经济而言，吾等海峡华人群众之前景实为黯淡。唯恐许多海峡华人就此或视吾浅见为现代卡珊德拉之狂言，因丑陋之现实常受憎恶。吾不特指若干富裕家庭，而乃市镇中为生活而工作之商户职员或雇员等大众。吾以沉重心情见证某地一度繁荣之社群。25 年前曾有活跃之商行。今其已处衰亡末路，而许多已告消失。该等商人之子弟多数受雇为律师、大进口商行或市政之职员。其庞大种植园已受忽略。农场主与经理已开启新关注点，或成为华商于海峡土生之子，或将其市场份额减至微不足道之比例。作为商人，吾等并不成功。除少数例外，海峡华人未能展现"照料生意"之天资，而若高利贷适可称为生意，颇有如"仄迪人"（贷款者）之成功者。唯于马六甲及槟榔州，其作为贸易商较为成功。而吾等须努力制止遍于全国之自毁政策，其使吾等之青年仅为商业之机器。所至要者，乃将青年自支配彼等之萎靡中唤起，并激发吾等青年之想象，热切审视商农矿业所需之尽责努力。吾等青年所受之学校训练，无疑欲其接纳看似理想商贸职员之生活：固定工作，固定时段，如同于学校之固定假期，无忧无虑之固定酬劳，下班之后无责任，夜晚无事且为欢！较之大多数昼夜忙碌、并无假期、航海探险常涉危难之中国商人而言，不知何等人生。吾确认于此特定地点，正是如此比照，驱使几乎一代农商子弟回归市镇账房或为政府服务，常平白放弃其察觉需过于费力维持之生意。

过往之回顾

吾虽绝非悲观者，亦不察赞颂过往者有任何过度之缺陷，唯严峻事实为顽固之物，社会进步之学生对此固应理解，若其急于找寻最佳方法，以解决妨碍社会进步之困难险阻。对英属马来亚华人于工业及社会发展之非常成就，一项匆促之调查表明，华人移民者自古素为耐心坚韧之工人，预备至为费劲之努力，并愿承担天气、岗位或环境可能所需之逐项风险。多数伟大商人已获得形成贸易之人物、地点与事物之第一手资料。彼等多数广为旅行，并拥各地所需之精辟知识。其于贸易往来中，均有高度荣誉感与正直感。而时至吾等之日，于马来亚全境内，华人言语之信用与其契约相等，实更优于今之烦冗及常显愚笨之证券，其上附有各位商人之签名。而过往世代之人，生活简约，且颇愿于各方面协助他人。华人社群之一项显著功能，乃每独凭德能，提携人自极贫极微之地位至显赫富裕。该事实予新来者极大鼓舞，并使其成满足及稳定之工人，因其感知热诚终将得报。

若以吾等今日之地位，与先辈或一般华人所处情形相较，吾等对自身之不满甚多。与其相较，吾等似为更劣，荷属东印度之峇峇蔑称其为"新客"。

由于普遍之蒙昧，保守狭隘之心灵，及天生卖弄与推脱工作之倾向，吾等未能善用置诸门口之机遇。陌生者似正升至高位，而吾等必缓缓沉沦！

所幸该等国民之弊，庶几可以补救。而吾等望将有真切之努力，以清除舛错，并将处处保证有利之地位。

吾实希望引领汝等至于某种精神上尼波山之高度，海峡华人可自此于该等富裕蓬勃之地区，见证未来繁荣喜乐之应许之地。吾等似见前路于短途内引向分歧：一条正确、狭窄、艰难之路通往全面辉煌；而另一条大道易坠入衰退之渊。

吾等颇似远东不同国家犹太人之政治状况。吾等人种为华人，唯自政治观点而言，马来群岛与印度马来半岛之土生华人，乃属包括荷兰在内之欧洲列强之子民。海峡出生之华人、荷属东印度之马来华人与严格意义上之中国人之间，存巨大且深刻之区别。吾等可宣称大英帝国之直接利益，不特依出生地之优势，由于正如德人发动战争后所表明之态度，此点将毫无意义；更因英格兰之理想及大不列颠之政治抱负，其以共同忠诚及共同语言之纽带，团结吾等及帝国其他人民，全然未计大战后必将到来之更为庞大之经贸关系。作为一个民族，今吾等依附大英帝国，无可分割。其利益即属吾等，其敌亦属吾等，而吾等当[①]奋勇慷慨承担，以

---

① 原文为 shonld，疑误，应为 should。——译者注

全力承其绝大之负担，斯乃大不列颠及海外领地颇欲乐受者。故吾以为吾等作为一项部件，不论于帝国中如何细微，可达致全面之解放，亦为值得英国赌上一切而获得自由与正义之一分子。于此国史之危机中，吾等乃适于受托以保卫帝国艰巨任务之人，并预备牺牲一切，如同吾皇广袤领土之各地其他人士。陛下之王国于斯地土生之民，将享欧人之同权，此日必将到来。吾等要求甚少，或至全无，唯宁符儒家之高标，因功绩获得承认之权利，而最终真理及正义必将得胜。

吾个人颇为自信，卓杰之领袖将于吾等民众中崛起，引领其于正道，以使吾等子弟踊跃，并续为同等喜乐、忠诚与繁荣之社群，而吾皇及大不列颠诸民族将引以为豪，列之于辉煌帝国众多成员之中。

战时讲演与随笔集
（1914—1917）

十

和平之探寻

人人须承认教皇之职乃擎教会之帜，并尽力于战斗之喧嚣中，使其微弱之声得闻。唯对梵蒂冈之和平讯息不特由教会利他精神所鼓动之疑虑，颇难隐藏。措辞如此，实似泄露匈奴人嘈杂之声。协约国为"道德力量"与"公海自由"而战，而若梵蒂冈切望"维护"正义，已发往所有交战国之该等观察，本应致送德皇，其乃负责战争中一切血腥恐怖之当事者。若基督教原则或平常伦理准则，对德皇及其军事党羽有任何影响，则今日超过敌对国影响范围之一切国家，便不会因战争而对德人高度憎恶。吾等颇能明察，德人于今所惧者，乃"战后之战"。故其甚为渴望仁慈与持久之和平，以恢复现状，因已全然发见泛日耳曼计划无可实行及无法实现，除非大胜协约国，斯乃今时不可能达致者，仅存于最狂野之德国幻梦中。教皇干预之时，乃常言所说压断骆驼脊背之最后一根稻草。于此情形之下，不可期望协约国热切接纳日耳曼主义之恶魔。梵蒂冈须充分意识此严重情由，斯迫使威尔逊博士领导之美国勉强对德宣战。世上最为和平之人民——暹罗人与中国人距实际战场甚远，亦已感知与协约国同患难之必要。能否想象若未意识与作为世界强权之德国维持永久和平实属徒劳，该等新老国度任意对德宣战？

威尔逊博士力图拯救美国于战争之苦痛史，精妙展现人类依赖道德正义，而非武力维护公义主张之绝望。中国与暹罗亦于过往苦痛经历得知，不欲守其荣誉之国，于强权之前实无权利，彼等唯知物质利益与优越武力之主张。协约国之希望，乃能斩杀物质主义与自私之恶龙，使正义于各国议会中充分挥洒，可能确保小国与无军备国家之自由与正义。若德人仍未得救赎，持续当权，则教皇之善意将对世界毫无影响。

历史已重复证明人类社会由个人组成，乃彼等性格之反映。于人类事务之施行中，无论公私，若自利仍发挥重大影响，弱小国家与更强政权存在任何重大意见分歧时，仅依靠正义乃属枉然。有关商业利益或政治权利之争端，强国对无军备国家所做让步，能至几何？强国人民自愿放弃可经武力强加于弱小或无防卫能力国家之主张，并无充分保障。某特定事件之正义，可易由最受称许及最为爱国之观点阐释，将使政府采纳媒体及政治团体所反映一般民众之观点，并自担风险。直至当前战争之爆发，国际法仅为理论存在，而当德人启动反文明之战，干脆将其完全抛开。若忍耐与两相情愿可裁断^①事端，而海牙法庭并无实务机构执行司法判决，发自该等法庭之道德制裁必为空文，并受德人公然无耻之漠视。

若协约国之目的乃实现永久和平之战果，获胜之协约国自身须组建国联，以维护自由公义之主张，固甚明也。最可行之法，乃该联盟将维持一段时间如约 20 年，其时协约国可考虑是否敌国得以平等条件加入。应树立之要点，非在裁军，而在摧毁军国主义精神，斯乃恶魔之化身。作为对文明残忍施暴之罚，同盟国应不得保留军队，除非为警察之目的所需。而协约国可通过安排，决定各国家应保留之武力，以作为国际之警察，推行各国议会之决定。该方案固遍布困难，并含无数缺陷，故于颇疑其为虔诚意见之外，也疑其于现实政治之领域能有机会看见曙光。另外，无超级强权之指引与威权，及充足武力之后援，于世上争斗之各国间维持和平并无希望。彼等皆满怀妒忌与习癖，各自渴望智取他

---

① 原文为 adjucated，疑误，应为 adjudicated。——译者注

者，并攫取可能之最大利益。教会已未能使人类依照伦理及宗教原则调节生活。人类仍存甚多野兽习性，纯由苍穹之星引导其路向。正如每一社群内，需警察维护和平及秩序，故对未来数代人而言甚明，欲防如德人对文明所造成之大祸，国际警察不可或缺。

协约国已加入圣战，反对恶名昭彰之暴政与野蛮。其应以正义、自由与律法之名持续联盟。若各国代表依平等条件会谈，并悉知其须以人类整体普遍利益之公义考量为引领，则有理由希望该试验可获显著成功。

大战已为世界揭开和平新时代。若非如此，各国所作一切牺牲将为徒劳。唯人类于思想方面将须悉知要害事体，并施各项可能之宣传手段，使路人重视所涉之道德问题。若民主政权欲使世间政府感知其力，每一民主国家之个人须能理会于人类进程中，所呼唤解决精神与道德问题之本质。

于有利于谈论和平条件之前，须认识所呼唤解决问题之本质。当前之停战使文明世界充斥骇人之危险，除非德国军力破败，及德人已意识其误并感悔其罪。德人颇为一致称其信仰以强凌弱之权利，若非惨败，并无事物可使军国主义之受害者信服，现实中有更为高美之世界，而非为生存做暴力争斗之竞技场，弱者于兹须得碰壁。基督教逾千年之宣传，未能使条顿人深知文明奥妙之精神洞见，斯使法英两国如此特别突出。实可驱人动问"豹能变其斑否"？

若文明世界未能使德人改其对社会之道德心态，如无强力后盾，将无和平。对付孩童与野人，终极之求助每为棍棒，斯乃致伤之物，并使粗暴感以足够强度由某些敏感部位接收。协约国颇无可能信任德国政客，彼每考虑其身其国之利，表明其无德依善意行事。欺诈、阴谋及叛变将诉诸每一可能之途。正派者于此氛围无可作为。正义要求惩罚该等人士之罪行。与其商讨任何和平条件，乃为癫狂。故依一般原则，须觅得协约国略存信心以打交道之人士。而该等人士须由德人自行觅得。若其信任德皇及文明之巨蠹，战争须持续甚久，因再次托付世界未来予无信国家"一纸具文"之保证，将属不智。

有关世界民主政权可接受之条件，协约国列强已以明白无误之语言，清晰阐述。而德人每进一步之可怖经历，仅是确认其为破坏与掠夺之罪行做充足补偿，并对未来做有效保证之必要。比利时事件凸显，并无需任何讨论。即使德人于其清醒时分，当同意贝特曼·霍尔维格先生所言，即德国对一伟大国家犯下大罪，彼唯一过错乃阻挡日尔曼扩张之路，斯与国际法之令及各国既有权利截然相反。包括美国之西方伟大国家，已矢言比利时须复兴，并尽可能复原及获偿。北法之大肆毁坏，与文明冲突之制裁相反，要求大量之赔偿。于防范未来摩擦与误解之中，乃国家与民族之疑问。所涉问题之性质影响深远。于任何努力探寻复杂缠绕问题之可行方案中，需各方面之诚意。美国可将内战作为先例，冒一切风险，代表受奴隶般役使及对待之后进卑屈人民，能于适当条件下应对文明渐进之环境。欧亚弱小国家均已类同，并高度组织。一旦脱于残酷商业主义之暴政，及自私民族主义之迷醉，其独立易得强国司法指引之保护。强国须永久放弃帝国之贪婪，并须准备为人类整体利益承担托管者之角色。

大战之恐怖与苦难，已使文明人士深刻意识人类家庭之真正团结与基本一统。地理区域之政治分隔，不论相关人民之意愿，已成烦恼不安之多产源泉。人类思维对束缚及压迫之自然反应，已引致残酷迫害及镇压措施，彼等仅助于种族间之仇怨，并渐增本为近亲民族间之忌恨。而勇对现实之际，当世仍几未预备实现人类自由之民主理念，甚明也。芬兰人、蒙古人、哥萨克人及其他各种部族组成俄罗斯帝国之庞大人口，俄国是否全面预备就其意愿自由行动？奥地利如何免于分离与肢解？唯或瑞士之例，及大英帝国与美国之经验，可表明根据民族可对国家进行任何重组之草纲。纵无德人之诡计，其并非易事。爱尔兰问题可对最佳景况下可能之陷阱，做最乐观之警诫。唯强国无畏行动之时机似已到来，将正义及自由之伟大理念付诸实践，斯为过往两年谈论甚多者。

中国现为参战国之一，唯正苦于胜者所订条约之效力，其正义呼声屈从于商业主义及自私之嘈杂需索。印度种族正期宪法修正，并信任英国政府之保证。于欧洲自身，种族与民族之主张正相冲突。世界和平不能得以确保，除非与种族厌恶及偏见相关之微妙问题，可觅得某种方案或妥协，并于任何情况下，有必要维持充足武力为国际理事会后盾，彼乃文明之仲裁，并增强文明人士之职权。至教育普及之前，及社会伦理与民主政治要素为世上伟大国度之大众理解，并成彼等日常生活之一般规则之前，将无满意之和平。即便如此，将耗费许多世代以遗忘种族、肤色及宗教之现存偏见。

战时讲演与随笔集
（1914—1917）

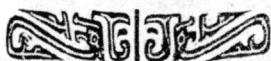

十一

从中国史观照大战之若干问题

于奥登堂文学社之讲演

大战如巨型箭毒木，遮蔽渺小人类之思维，并使一切思索与当前重大斗争相关话题以外事物之尝试，归于无用。日复一日，德人无情之怒火与不智之绝望，促其铤而走险，处处牵涉不必要悲剧与损失之恶行。世上史无前例者，乃一国自外部迹象好歹而言，似已达至物质进步之顶峰，突失其神智之平衡，并展现一切残暴与野蛮，斯曾为德国森林中其史前祖先之特质。世界骇于普遍之掠夺与毁坏，及跨越阶层、性别与年龄之数百万人之并发灾难。欧洲一世纪之和平与教育之推广，连同科学之进步与商业之成长，已使许多人士甚难明了，一场几乎卷入世上所有主要国家之全面战争，可使文明骤然降入混沌。而彼乃德国所为，欲使德人手中"世界权力"之理念，于指定"日期"之心理时机，化为实际政治之规则。

突如其来，各国面对诸多政治、经济、法律、商业与伦理之难题，均由不择手段与不计后果之德军、密探与官方特务之行为所引致。历史告诸吾等，令人生厌之腓特烈，痴迷于马基雅维利尔虞我诈之政治及谋划，斯用于文艺复兴时期小公国之极端腐败及邪恶法庭。唯其足为狡诈，撰写小册一本，反对马基雅维利主义，以缓其邻可能之疑虑，而欲对之施以毒手，以夺垂涎已久之领土。

今德皇已准许政府重演 18 世纪之阴谋,而乏其先人可申诉之借口,亦乏霍亨索伦王室大恶棍之天资。整体文明世界蒙悲苦之打击,常不知横扫全球所有经济灾难之缘故。受难者未能客观思索需解决方案之棘手问题。

多数问题作为战争之果,幸已吸引普遍关注。其并无新意,而仅为种族利益冲突世界中自然生存之旧难题,彼等精神发展程度各有不同,为霸权而争战。借镜中国史可见,自太古昏暗时期出现之文明民主,持续奋斗,历嘈杂动乱之周期,直至最终建立中华民国,[①] 推翻蛮力与不负责专制之代表。中国人民过往所面对之同等困惑,不巧正立于当今文明国家中战争状态与实现永久和平之间。历史之公断,为探寻国际关系合理重建之更佳指引,胜于争权夺利党徒忐忑歪曲之观点。于此根本问题之宏大与冷酷冲突中,并无中立可言,正如不断揭露之德人阴谋完全得以证实。中国之经历或为有趣及有益,以尝试解决国家独立与猖獗军国主义冲击浪潮之谜题。中国如同比利时,已成交战国之斗鸡场。每代军事冒险者之纷争令其受难。对东方之耳而言,新战争之呐喊,如闻千载以降相似声音之回响。自由,自文明第一抹曙光以来,已成扰动人类之问题。其乃小国或弱邦以自身之方式,过自身生活之权利,并为秉持以民族特质动机为根据之正义、宗教及哲学理念之权利。自由之爱乃精神化身之初果。正如生存之斗争给予吾等官能之进化,及现世个人与种族器官之差异,精神之解放已成人类发展进步之主因。人类精神要素之提升,诚使战争无可避免,唯战争本身实非文明持续深入发展不可或缺之条件。而只要存于人身之动物本能及冲动,压制人类实现更高精神理念之趋向留存,则更高级生命体便须预备与强加其身之侵略搏斗。此为国际冲突最后阶段之简明含义。长期争战之后,中国人已痛恨战争,并热爱和平,唯仅当其发见一生活模式后,并经其合意得以维持

---

① Chunghua Republic 为中华民国之官方名称。——原注

和平。中国史呈现民主重要性之动人景象，以及随和平而来之危机，彼并不能确保精神发展之基本条件。世界不欲以任何代价换取休憩与和平，而和平之代价乃停滞与死亡。大略检视中国史可见应避之陷阱，及可保障民主进程之方向。

上溯至孔子时代，军国主义之恶已吸引道德主义者之注意。儒家体系乃有意尝试将一切邦国政治行为，建基于明确道德及人道之结果。儒教乃中国古文化之延续，经后继哲人政要修订及诠释。虽有内战与蛮族之征服，其已成不可变更之根本大法，并为纵贯千百年来人民之最佳支柱。暴君霸王虽已竭力以所谓君权神授充分自利，唯已无力压制基于古代共产及民主制度之伦理与政治原则。儒家反对民主政体乃普遍接受之观念，实无其他共同基础，唯有明显延续千载之独裁。此归于超逾儒者所能控制之缘由。且儒家所愿授予无上权力之君，于品性及职能与美国之总统更能紧密呼应，胜于"龙座"上无力无知之暴君。"国王不应仅凭权力长据其宝座，而更应倚赖其显德。其愿为人民自身利益而治之，而不欲害其福利以逐些许徒劳之野心。其欲与境内智者善人之意愿协商。其欲鼓励学习与产业，并使国家获得保护，亦为食物生产及分配提供措施。"① 此为儒家理念下之理想君王之职。孟子以平实言语谴责独裁，并赞颂反抗暴政乃为人类及文明利益之善事德行。孟子之原则即暴君不配统治。据孟子之见，国君须由民意引导，并须仅依人民利益行事，与人性及正义之需严格一致。孟氏之国度如柏拉图之共和国或莫尔之乌托邦，迄今犹为空想，唯其激发思考，并促进民主自由之理想，斯已可使中国人民赞同共和政体。

自周公聪敏能干之指导所设周朝制度，中国人民已从中汲取政府与政治之原则观念。人民之福乃政府唯一目标。其奉行之结果，与现代民主志在所得者并无二致。若其非"民有民治之政府"，则必为致力于全体人民利益之政府。其乃为人民福利工作之贵族

---

① 疑此处缺一下引号，出处待考。——译者注

阶层，唯贵族须拔自品优贤智之人。如前所述，国君须做本邦之首要仆役，并对任何降临该国之悲惨灾难负个人之责。如此慈父般政府，并非由周公之天才所创，《史记》无疑载有平实之明示，此根本思想源自更为久远之时代。唯周公之努力，无疑梳理上古政治及伦理观念，并将其结合为一致及实用之统系，其为远东政治伦理一切相关事务中后续修补之框架。唯该计划显然过于理想化及乌托邦。

孔子时代许久之前，周朝之伟大国度化为碎片。封建领主自相争霸，而敌对派系常卷入内战及阴谋，其时周室正丧失影响及领土。是为无政府时代。正义及律法受公然藐视，并于不断之争战中，生发各种政治权宜，势力平衡，裁军、中立、攻守同盟、和平公约等，于吾等时日至欧洲大战前吸引公众注意达四分之一世纪。历史正自反复。中国之"战国"富于建议计划，依确保永久和平之观念，以复原社会及规范邦国关系。

王诩为当时隐士。其退隐于山谷，享其恶名"鬼谷"。吾等不知其名是否因该地之古怪及难以接近而得，或得自此政治投机者之背信弃义及恶毒教条，其于该遥远之孤寂中，细定残忍之密谋。虽然，后人知王氏为"鬼谷"之哲人，第一流之机会主义者，其似已预见马基雅维利之主要原则，并已夸耀其弟子可于任何政治角色成功，无论是战争鼓吹者抑或和平领导人！其拥趸奔波于各朝廷之间，献计献策及襄助谋划，并预备加入每一派系，因宣称诡辩不论对错，皆可适用。又有他人兜售各种政治方略，断言此为缓解当时社会及经济危机之完美措施。

儒教师长之门徒，反对此学派之物质主义及机会主义。孟子于乱世哲人中卓杰超群。其一贯要求君主政要深入检视事物准则，并使政府立于人性之基石，而非暂时之利益。如其恳请梁惠王更为妥善理解一切政治行为之基础，宣称人民与国家之福主要倚赖对诚信意涵之全面理解，彼存于公正及仁慈政府之正义中。其与

106

盛行对权力及影响之贪婪论战，并妥当辩称，除非敌国君主依人性及正义之主张调整其行为，否则将以身为则，鼓励违法及争斗，以放纵之野心及肆意之冒险保障其自身私利之结果。孟子否定人须如兽斗，并灭绝较弱之同胞。无人理会有更高使命等待人类之教诲。自私贪婪之政策，导致无穷战争之预言得以实现，而封建君主之间战争不止，将古老国度带至纷乱毁灭之边缘。鉴于军国主义所能达至之物质利益，道德考量轻易搁置。故煽动者及聪明人"鬼谷"之弟子尤为成功一时，而周人伟大遗产，经持续战争及剧变已撕为粉碎。经长年之悲惨及无政府状态，原本孤立之秦国崛起，声名显赫。其经秦孝公明智之策，欢迎战地难民来归，故使其国成商业、艺术及产业中心，而其邻因长期战争疲乏悲苦以致凋敝。秦免于政治纷扰约二百年，致其邦于公元前约400年之初相对富足。当时有两位杰出人士，即张仪与苏秦。其皆为鬼谷恶名昭彰隐士之弟子。唯其循各自政治信仰，成为对手。张仪拥秦之大业。其曾经之伙伴于封建邦国间奔波，宣扬对此崛起政权之战争。终于，其成功组织六国联盟，以图粉碎如雪崩般接近之秦国。苏秦获任纵约长。历史及传奇皆载甚多光耀场景，是日其为英雄人物，当时诸代表于盛大检阅中会谈，授其代表合纵六国之完全权力。至今中国舞台对此伟大事件之呈现，乃中国戏剧世界至为如画风景之一，以写实手法反映漫长中国史中激动人心之一事件。秦于诸多方面乃今日德国之蓝本。由苏秦先见所致成功备战之警示，秦王运用每一可想见之方法破坏团结。所用手段之一乃向各国派出使节，并于合纵国之间激起不和。而张仪引发缔约国间之内战，成功破坏合纵，而不幸之投机者苏秦见弃于其凄惨之支持者，流亡邦国之间，最终乃为追获及刺杀。秦所传之谣，令合纵国先为相疑，如今日之德人，张仪之君主屈尊以行各种欺诈、谣传及贿赂，以成其野心。合纵国陷入自身之内战，而秦国各个击破之，并非不可完成之事。封建体系废墟之上，崛起中国首个统一帝国。其王自称秦始皇。如德皇威廉，其为幻梦之梦者。唯其人亦为天才，不似德皇。其更似亚历山大大帝或拿破仑，而非平庸之德皇，引领其国人至于毁灭。始皇兼为政治家及武士。其摧毁分封制，改革政府，并建造中国长城。其亦似德人，喜宏大之建筑。其所建之阿房宫可坐万人，阔敞如此，乃当世奇观之一。若人获知其系统教导之恐怖计划，便知此相似几为完全。其以冷酷专制为人民彻底痛恨，而至今日对其记忆仍为诅咒。足可诧异者，乃当时一悲观者名荀况，尼采哲学似为对其原则之模糊回应。其弟子李斯为秦之冯·特莱希克。其于编史之书斋，详述某种"军国主义"，欲以迫害及强制取代孔子之体系。荀况为尼采之原型，提出恐怖理论，因依其观点，需暴力断灭人之兽性。其信仰冷酷之原则，而荒唐推想经残忍捶击之手段，可将野蛮打造为适宜之形。其厌恶儒家学说之保守，建议焚烧一切史哲及伦理文学，以便国史可始于首要君王之成就。普世帝国之梦想扭曲其生活观念，并感染其弟子李斯及其君王之意见。专制成新帝国之要务，而爱国者须忍受迫害及暴政，直至普遍之反抗摧毁压迫者，并实现汉代之文艺复兴。

于政治动荡中，一笃实之爱国者屈原，乃楚国公族之子弟，颇不为时人马基雅维利式诡辩所动。"和平论者"及狡诈奸人入于楚王之耳，而彼之警示受忽略。彼为其君流放时，所著荡气回肠之挽歌《离骚》乃中国文学至纯宝玉之一。于本哀诗中，此爱国者溯源文明，揭示治主所能追寻之唯一路径乃正义，并证明正义与荣誉之联结乃君民间唯一纽带。怀王为阴谋者之诡计所害，于欲建立均势与和平之某次战争中落败，并死于囚禁。其子亦罔顾屈原之申述。诗人与政治家屈原归隐于鲜为人知之处，并终自投于河，因其不忍见降临其国之灾，而无能为力。此史事发生于农历五月初五日。此重大之日作为全国假日，以示感励之盛景，中国全境之民举办龙舟节以追缅逝去之英杰。

至此仅述自相残杀之概况。当文明邦国执意自毁，北方蛮族已不断自寒冷西伯利亚风雪中南进。始皇建造长城乃伟大贡献，使农民得以抵挡狂野骑兵之躁进。因对军国主义及其后续专制之普遍斥责，此宏大成就之意义尚未得适当认可。唯今日自当前大战而言，人民将知全面服役乃唯一充分措施以应对野蛮入侵之可怖危险，而后世必将修正其对秦始皇所完成伟大工程之评价，其以国家强制之牺牲，使文明抵御蛮族之冷酷暴行。自该世至清朝覆亡，中国人为守卫文化及文明斗争不息。匈奴人、鞑靼人之蛮潮接续消长，袭击中华繁华城市及文明平原。于其爱国义士徒遭屠杀之后，中国人一再让步于蛮族侵略者之军事威力。唯于每一事件，文明力量实终得胜。因蛮族开始衰堕，而理性、智慧与想象之互动，总使文明致胜，正如武力与正义之争所切近者。一旦文明邦国之个人知悉于举国斗争中，一切琐碎之自我考量须从属于国家利益，文明邦国之资源终将足以击退入侵，或至少建立若干程度之自由，因能赏识自由之价值者，宁取灭亡，不愿受奴役。暴政与压迫从未粉碎任何国家之精神。身心灭绝，一切激励国家之资源消亡，或可最终发生。唯各国历史并未助长该观点。无论迫害及灾难为何，中国人及犹太人已生存数千年。故保国家生存已成哲学及政治之永恒问题。蛮族终已屈服于高等文明政权，并与一般人民结合。无论事实如何，一切民族间之该等竞争，于爱国者及斗士牺牲后，屈服乃力竭之结局。若受征服者更为文明，将不断力图摆脱外来桎梏；而若其正处文明较低阶段，将不时持续爆发暴动与反抗。故自由精神永未根除。于宋代最为黑暗之时日，当蒙人涌入华北及华中，文天祥坚持国家一统，并要求一切彻底之牺牲，以遏制蛮族之侵袭。1260 年，其无畏弹劾居高位者，尤在朝廷之红人。无论其懦弱无能，仍见容为高级指挥。中国不幸，命运对其 ① 残酷。此伟大爱国者于英武力行、重整国力之际，

_____

① 原文此处为逗号，疑误，应为句号。——译者注

一再遭遇厄运。经历诸多遭遇战及险难之后，其终落入蒙人之手。其蔑视主将巴延所示一切善意，彼冀其劝说皇帝投降蒙人。唯文天祥不为所动。关押三年后，传唤其至忽必烈汗之前，并令陈说合其自期之待遇。其个性之回复为："安事二姓，愿赐之一死足矣。"呜呼，其不可动摇之忠心落空，因国家经长年分裂及暴政，颇为无力，并尤以一切爱国志士，为敌军及内奸之政治阴谋所消灭。

当时另一著名政要之命运值得回忆。王安石已预见蒙古入侵之危。其学识，其于朝廷之影响及其热忱，颇助其庞大民主计划初见功成。国家资源依此为公众机构所俭用，国防由全面服役确保，公帑由国家专营及控制而得保障。惜其为当时所有伟大人物反对，而人民并不认同自我利益之牺牲，因其不能想见举国将受奴役之险。其全面受挫，见其宏伟计划正入歧途，而未能实现其以极度热忱向皇帝所许诺之善果，而皇帝为予其所有可能鼓励之庇护人。唯当其宏伟经济革新不成，皇帝近乎勉强让步于政客与大众之请，斯视其为野心阴谋家及儒家经典之异说者。皇帝之眷顾未能使王安石免于失宠及流放。唯后世须视其为天才及爱国者，因若其经济与军事改革得以公平试行，蒙人之入侵或不能使一度强盛之宋室完败。战前十年之大英帝国史，包含与此奇似之惨事。若非海军之筹备及命运之手，德国入侵很可能使大不列颠产生巨大损失。无论如何，大战已充分证明此宋朝杰出政治家目标之合理，其尽力落实古代经济理论。产业之维持，农矿资源之开发，及全面训练国家刚毅之气应战，皆与广泛国防组织紧密关联。

王安石之模范为著名之管子，其活跃于公元前 7 世纪。此政要及哲人预先使用俾斯麦之原则及政治方法，并造就巨大产业发展，致国富强。其以所创巨富赢得伟大声名。孔子虽承认其达至甚多物质进步及推动国防之大功，唯不能完全认同其物质计划为人类社会之理想。将其所属齐国之完败归咎于彼，正如今日吾等固能追溯德人之狂妄自大至俾斯麦，并令其亦为奸邪外交之现状负责。

今转离战斗景象及阴谋诡计，乃闻军事荣誉，[①] 及对奖励分功之抱怨。当某些战士之英勇或文员之特别功劳未获适当嘉许，便直率表达怒意。怨者或可由公元前 7 世纪介子推之事例启发，其甚自傲，不求回报。公元前 635 年，其随公流亡。其曾濒为饿殍。此忠臣以自身一块肉饲其君。公得胜归国之际，忠心介氏之功劳乃为忽略及忘怀。其并不吵嚷求赏，悄然隐居，默然生活，而贡献较少者得势。虽友人促其示公以劳，因宫廷之喧闹及辉煌，暂使公忘其忠仆。介氏对政治世界不屑一顾,因见混乱[②] 诸事中,"上赏其奸，上下相蒙"。唯一日有人于宫门张贴，提及介氏。公即为悔责所动，乃始寻其流亡之伙伴与大恩人，而介氏并无觅处。公便赐其原籍一片封地，以追念其忠谦。于当前战争中，各国必有多人甚为自傲，不求赏酬，唯掌权者理应于事成之后记取出力之人。当值得嘉奖者抖落足尘，并向忘恩之国与负义之民诀别时，自责及后悔并无用处。

讲演已甚冗长。唯于结末，吾且须暂提现代中国之悲剧。于中国,中"外"居民之间许久之系列误解,终有"拳乱"。其真相为，直至此世界史特殊事件之前，白人国家一直试图创设国中之国。中国"门户开放"，而中国人却于"白人之国"见拒。中国人实见白人基督徒于其政商交易中，全无登山宝训中伦理及利他之信仰。忽略国际关系中之公义，于今已得天谴，而正如孟子两千年前所预言，国家之对抗乃因其以赢"利"或物质利益为国家繁荣

---

① 此处原文为句号，疑误，应为逗号。——译者注
② 原文为 tursy，疑误，应为 turvy。——译者注

之准则。中国圣贤已宣称，仁义乃幸福国家与文明世界唯一可靠基础。大战已将欧洲自道德冷漠中唤醒，彼正削弱社会之柱石。野蛮战争之恐怖中，德人已将物质准则真切付诸实践，并已成指导统治者及外交官伦理原则之构想。其与既定儒家学说之准则大体一致。若能成功阻止"人类相残"并于世间树立正义，大战将自证其身乃因祸得福。

战时讲演与随笔集
（1914—1917）

十二

种族与帝国，兼谈英属马来亚

　　种族与国家之问题曾于史上紧密纠缠。自上古时代，每一帝国总有种族对国君尽其臣节，彼经战争或和平协商树其霸权。不特如美利坚合众国之例，异国人民常常迁入新商贸及工业中心。

　　古罗马就贵族与平民区别之争议，仅为同一问题之另种形式。大众为平等自由之痛苦斗争仍在持续，经诸多政治剧变时代之诸多干扰，而于每一时期，虽常得微功或徒劳，征服者力图强加不可逾越之障碍于其自身与人民之间，既为其所征服，故以臣民治之。英国历史上，诺曼人之征服一度建立法国贵族统治，其毫不同情撒克逊之"恶人"。此为历史一奇特讽刺，即受鄙臣民之语言存留，而征服者全数为受征服者吸纳。

　　当罗马人继续扩展其军事冒险，一时罗马文明似将吞并欧洲所有部族；亚非已臣服于罗马之势力。而形势置野蛮异族日耳曼人于神圣罗马帝国之王座，并于欧洲种族甚为高度同化之前，造成帝国之瓦解。唯现代罗马国家与英国民众为罗马文化多方面之代表。故英国可追溯其发轫至不同源流。而罗马文化之影响，显然仍存于大英帝国之法律、语言及制度。虽英语现为全国之语言，今日主要血统之"国民"如旧时一般，矜其个人特质。苏格兰人、盖尔人、威尔士人及爱尔兰人毫不担心以英国人之名融合。留意自傲及得胜之诺曼人如何全为吸纳。努力不时做出，以振兴威尔士、爱尔兰及苏格兰高地之古语。故凡就英人而言，其显著种族之要素于今清晰界定，如当年彼等与共同死对头罗马人各自为战之时。

经受自身内部之腐化，及北部与东方蛮族之外界压力，罗马帝国终于瓦解，史前种族最重要之血统再次自籍籍无名中现身，罗马文明曾为其蒙上阴影。伊比利亚民族，高卢人、比利时人及日耳曼人之后裔，更遑论其他民族，于今展露与其先人相同之特质，彼等为罗马史家忠实描绘。若现代意大利人并非全然等同古罗马人，其或不再为同一拉丁种族或血统，因多次入侵及经吸引至意大利土地之种族杂糅后，现代意大利人必为高度混合之种族。

西班牙帝国未能于美洲摧毁诸多部族之当地特性，虽已强行加诸西班牙语及天主教。于菲律宾，西班牙语未能完全取代群岛之土话。

于大英帝国内，法籍加拿大人完整保留其法国特性及其语言。布尔人将永保荷兰方言及情感。印度全境内，种族区别将予保留。彼等将发展自身之语言及文学。

此简述及摘要足证无论帝国政治若何，种族要素将趋于存留。奥匈帝国乃名副其实之混合，并未能成功诱使非日耳曼民族为泛日耳曼运动之利益，同意去除自身国籍。大战为种族阴谋之直接结果，奥地利希冀用以骗取塞尔维亚人民默许奥匈帝国之治。匈牙利人、捷克人及其他国民继续精心守护其自身曾有之民族观念及古语。

虽波兰人于今无国，其从未停息对自由之鼓舞。德人尝试所有可想见之计划，以诱波兰人转为日耳曼人，唯其几无成果可得。整体而言，英国之政策终究乃最保险之方向，其以英语教育异国分子，令当地人通晓英国方式及思想，并绝不欲干预土话之运用。此必定聚合不同种族以相互理解，并认同帝国之价值。经适者生存之法则，英语以自然平和之道取代较不适宜之语言。

拓展英国民主原则至帝国全境，是否可行之问题浮现。

战前所进行之一场强力运动，欲维持白人种族之显著地位，不利于有色种族。显然该歧视亦完全基于肤色之问题，罔顾相关个人之社会地位、教育或文化。统治阶层欲驱逐全部有色种族，而致印人于严苛耻辱之境遇，令居于该等英国领土令人生厌及无可忍受。于南非，印人有意不遵歧视彼等之法律，并宁愿入狱，胜于屈从耻辱之对待。唯总督及帝国政府均无所作为，以改变殖民者之观念。毫无疑义，帝国政府未能为其真正属民于帝国内提供全面庇护，乃极度不满遍布印度之缘由。印度以外之英属殖民地内，官员与有权势欧洲商人间达成一项心照不宣之理解，乃所谓"肤色隔阂"须猛力推行。

认为该等种族厌恶无关紧要乃属无盖。因其为当前多数不满之根源。帝国政府已普遍接受正确态度，唯就统治种族与英国有色臣民间应存之适当关系，殖民者及英籍印人之顽固意见使问题复杂。于过往时日，白人惯于接受极度之顺从，而土著自为谦恭，并以亚洲礼节要求之方式，屈膝于"主人"之前。如当地仆役俯卧并亲吻盛怒主人之脚。较低阶层将因最细微之缘由双膝跪地。于今日爪哇岛，当地仆役与其主人对话或等候任何指令时，甚至伏于地面或蹲坐于腿上。若干年前，当欧人于爪哇岛乡村道上经过时，土著蹲坐于地并摘其遮阳帽之景象既常见又耻辱。旅行及教育已为整个东方带来改变。旧世界有关何谓适宜之理念正迅速消逝。较新一代正放弃亚洲古老迷信，并吸取欧洲之见解，模仿欧洲之风俗。其于学校习得诸多东方观念已属过时或招厌，并终自然运用现代文明之一般原则于所有事物。唯诸多欧亚混血或亚洲人发见，当其离校之际，并按欧洲礼节对白人行事，其行为常受憎恶。一位"土著"期望受待以绅士，初似荒谬，而后有"奚落他"及"让他看看何谓得体"之冲动。若白人其自身为"一名新贵"，以粗暴无礼表露其不快，而若其并未将"土著新贵"逐出办公室，其对有色人种无尽懊丧挫败之社会优越感，亦常常予此不幸土著留下深刻印象。于印度之欧人，每疑缘何较低层级之欧亚混血倾于恢复土著衣着及习俗。此处所言如此之待遇，苦痛于心，并驱使有色人种至于绝望。其受必需之迫而实行"叩头"，唯其已失对白人之一切尊重，彼等以如是行为表明其教养及举止并未优于至恶之暴君，至少其行径乃因无知之故。诸多肤色问题引发之反感，由土著与欧人交往之种种细事而产生。若欧人常由不充分之根据，得错舛无理之结论，土著亦当常由其自身之不幸经历及白人之败坏声名，做彻底之推论。以若干个体之表现，不能可靠归纳全体部族或国家之相关行为。社群非全由无赖及愚人组成。害群之马在焉；唯群体由平均个体组成，其于遍世之中大体相同。于不同社群中，或有特别之观点、教条及迷信，似各自决定行为。唯因模仿本能之规律，人类易于模仿同类，大体而言为环境之生物。至此，甚至如古时所知，人类常抛弃其所属阶层之缺陷、劣势及舛误。同时，良好社会素质及道德属性非白人种族专有。一项对人类伦理行为之公正调查，须揭示其过失、愚蠢及罪行中颇为震惊之事实。不论其肤色如何，一切种族显示奇妙之相似，自身体组织而言，不特足以证实其实际之密切关系，亦可确证其同源以及精神与道德定命之信仰。

对英属殖民地土著任何此等之歧视，完全为一退步，并与皇家制诰所载承诺存有分歧，彼将海峡殖民地由东印度公司治下让与英国。英国政要一向轻视英格兰应着力利用殖民地土著之建议。甚至英格兰之敌也当承认，大英帝国之伟大成功，基于对所属异族臣民公正自由之待遇。大战确证英国殖民地及其各种族与部族，已表明其忠爱母国之欣慰实据。

若吾等考虑大英帝国内土生种族之无穷多样，须即刻意识其社会、伦理及智识情况差异颇大，而仅凭常识可知绝无可能将治理彼等之原则减至一条普遍规则。巴苏陀人、美国印第安人、太平洋岛民、巴布亚人、迪雅克人、沙盖人，遑论其他土著，所达文明阶段仅视为婴儿一般。唯即使于彼等之中，智识与社会知觉之发展各有程度，故或可证实适于野蛮之巴布亚人者，恐颇不合于进步较多之巴苏陀人。如强迫肤色黝黑之印度种族，服从为管治某肤色黝黑之非洲殖民地而制定之规则，则为招厌之愚行及粗野之不公。此理甚明，似无须指出。唯于若干欧人中，存流行过甚之信念，即一条肤色界线及一条普遍规则，可满足一切实务之目的。虽于英国殖民地所知律法中，并无此处所提及之肤色差异，唯土著于现实中察觉所作区别，故总体印象乃有排他规则。海峡殖民地之亚洲人要求平等机会及平等待遇。表面无作二致，唯实存摆明之歧视。幸吾等之出色当局一贯恪守严正。除一二例外，殖民地幸有长官，能维持英国之崇高理念，并为帝国赢得英属有色臣民之忠爱。于和平、良善政府及帝国团结之利益中，一切琐碎及不必要之区分皆应废除。英国之统治基于正义及道德劝诫。白人须以内在智慧及道德素质赢得尊敬，而非由警力执行之专制命令！再者，亚洲人一词于殖民地中已用作轻蔑之称呼。唯无合法依据暗示亚洲人天生劣等。有大量反证可说明，亚洲人脑容量颇大，因而神智之适应力与任何白人种族相等。犹太人为亚洲人，及白人种族自身发源于亚洲之确凿事实，表明帝国治理基于不同种族及单纯起源地机遇之荒谬。"亚洲人"无须耻于斯名，而自其先人过往之辉煌纪录而言，至少未来可期。

　　于任何帝国内，对异族或可取三种方法：1.灭绝或驱逐；2.同化或吸纳；3.某种形式之奴役。该等方法亦为邦国间争夺政治霸权或扩张领土时运用。所有侵略帝国已运用该等策略建立君主专制。如罗马历长期经验后发现，其维持拉丁种族霸权所有可行之事，乃摧毁迦太基之势力。今日德人于攻击英国之前，欲瘫痪法国。此为世界灾祸之真实原因。塔斯马尼亚之殖民者惯于杀尽土著。唯此行动除恶毒之外，晚近方见其愚。于西非之德人依相同原则实已屠杀赫雷罗人。俄罗斯人与土耳其人一再付诸此不人道及野蛮之实践。今吾等所言，并非狂徒之暴行，而乃政府深思熟虑之政策。大战期间，土耳其人几杀绝亚美尼亚人；而若非协约国之助，德人已消灭比利时人、塞尔维亚人及罗马尼亚人[①]，并接收各国。于东印度之荷兰人，及于台湾之日本人，面对不和解之部族，平定其域，常为不折不扣之屠杀。因冷血灭绝人类对文明国家之考量而言，乃过于恐怖之事体，近年白人已求助于各种方式，驱逐或排除不受待见之种族。此为古老亚洲国家之野蛮旧政，欲驱逐其国民，彼等已受欧洲列强严惩。中日原为排外者，唯西方雷鸣于其门，迫其对所有外来者开放。今该等国家对欧人开放，唯来自该等国家之亚洲人，现正要求于美国、澳大利亚及加拿大居留与工作之相同权利，如白人已获于东方者。俄罗斯之犹太人已蒙受残酷之恶行，直至最近于欧洲全境遭遇颇多迫害。即使现今于欧洲各国，反犹主义为须认真对待之势力。恶名昭彰之德莱弗斯事件中，所犯严重不公引起全体文明世界之轰动，并最终成功唤起法国公众之情感，毕竟其为解放与自由先驱之地。

于有色种族占多数之殖民地，同化或吸纳为英国、法国、美国所好之方。小群个体易为同化。唯于庞大社群之情况下，经验证实不施高压，几无可能实行同化。强制同化与统治种族同源之民族，已引致于一切政治史上极大之恶行。日耳曼人、奥地利人、俄罗斯人及土耳其人干犯最多罪孽。英国人许久以前未能同化爱尔兰人。法籍加拿大人及布尔人将保留种族之完整，而仍为尽忠之英人。故于印度及英属殖民地，种族与部族将继续完善其自身语言，并维系其于英国国旗下之社会及宗教制度。于帝国内对异族之宽容宣称为吸纳。法人亦成功探寻吸纳政策，并赢得诸多不同种族之信任与忠心。此战期间，法国殖民地给予之极大支持，证明吾等勇武之法国盟友，已以广大之民主解决帝国之问题。于菲律宾之美国人，已于种族间政治开展重大实验，并已得超逾所

---

① 原文为 Roumanians，疑误，应为 Romanians。——译者注

有预期之成功。经与坚定混合之正义及仁慈，西方伟大白人共和国已减少纷乱，趋向秩序，并已提携半野蛮之种族至文明开端之处。美国正为菲律宾人建国，虽于该等辛劳结果可得公正预期之前，此工作至少须持续百年。西班牙人失利，荷兰人未得成功，因其有根深蒂固之偏见，以土著诸事不配与白人平等。西班牙人得其教训过晚。荷兰人正开始体会历史之实在教诲，而恰可言近年来，彼等正努力收复失地，并适时将向荷兰治下之马来人及其他种族，提供一切现代培训及教育之福利。

于海峡殖民地，英国政府已准许传统之放任管治以容忍吸纳，唯吾等随波逐流，并无任何明确政策。而居民开始经历肤色隔阂政策之执行，彼正激起全体阶层各方面相当之怒火。英属马来亚全境，于大量欧洲种植园主及商人到来之前，吸引世界各地之白人，其生命最美好之部分留置于此，故而与土著交友并努力了解彼等，最终其可欣赏彼等。土著习得敬爱白人。故无任何肤色偏见之余地。唯因教育及旅行已造成土著方式之改变，并因自欧洲新来者数量增加，隔群之鸿沟每年见宽。土著发见杨、汉密尔顿、里德、司哥特、柯里及诸如此类之英人，为并不甚友好之他人取代。彼等发见，未于该国生活且未与彼等往来甚久之人，对彼等了解不够充分。该等新来者妒于权势及地位。某些来自印度、非洲及中国，并欲引入歧视，于该等国家内加诸有色人种。于海峡及马来联邦，该等歧视从未得宽忍，故而此等欧洲势利者之行径引起极大恼怒，因此等欧人意欲排外；唯自由之土著不愿于己国为奴。吾等就其所习之自由，应感激斯坦福·莱佛士及其出色继任者等英才。

印度帝国为英国吸纳政策成功之特例，无论有何种可能之缺陷，开明官僚机构从未忘所托之职，在于为数百万众之利益而管治此伟大国度。虽有所谓印度国民大会党极端分子之牢骚，及其外之狂热分子，总督确已于各种族之混乱中，出色实现国家雏形之创造。不久之前，彼等忙于无休止之冲突，并仅能于暴君征服利剑之强制下享有和平。大不列颠已为印度种族解决诸多问题。其已赋予各种族及部族大英百科全书式之礼，斯为文明之通行语言，并成印度及帝国之语言。其已授予印度精妙法典，虽令人想起古罗马引人注目之制度，亦已并入其包容一切之网络，包括中古及现代欧洲经验，以及印度所有最佳之法律学识。其已给予所有阶层和平、正义及繁荣。其已使宗教差异得普遍之容忍，并已提携低等及受抑之种姓，摆脱古老风俗之束缚。其已于迄今仅惯于暴政与专制之异族中，将英国民主原则相当之部分成功转化为实务政治。统而言之，其已成养育印度部族与种族之真正母亲，并为人类之伟大女施主，以其社会、商业、工业、教育及博爱之广泛努力，提携及救助数百年来暴政之受害者。为使该等宏伟目标产生实效，白人已为帝国做出巨大牺牲。战争必须发动，而骁勇民族每次均为帝国统治最可靠之支持者。自尊之拉其普人、尚武之锡克人、好斗之廓尔喀人、急躁之帕坦人及诸多人等，于今正为帝国及旗帜忠心奋战。非作战民族亦正千方百计履行其分内之战事工作。大战已向世界证明英国统治印度之极大成就，因英国不特赢得印度百万民众之感激，亦得其爱戴。叛乱之存在，仅表明印度政府已广播自由之种。麦子与稗草之寓言①，对狂热分子及总督皆有意义。善无恶报。故当零星叛乱突现，当局须明察其因并除之，而非求助基于肤色隔阂之拙劣一般手法。事实上，印度总督近已采纳明智及调停之策。所建议之改革将为伟大建构添增一项基础，而战后新时代将睹欧人与土著之间开创更深理解，故所有人士将会为帝国及文明之更大利益而消弭种族偏见。

对付异族之另一途径，乃任其于各自黑暗中摸索，并以武力为后盾对其进行各种限制与约束，以压制彼等。可许其于主人控

---

① 见于《圣经》马太福音 13：24—13：30。——译者注

制下，作为纯粹工具从事机械等工作。旧时西班牙人于其美洲殖民地，惯于雇用土著，尤于银矿及其他矿山，彼等如野兽般工作。兰德矿山中国苦力之雇佣条款，否定其自由人之权利。斯为极端之例。而已有阴谋，欲于所有政府及市政部门之职位限制土著。一般之托词为土著不能胜任，且不值信赖。唯若当局不力行安置人民于可得之最佳岗位，反而于职场拒用彼等以沮丧之，则不胜重大责任之职，几非土生种族之责。土著中并无人要求与所需德能未充分相符之委任。抱怨在于，法律规定无论土著之可能如何，其必永属纯粹之机械，并不得立志极高远之处，斯为素养可令其如此行事者。吾等且看职业。于"肤色隔阂"治下，并无土著可获其或有之"肥缺"，除非其具有利之肤色。即便承认亚洲人存有缺陷，其是否可能乐于永处次等地位？指责其为低劣者，而不愿着手改善其境遇之政府，将得爱戴乎？显然，冲淡肤色之唯一别径，乃经通婚之历程，此较单纯平等宽待有色人种更会引起反对。

到处所发生者，乃以彻底之偏见视欧亚混血为土著，而彼等时受驱迫，发现其社会需求之满足在于土著之圈子。于上流阶层，时有对欧亚混血不合情理之憎恶，其以傲慢之识见，纡尊应对较高阶层之土著。普通之薪水及社会之排斥，实已限制欧亚混血之机会，其已发现置于路中之障碍，阻其向上前行，欲克服之，任务甚艰。并无书面法律特为引导对彼等之反对。唯其发见于现实中，其未受喜爱，亦未得信任。此同一白人阶层，夺其运用毋庸质疑天资之机会，掉头宣称欧亚混血与土著不值信赖。怀疑全体阶层之笼统说法轻易做出，造成反感与不满。两项课程正开启，欧亚混血及有色人种皆可适时受教并受纳为市民。大英帝国政府自麦考利时代以来，此素为对印人公开声称之态度。否则其必受抑，充当某种现代反面人物，永为职员，或任白人主管下次要之普通工作。若后者成为政策，则所吹嘘之自由安在？奴隶或受限于锁链，而有色人种深知，该等锁链无须铁锻。社会及政治禁令远恶于图

123

固之墙。当帝国之有色臣民知悉，该等阻碍主要由恐失声望之无知偏见怂恿所设，其必大觉不满。尊善崇贵乃东方既定习俗，而礼貌为双方之间共识之良好举止，乃恒受认同。贵贱贫富、雅俗主仆之间，有清楚明确之礼数，斯为全体文明国家所知。若妥当遵循此尊崇之规范，并无理由抱怨土著之"放肆"。若白人自身不愿施展礼节，其不得期待客气。有色人种，如蒙特苏马之不幸臣民，倾向于相信"白脸孔"者乃上帝肉身之时代已逝。若其无故粗暴对待土著，且自身举止如自傲自大所膨胀之蠢人，则不必惊见谦卑之亚洲人忽忘我而现勇武气概。某些欧人已见于中国内地旅行之危险，唯愿待亚洲人为明理者之人士，于中国到处活动时，从未见配备武器及使用武力之必要。故于东方殖民地，一切肤色之歧视并无正当理由，欧人于斯仅仅只是漂泊之客。

于马来亚地区殖民之英国拓荒者，精神广博，且本性富于同情。据与斯坦福·莱佛士爵士等人相熟之阿卜杜勒导师证实，每一对土著所示之礼节，均得有益之客气回报。

一般欧人之态度，无疑迟早渗入社团，而及全体社会。随后影响施于政府。已故金文泰·史密斯爵士所设高等奖学金或女皇奖学金，使殖民地与母国更为紧密，而受人瞩目；具更广博精神之塞西尔·罗德斯，于若干年前受罢免，因某些有权势之欧人，不喜派遣亚洲人赴英之主意。教育委员会报告内发布之表面原因纯属婉辞，而真实缘由正如所述。同样之憎恨，已使陛下于殖民地之行政机关，仅对"纯白人血统"之欧人开放。谎言传布，即有色人种不信任居官位之有色人士。此等断言并无丝毫基础，反而土著社群深恶于政府服务之有色士人受不公正之狭隘侮辱。某位地方法官，不得不忍受其同僚诸多"冷落"之烦恼。另一有色士人，于得以准入某必须加入之俱乐部前，难免激怒当权派。人人相信该等士人为权利之躁动，间接开启一运动，导致剥夺殖民地土著加入地方行政服务之权利。虽印度土著于某种条件下有竞争行政服务之权，国务卿以专制法令，禁止任何条件下斯土之子民参与本国行政服务，苟其非纯种欧人之后裔。战争已使于马来联邦高等职位聘请马来人成为必要，而今年11月高级专员于联邦议会近期之演讲，已给予该等马来士人履职良好之评价。若于马来邦如此，则无理由为何殖民地土生之英属臣民最终不能同样成功。

为殖民地及帝国之利益，吾等须期土著人民完全忠诚爱国。人民须以其国为傲，并须感佩政府。今吾等不得拒绝教育民众。且不论政府，教士将为其带来曙光。土著自身正尽力教育其子弟。故政府将须提供充分教育设施。教育总为觉醒之过程。为何一面唤醒政治与社会意识，一面如墨鱼一般混淆^① 环境，于青年接近抚养其之父母，寻求更多帮助及指导时，于其进步之方向划下肤色界限？

显而易见，不可能于印人自身之国，以如此微妙之肤色隔阂抑之，实可证除暴力方式之外，彼有害于社会、政治及道德利益。莫利勋爵与哈丁勋爵切实把握印度叛乱之真正意涵，使印度种族相互对抗之老把戏，于今仅可能施于无知蒙昧之民众。唯于印度之白人政治推动者，每提示总督及帝国政府，斗士不愿服从空谈诸公所订之法律，斯为武士阶层惯所蔑视。唯斗士者何人？其行列中多为目不识丁之佣兵，不为一项事实乎？帝国土著对政治及社会正义之需，基于道德之理据。文盲糙汉之陈腐观念，须依据身份、教育及其他素质，让路于深思熟虑及合乎情理之平等主张。真切之怨怼，在于政府实以肤色作为划分人类阶层之表征。

尔常闻欧人管治之必要。一般而言，只要白人创造及维持条件使该等管治必不可少，则无疑如是。汝等未提供适当教育设施，将土著及欧亚混血限于社会及政治藩篱内，并抑其于政府服务之

---

① 原文为 offuscate，疑误，应为 obfuscate。——译者注

职，而后汝等疑惑为何该等人民如此无助，并如此无骨。须记脊椎乃激烈竞争进化之果。南非鼹鼠及无眼泥鱼乃于黑暗中长期生活之结果。土著不得已之生活条件，要为其屡屡失败负责。若政府努力补救破坏社群品性之错误，其将协助去除造成土著品质不良特征，及阻碍充分吸纳土著身份之人为帝国公民之缘由。

于自由与奴役之间，似无中途之旅栈。大英帝国已着手于民主之祸福，并以绝大牺牲，永远根除奴隶制度。故理论上，英国政要已于各处接纳教育土著之善政。于果熟之前，土著或已为此同化进程之果而呐喊。另外，诸多欧人视煽动者为危险及过于自信。于此二者冲突观点之间，或有真理潜藏。唯大战已提供重新检视整体问题之机会。

于半野蛮及野蛮之殖民地，某种形式之专制无可避免。即使如此，依民主理念之正义，帝国政府须取最宜发挥土著人民最大长处之政策，并为人民预备更高形式之社会生活。须有诚恳之努力，以教化该等后进之天真孩童，否则该等人群必于现代文明环境内退化。自然运行之伟力将不再存在。适者及不适者将生存。而落后种族将发见难以抗拒饮食之诱惑，遑论其他事物。目光短浅、无知贫穷、缺乏政府父爱之"次等种族"，迟早必为逐入贫民窟，并于贫穷、堕落及疾病中消亡。此种社会之堕落，乃无情之商业主义强加于全球劳苦大众情形之一，甚至奴隶制较其更为可取。

就亚洲人而言，其已继承东方古老风俗及理念。无论其当前或未来之地位、教育、品质如何，必彻底排除彼等于自身国家政府中受信负责之职，此种观点同时令人生厌及无可忍耐。有色种族并不于筹划阶段抱怨，唯其要求做出诚恳之努力，以发动初步之训练，并于一旦存在体面机遇时，给予其子弟公平机会。此为有色人士吁请之重任。若民主即将实现，并成帝国内生命之力，则此种族之声音须得白人统治者内心负责之回响，尤对在场人士而言，沟通君民间之海湾乃职责所在。此战已向每人证明，有益及理想之社群能有效联结最不同之种族，做出最大之牺牲。故仅按肤色区分帝国人民不再合理。且此战亦已展现，所有人士皆处同船之上。军费将由所有人士负担，将须于社群发现人力，国家须充分倚赖人民。若印度及殖民地为帝国必须之部分，其有色人口必不乐为奴役，而须进至自由公民之地位。中国"门户开放"政策之讨论甚多，而所亟须者，乃大英帝国内，为英国有色臣民"开放门户"之政策。

不可能于单一文章之篇幅内，妥当处理此重大且具争议之问题，而仅可能有所提示；唯时机已至，所有相关人士当认真考虑事实，并认识其与帝国相关之道德及精神意义为何。

有色种族就自身而言，须为自身选择将遵从之路。若政府明智开启道路，以解放及有条件去除不义、招厌或明显之无能与不公，异族必将于适其充任之处，获该等习俗与理念。其将立志为自由人士。其将习得以自由民主政权之经验付诸实践。其将以行动及牺牲证明，其乃大英帝国合格之公民。

唯若政府拒其一切进步之机会，并阻其一切担险负责之任职，如何证明其诚意或素质？自尊乃民主人士之基础。吾等须就此教化，否则将不能带领土著走出传统公社。

"吾等并无用处"，乃海峡有色阶层中所闻之怨言。其有一深沉之沮丧，冷却所有热情。对志向远大与理想高尚之社群而言，若"安全"仅以拒绝分担英勇行动之自由而换取，斯乃何种之"安全"？其可否独自赢得拯救？对自由人士而言，强制之安全如狱中强制之休息，令人难忍难堪。

如今寰球真切渴望基于公义之持久和平。普世亦知未摧毁军国主义，不得臻此。作为此主题之推论，增添种族与国家之独立，乃须解决问题之一。故于帝国内唤起对种族问题之注意似为恰当，并要求各方面详考所涉复杂问题，俾为世界有色种族奉献良多之大英帝国，可于战后启动公义方案之详订，以助注重实务之政要于实际治理中，解决为输诚于大英帝国之所有种族与部族落实大英帝国宪章原则时，所面对之艰难困惑。命运已眷顾大英帝国。英国之天才人物，已勾画即将导向成功之路径。今日之帝国，乃世界史上最伟大人类事业之丰碑。其不再为独裁所制。虽有错误及缺陷，吾等强大帝国乃屹立于世间最伟大之民主政权。公义为吾等信奉治理原则之基础。唯所需乃同情与智识，以完成帝国之非凡宏构，斯为众多种族之团结、协作及热爱所培育。彼等献纳一份忠心，并认可唯一母亲，其高尚范例适可为世界大同之序曲。

跋

　　林文庆博士此书出入经史原典，洞察当世乱象，举凡政治、历史、宗教、伦理、军事、经济、艺术、文化、种族诸项偌大问题，均在所论之列。深见志趣之远大。而又创发睿见，多中肯綮。即应时局为中国政府而谋为例，对德宣战、以工代兵、举措依据等条理，无不证于后来。其他又及大英帝国高明治策之借境、对海峡华人处境及前途之关切等内容，皆属研究其功业进阶之要素。而因外乱而内省，致有力者倾心传统，确属现代思想史之一大关键，幸毋小觑焉。

　　初读本书，意思无不豁朗。而译笔难下，辄沉吟踌躇。每稿甫出，觉处处未安也。予视译事，素以"忠信"为第一要务。钱锺书所言之翻译家天生保守，乃谦谦君子，"抵抗得了种种诱惑，手痒难熬而不轻举，心痒难搔而不妄动，端的是有克己功夫"。吾不敢言才情，故斟酌用舍，宁取丑拙，避妍以求真，不敢虚饰而媚俗。可谓略伸吾志乎。

　　辜鸿铭曾于《英译中庸》1908 年伦敦初版之序言内，云其本拟以英译《中庸》及《大学》为一合集，唯《大学》之译本，未能达其自设标准，姑且置之。续云译者欲追摹先贤，与其同情，实乃现世之难事也。虽然，小子不敏，请敬事之。译事亦雕虫之一道也。若大而言之，举一切事体，以先儒所倡之力行，加克己工夫以纠时弊，则何不可臻贤而至圣也。惜时人未能克己，而孜孜力行，遂致于南辕北辙之地步，无可挽回。痛哉痛哉。

本书校稿，仍承章木良小妹悉心照料，时有削补；又蒙同窗李夏凌女士妙手制版，长留仪范。二人贡献尤多，并此致谢。而家人多年一日之力助，又无庸待言也。

译事告成，感赋一律：

如梦人琴哭子献，坊间孤本本潜幽。

溯源遥忆儒知战，排劣垂成民守柔。

溪壑百年遗绝曲，天仁三策老横秋。

力行克己近乎圣，继往从兹唯内求。

偶堂

2019 年 4 月于珠海

THE GREAT WAR

FROM

The Confucian Point of View, and Kindred Topics.

BEING LECTURES DELIVERED

During 1914—1917.

WITH AN INTRODUCTION

BY

A. W. STILL.

BY

LIM BOON KENG.

SINGAPORE:
THE STRAITS ALBION PRESS, LTD.

1917

THE GREAT WAR

FROM

The Confucian Point of View, and Kindred Topics.

BEING LECTURES DELIVERED

During 1914—1917.

WITH AN INTRODUCTION

BY

A. W. STILL.

BY

LIM BOON KENG.

SINGAPORE:

THE STRAITS ALBION PRESS, LTD.

1917

DEDICATED

TO

THE MEMORY

OF

THE LATE R. W. HULLETT, M.A.,

FOR MANY YEARS

Principal of the Raffles Institution

AND

Director of Education

IN

GRATEFUL REMEMBRANCE

OF

His Sterling Qualities

AS

A TEACHER AND A FRIEND.

PREFACE.

THESE lectures and addresses were prepared by request of different societies during intervals of other onerous duties. As some of the articles were written from memory after the lectures had been delivered, exact correspondence between any report of the speeches and the present essays could not be expected. As there has been neither time nor leisure for re-writing, the overlapping and imperfections are unavoidable. The main object of these addresses and of this publication, is to direct attention to the solidarity of the common civilization of mankind and to "the eternal verities" of human existence amidst all the noises, the wranglings and the vicissitudes of a troublous time. The success of "Pacificism" in some quarters shows the need of a sound theory of politics, in harmony with modern views of life and its destiny. These old aphorisms of the East in their English dress may serve to press home some common-place truths, which have been overlooked because they have been too familiar!

In the concluding chapter, the principle of justice and liberty which is the basis of the Peace terms of the Allies is applied to the British Empire with reference to the many races bound together by a common loyalty to the mother country and to His Majesty the King. The future must discover a satisfactory solution of the racial problems within the Empire. This can be found only by a sincere application of British democratic maxims to the needs of each individual community, with such modifications as local conditions and actual circumstances will necessitate. Mutual concessions and sacrifices are required but the experience of the ordeal of the Great War will have been thrown away, if we fail to realise within the British Empire, the ideals of race independence and of individual freedom, for which the bravest sons of the Empire and of the great democracies have so freely sacrificed their lives.

INTRODUCTION.

THE characteristic of Dr. Lim Boon Keng is his duality. I have seldom met an equally well read, courteous, and broad minded European, and I have never met anyone who was so perfectly typical of all that is best in the pure Asiatic. One other quality has always warmed my heart towards him. He is as proud of being an Asiatic as I am proud of being a European, and he has given far more deep, earnest study to the justification of his pride of race than I am capable of giving to the justification of mine. No one can overstate the value of the service he has rendered to the Chinese by his study and exposition of their ancient classics. The greatest work that any man can do whose mind has been broadened and enriched by education and experience in the East and the West is to shew how closely linked are the best thoughts of the greatest minds all the world over. Many times during the past nine years I have shared in discussion of literary and philosophical topics with Dr. Lim Boon Keng, and often I have been mentally startled by a new brilliance of illumination given to a theme that seemed modern by some gem of thought called from the ages-old classics of the East. Such experiences are good for Europeans, who are too apt to assume that the Sun of the intellectual sphere rose in the West and moves but slowly Eastward. Of a truth it rose in the East, and shone there with noontide splendour while the West was still in darkness. Shadows may have fallen, yet they do but temporarily obscure. and there is dawning a new day in the East which will reveal again all that has been and is.

In the Lectures and Essays to which I am permitted to write these few words of introduction, Dr. Lim Boon Keng has brought out the facts of the World War vividly and clearly. More particularly, he has stated them in a form, and with references to the great Chinese classics which make a strong appeal to the thousands of educated Chinese, many our loyal fellow subjects, others immigrants who are living contentedly and prosperously under the protection of British law and justice. He has, indeed, rendered a service which no European could have rendered, since few Europeans possess his knowledge and none understand as well as he does how to state a case so that the full force of it gets right home to the Asiatic mind. And to readers in East or West there is food for deep gratification in the revelation that an amazing antiquity can be claimed for the fundamental principles of duty and justice towards individuals, towards small nations and towards

INTRODUCTION.

mankind in general which are the basis of the Allied Cause. Gross violation of these principles by Germany makes it most fitting that the Chinese Nation, oldest of all surviving civilisations, should have ranged itself with the comparatively young Democracies of the West in the struggle for Right against Might.

By such lectures as this book contains and by his speeches as a member of the Legislative Council of the Straits Settlements, Dr. Lim Boon Keng has broadened and deepened the sentiment of loyalty among the Chinese, and we have the proofs of this in the splendidly generous response which all classes of Chinese have made to the many war fund appeals issued here since 1914.

By his strong personality and his earnestness, Dr. Lim Boon Keng has exalted the political and social tone of the great community of which he is the acknowledged leader. On all public questions he is an apostle of progress, but a statesman's caution tempers his zeal for reform. The closing essay of this series deals with "Race and Empire" in a spirit which I would most earnestly commend to thoughtful men of all the races living under the Pax Britannica. To-day our sons are dying for liberty; to-morrow we shall have to demonstrate by our actions that we understand it fully—not in any insular or narrow racial sense but as the principle upon which we confidently rely for the future stability and internal harmony of our vast and complex Empire. Difficulties are inevitable : let it be our pride to conquer them. Prejudices die hard, but they are stronger in the individual than in the nation, which, as an aggregate, is wiser than the wisest of its units. Precious help in the task of solving colour problems is available if we are ready to welcome the co-operation of men like our essayist who, being different from ourselves, are greater than ourselves for the purposes we have in view.

The world war has proven that the British Empire does not rely upon force for the maintenance of its internal stability. It is held together by the silken cords of loyalty, not by the iron fetters of subjection, and our task is to deepen that loyalty by daring to move just a little ahead rather than to lag just a little behind the fitness for full citizenship and responsibility of the various races which honour our flag.

A. W. STILL.

Singapore, February, 1918.

WAR TIME LECTURES AND ESSAYS.

A CONFUCIANIST VIEW OF THE GREAT WAR.

In order to be able to state the Confucianist view clearly, it is necessary in the first place to show what Confucianism really is, and what its attitude is towards War in principle. Then it will be possible to review the Confucianist outlook upon this war of the nations.

I.

General Principles.

Although the Chinese classics have been translated into all European languages, yet it is safe to say that the general doctrines of Confucianism are known only to a small coterie of philosophical students. Most educated people know something of the axiomatic thoughts of Confucius, but beyond a few common places, the outside world's idea of what Confucianism is, consists much more of the unfriendly criticism of its alleged defects than of its intrinsic quality as a religion and a system of ethics, philosophy and politics. The Chinese Classics are comparable to the Bible, and are not suitable as text books for the uninitiated to cull from them any consistent system of doctrines, since they present a bewildering mass of materials much as the books of the Scriptures do.

Confucianism is a Religion.

European critics have often attempted to prove that Confucianism is a mere philosophy and is not a religion. This idea has come down from the Catholic discussions of the 18th Century, for the Jesuits at one time succeeded in gaining favour in the Chinese Court, and nearly succeeded in absorbing Confucianism within the all embracing folds of the Church. It is not at all necessary to go into this notorious controversy. Chinese history is quite clear on this point. Chinese traditions associate Confucian teachings with the oldest national religion— a sort of nature worship sufficiently advanced, however, to admit of a conception of God as the Spiritual Ruler of the universe in terms quite indistinguishable from those employed by the Ancient Hebrews in the Old Testament. The ancient Chinese believe in a Divine providence over-ruling mundane affairs. But this truth is not the outcome of a miraculous revelation but rather the result of intuition at and ratiocination on the part of successive seers and sages.

THEISM.

In the Classics, there is very little theology. The utterances about God are axiomatic. The belief in God is never discussed. The rule of Providence is never questioned. Atheism is unimaginable! In connection with the belief in an Omnipotent and all benevolent Father in Heaven, is the theory of immanent goodness in human nature. An evolution of the races of mankind is tacitly assumed, bringing about social progress and intellectual enlightenment, and ensuring the steady ascendancy of righteousness in human affairs. Altruism is the criterion of Truth, and is also the differentia by which mankind is to be distinguished from the beasts of the field. This absolute faith in Divine wisdom gives rise to the highest optimism, and has led every Confucianist thinker to indulge in visions of a future Millennium similar to those of the Israelite or the Christian on the advent of the Messiah. These fundamental ideas are all pre-Confucian. They were already crystallised in thought in the ethico-political treatises attributed to the royal founders of the Chou dynasty (B.C. 1122—255).

THE NECESSITY OF PREPARATIONS FOR WAR.

From the earliest ages, the Chinese have abhorred the evils of war, and have regarded them among the calamities with which Heaven punishes a nation for her iniquities. War is according to such a view an act of God. But the historical lesson deduced from the annals of China does not agree with the vulgar notion that God is with the big battalions, for the Chinese allege with firm conviction that righteousness always prevails, at least in the long run. The house of Chou was founded as the result of a great rebellion against the tyranny and oppression of the preceding reigning dynasty. In the reconstruction of Society, the needs of military preparation occupy a prominent place. Feudalism is introduced with five grades of nobility and with military equipment proportionate to rank as compared with that of the chief of the State. Communism is carried out successfully and every family is required to supply conscripts for the national army in return for the allotment of land. The state is maintained from the revenue from the crown land cultivated by each unit of the commune

Confucius extols the efficiency and social benefit of this patriarchal system, but unfortunately long before the time of Confucius who was born in B.C. 551—internecine wars, and the encroachments of barbarians have brought about great changes in the form of government, and in the relative positions of the feudal nobles.

The age of Confucius marks the beginning of the disruption of the Augustan age of China. Chinese culture may be said to take its rise from the social and political institutions founded by the first rulers of the Chou dynasty. The Duke of Chou in his famous "Treatise on the Institutes of the Chou dynasty" (Chou-li) describes in detail the various departments of civil and military administration. The duty of a man to fight for the honour and the safety of his state is strongly emphasised. Confucius is recorded as having reprimanded the employment of untrained men in war—thus giving the weight of his authority to enforcing military training upon men who may in an emergency be called upon to defend their country from invasion.

In the annals of the Bamboo Books, the Patriarch Yao is mentioned as having established the first standing army. His reign begins from B. C. 2145. Wild beasts are said to have been employed in War at that period.

The Cannon of History contains a fragment on military preparations, with the expression of an optimistic view of the possible military achievements of the House of Chou. Commentators argue that it really points out the importance of military preparedness as the best guarantee of peace. In the same classic, the right of the people to rebel against tyranny is defended, and the unanimous opinion of the multitude—the vox populi—is regarded as the vox Dei. Wickedness in high places brings calamities upon a country, and High Heaven sends His avengers to punish these evil-doers out of pity for His people whom He loves. Throughout the older classical books, the belief is emphatic that God will punish rulers whose acts bring misery hardships and suffering upon those entrusted to their charge as shepherds of their subjects. King Wu— the Martial King—who really consolidates the dynasty of Chou styles himself "the instrument of God."

OPINIONS OF CONFUCIUS.

When we come to examine the opinions of Confucius more particularly, we are struck with the remarkably modern spirit which they breathe. He is asked about the essentials of Government. (Lun-Yu XII—7). He says in reply that these consist in three things—(1) A government's first duty is to ensure sufficiency of food for the people. (2) There must be adequate military preparation. (3) The government must have the confidence of the public. He goes on to emphasize the fact that without the last, government is impossible. He is also of the opinion that if a country enjoys the leadership of a good man during a period of seven years, the people will be fit to take up arms for the defence of the country. Lord Kitchener has shown the world what he could do in eighteen months. Confucius lays stress upon military training but he himself will not give advice on military matters, pleading in terms of Socratic logic as given in Plato's Republic, that he is not a fighting man by training or profession and that he has no actual experience. But he emphatically asserts it to be a crime to lead an untrained mob to war—for it is " to lead the people to destruction."

According to the ethical principles of Confucianism, the good and the wise sometimes meet with trials but these they always bear with patience and fortitude, and show by their courage and heroism an implicit faith in righteous conduct. In times of anarchy and disorder such as now prevailing in Europe, the man of principle according to Confucius prefers death to dishonour or rather welcomes injury to his person and death itself than seek to live at the expense of truth and right. (Lun-Yu XV. 8.) This reminds us of his famous saying that it is cowardice to refrain from doing what is right, and with this must be associated the teaching that moral conduct is a duty that cannot be shirked on any account.

In the Discourses (Lun-Yu XIV 13.) Confucius tells us what he considers to be a perfect man in his day—such a person when confronted with the view of gain places righteousness before private interest and when placed in a position of danger, is ready to sacrifice his life for a good cause, and moreover such individual does not forget his plighted words however long ago they might have been uttered. These fragments of opinion expressed more than two thousand years ago are enough in themselves to show how a Confucianist must absolutely condemn and abhor the attitude of the German nation towards Belgium and the Powers which have stood by her during the present ordeal by battle.

Confucius is no believer in the doctrine of non-resistance. He is more like a Roman Stoic in his attitude to evil-doers. He believes in striking hard, and in punishment, but he pleads consistently and always for justice. Although he is never tired in singing the praise of peace, he teaches as the lesson of human history that bad rulers must be chastised, and that every state has a duty to perform in the interests of civilization in bringing evil-doers to repentance and to justice.

MENCIUS.

Mencius who has justly been called the St. Paul of Confucianism, is a great protagonist of democracy. He is a disciple of the grandson of the sage. His experience of the prevailing lawlessness of his times and of the turbulent anarchism of the age, lends force to his powerful indictment of militarism, and to his unmeasured condemnation of despotism. "The Virtuous" says he "has no enemy in the world." He grieves that the wars of the Feudal age are all unrighteous for they are all engaged with the view of gaining some material advantage or other over adversaries. Mencius was unsparing and vehement in his protest against an aggressive War. What modern European politicians and diplomats have styled "military expeditions"—Mencius denounces as plundering and murder. He reminds us that Confucius reprobated one of his disciples for helping a tyrant to become powerful and wealthy, and argues that those who wade through slaughter in order to possess themselves with booty and territory—are criminals for whom death is not an adequate punishment.

Those who encourage militarism and form alliances for defense and offense are called "Robbers of the People" by Mencius (Bk. VI ii. 9.) for they mislead the rulers and encourage them to think material resources—wealth—trade and military power are the main objects of successful government, forgetting that righteousness and the love of mankind alone constitute the right path to real dominion over men. His words seem almost prophetic of the state of Europe before the Great War. Mencius in his time discussed politics with tyrants and did not mince words in pointing out to them their grievous errors.

War is a necessary evil under the existing conditions of civilization. Confucius and Mencius would fain regard it as serving the function of a moral police for the world. Mencius plainly says that a military expedition against a recalcitrant nation or State is clearly a means of correction in the general interests of mankind.

CHIVALRY AND HUMANITY.

Confucius advocates that a man must exercise his humanity in every possible situation even in War. He carries this principle in his private life, thus while he will angle for fish—he will never use a net, and though he is an enthusiastic hunter—he will only shoot at birds on the wing, and will not shoot a bird on the perch. Confucius is anxious that under no circumstances should a gentleman ever forget his chivalry and we may infer from Chinese history the greatest soldiers have been noted for their magnanimity and their chivalrous conduct towards the enemy.

WHEN IS WAR JUSTIFIABLE.

The general view of Confucianists in regard to War, may be summarised in the words of the essayist Ssu Ma Fa : " The ancients base everything in conduct upon humanity. Right is the regulations of human affairs by means of righteousness. Right without compulsion is Power, and the latter is the outcome of War . . . . Therefore if killing is to give peace to mankind, killing is justifiable. To attack a country on behalf of the population is quite justifiable for the onslaught is with the view of stopping misgovernment. If War is enough to bury national animosities and to lead to their suppression war is justifiable ! Humanity sees kinship ; righteousness appreciates explanation ; wisdom discovers trust ; courage finds the way, and sincerity meets with sincerity. While love reigns within the army, the defensive can be maintained. When the superior prestige of the forces become obvious, then the time is ripe for the offensive. War should be conducted with due regard to the seasons and without shifting the non-combatants from place to place . . . . Although a state may be great love of war will surely lead to its destruction and though a country may enjoy years of peace, to neglect preparations for war is perilous."

From the practice of feudal times is derived the principle of employing force to chastise a ruler for oppressing his people. This is one of the most striking features of the politics of Confucius. Government must be maintained for the good and the happiness of the governed and not in the interests of autocrats and their parasites. The Ruler is the shepherd or pastor

of his people and is responsible to God for the faithful per-
formance of his duties. Neglect of these is punished indirectly
in numerous ways through the agency of natural causes—such
as droughts, inundations, famines, pestilences. War of course
has in all countries been regarded as a curse inflicted upon a
country for the sins of its ruler or people. One can deduce,
however, from the teaching of Chinese sages, that all rulers are
or should be interested in the maintenance of righteous government in the world, and that it is the duty of every government
to punish any ruler who oppresses his people and who commits
acts contrary to justice, right or humanity. Thus Confucian
politics distinguish a war of aggression from a military
expedition with the avowed object of punishing a wicked ruler or
people—such for example as the British punitive expedition
against King Theebaw. Confucianism condemns militarism as
the means of aggrandisement, and vehemently detests all despotic interference with the social life of nations.

MILLENNIAL DREAMS.

Another great principle of Confucianism intimately connected with this subject is the recognition of the oneness
of the human race. The object of culture is to embrace all
mankind within the fold of civilization, and to ensure for all
the blessings of good government. Confucianism in its three-
fold divisions of ethics, politics and religion strives to prepare
the individual for his place in the family—to educate the family,
to understand its role in the state, to guide the ruler of each
state to comprehend his duty to civilization and humanity.
Peace is indispensable to the propagation of this great and
noble ideal. Man does not live for himself alone. He is a unit
of the race and must live to benefit the race as a whole. The
Confucianist millennium called the Great Communion (大 同)
in the Canon of Rites, is an era of universal peace, in which
law and morality are both superseded by love. Until this is
achieved the art of war must be cultivated in the interests of
right and of justice.

But in the "Great Science" one of the classical books of
the Confucian School, is foreshadowed the Federation of States
as the result of the spread of civilisation. The ancient history
of the Chinese affords abundant materials for showing the
futility of arranging a balance of power by means of intrigues
and alliances. The general conflict arising through failure of
such artificial arrangements is always worse than an ordinary
war because it lets loose long bent up animosities. All these

ancient and modern alliances fail because they are primarily
based on a tacit acknowledgment of force as the ultimate resort,
and they have for their main object the presentation of material
advantages to the stronger, irrespective of the claims of right
or of justice. Arising from this dissatisfaction with current
politics of the olden times, which curiously does not differ in
material aspects from that of our own day, the statesmen of
ancient China in the year 546 B. C. arranged an inter-state
Conference to arrange for the cessation of armaments. The
meeting came off but as in the case of the Hague Conference of
our day, no one was prepared to begin the task of disarmament.
The Confucian School, always with a keen eye to practical
measures, has not attempted again to trust upon such an ideal
arrangement, but it does teach that every state should have its
military preparations in the highest state of efficiency and
readiness and that the ruler of a state should ever be ready to
use his army in the sacred course of civilization, and human
progress. Of course the ideal of utilizing man's dormant
energies in the interests of peace, and of turnings words into
ploughshares is shared by the Confucianist idealist with the Jew
and the Christian—Yen-hui, the St. John of the Confucian
Church, expresses the desire to serve a ruler who will turn men's
thoughts to the arts of social life and of husbandry so that the
martial spirit and the eagerness to exhibit feats of prowess
may give place to endeavours for the general progress of mankind. The great Ruler and Despot—who built the Great Wall
by means of conscript labour—cast the bulk of his weapons
into bells and statues after his final Victory.

A RIGHTEOUS WAR.

In short war is in itself a great evil, but there is a greater
evil in a tame acquiescence in evil and in a silent submission
to brute force. As a means of defense, armed preparations are
essential—military service is an indispensable duty, and to die
for home, king and country is the highest duty of the good man.
Military strength, however, should also be employed by a state
in the general cause of civilization for the chastisement of evil-
doers. No Government has a right to oppress its subjects. A
neighbouring state has the right to interfere in the cause of
humanity and right but must not employ such a pretext for
self-aggrandisement.

These are briefly the general principles, from which we
can now understand the Confucian view of the Great War
which Germany has inflicted on the world.

II

WHAT IS CIVILIZATION?

The next subject for consideration is what is the Confucian view of culture and of civilization. Upon this will depend its criticism of German methods.

We have seen that the Confucian view of human Society is purely a secular one, and does not attempt to bolster up its ethical precepts by divine sanction. Confucianism, however premises two great principles (1) the unity of the human race and (2) the universal validity of the law of righteousness. It constructs its whole system of ethics, philosophy and politics upon the basis of altruism. The whole world is under the spiritual rule of God, and the rulers of the different Nations must promote the general welfare of mankind as the ultimate goal of the individual efforts of each national group. The laws regulating the intercourse of nations should be founded upon the same moral ideals in harmony with the aspirations of the sages, and the wanton aggression of one nation against another is as much a crime as the act of a robber or a brigand.

Civilization is therefore a corporate unity, embracing all nations, and requiring the faithful service of every individual. In order, however, that such a view of the moral order of human society can be realized—it is essential that ethical education should be universal. Confucianism aims at preparing this most desirable condition by inculcating filial piety, patriotism, loyalty, fidelity, courage and benevolence.

Love all men is the highest teaching alike of Confucianism as of Christianity. But there is this difference: whereas in Christianity there is no limit set to altruism and non-resistance, Confucianism on the contrary insists that it is the right and the duty of every man to oppose a wrong and to punish an evil-doer. No human authority can excuse itself for a wicked and tyrannical act under the cloak of religion. The Emperor or President or Priest who has committed a wrongful act must be punished, and justice must be done. This uncompromising attitude of the Confucian teaching has in the course of history made many martyrs. Of course in degenerate times men eulogise crimes and make virtues of the wicked deeds of their masters. Still Confucianism endeavours to subordinate force to reason and good-will, and in the end, the human spirit must come off on the top.

In fact civilization is the outcome of the confluence of many forces acting and counteracting upon diverse races from the beginning of human history. It is a continuous current but its strength and direction are determined by the factors that count in the dynamics of social life. Its manifold variation may be compared to the endless transformations of the figures presented by the kaleidoscope—in which though the forms seem infinite, we know that the elements are always the same. Shakespeare is adored in all countries and nowhere more so than in Germany because he thoroughly understands human nature, and in spite of the intense hate of the Germans for everything English, no one has yet thought of "*strafing*" the immortal poet of humanity. In Confucianism and in Christianity are to be found these rudiments of truth. The Germans in the eighteenth century have formulated the laws of civilization. From the Kantian categories are deduced the Hegelian Idealism with the apotheosis of the State and the defence of war as a moral agency. The whole world had been captivated by the depth and the breadth of the Philosophical questions profounded by the Great Masters, whom Carlyle, Ruskin and Haldane had belauded, forgetting that Kant and his disciples had really built upon the great foundations laid by the philosophers of China, India, Rome and Greece, and upon the illuminating thoughts of Rousseau and the French Encyclopœdists. In fact Kant's Essay on "Eternal peace" might pass very well as a disquisition by the most orthodox Confucianist although even Kant eulogises the moral value of war (Critique of asthetic judgment Eng. Ed. 1911 p. 112) what is admirable in the old German philosophy is this emphatic recognition of a moral order in the universe, necessitating the conformity of human conduct with the ideals of ultruism. Unfortunately for Germany, the cultivation of science had predisposed many of her thinkers to those ideas evidently derived from the investigation of nature. There is no doubt that the speculations of two insane though wonderfully gifted minds—those of Schopenhauer and Nietzsche have led modern Germans to elaborate the elements of *Kultur* and have provided the materials, which have been used to such great effect by Bernhardi, von der Goltz and others. The Kaiser may justly be called the father of the modern *Kultur*, the ethics of the Tiger and of the universal Teutondom.

In his prepared speeches and letters to persons interested in teaching and education, Kaiser William has left clear indications of the high ideals he has on " the co-ordination of physical, intellectual and religious training and discipline " History is to be taught so as to show in relief " the great achievements of the Fatherland." Duelling is encouraged in high schools and universities so that the young educated Germans will be provided with the degree of fortitude which is necessary when they go out into the world." The school is to be the recruiting ground for the devotees of Germanism.

The Kaiser confesses that the "glorious transfigured image" of his mother " whose every thought was art " has led him " to foster the beautiful, to develop art in the life of the people on strictly defined limits which are to be found in the sense of mankind for beauty and harmony." He also claims that the Germans alone possess the great ideals that " the working and toiling classes may take pleasure in the beautiful and work up and out of their every day range of thought." So far there is not much to quarrel with the objects of Kultur.

But another force was growing steadily in strength in Germany while the Kaiser and his diplomats were assuring England of the peaceful intentions of the Imperial Government. Bernhardi's programm of world domination as the climax of the Pan Teutonic league was regarded in England as the irresponsible vaporings of a rabid jingo. Only after the outbreak of war, did the world realize that the German nation had secretly embraced as part of Kultur the pseudo-philosphy of von Treitsche and had adopted its religion, the worship of Force. Treitsche's idea of the absoluteness of the state which is stolen from Machiavelli is made to justify the utmost despotism. His identification of the State with Might gives a moral sanction to the militarism of Frederich William IV, and to the most unjustifiable aggression. The Peace propaganda is not only foolish but also immoral. Fear is to be the means of imposing upon inferior and backward races the immaculate Kultur of Germany. So says this apostle of the German civilization—"The historian who tried to Judge European politics in Africa or in the East by the same standards as in Europe would be a fool. He who cannot inspire fear over here is lost." (Die Politik.") Thus it will be quite evident the Germans have not been shocked by the atrocities and excesses of their soldiers, as they have been taught to regard " fright-

fulness " as the proper thing in war. For Germany, according
to Bernhardi, there are only two alternatives—world domination
or ruin—(" Welt macht oder niedergang.")

From the Confucian standpoint, a state has no more right
to consider itself above the law of humanity or the moral law
than an individual to claim his independence of all his fellow
citizens. A state is a unit of the social order of civilization·
It has to conform with the land of nations, and it has to submit
to the ethical ideals and the moral restraints of civilization.
No man should live for himself alone. Confucianism enjoins
him to live for his family,—for his country,—for his race, and
for the good of mankind as a whole. Likewise an individual
state cannot be indifferent to the fate of its neighbours, and
has a moral duty to repress evil, and to foster virtue in the
interests of mankind and of culture. Consequently Confucianism upholding the principles of liberty does not approve of
any form of racial exclusion, though it justifies attempts
to ameliorate the state of inferior races and to impose conditions so that improvement and enlightenment may in time per-
mit all nations to live on terms of amity and equality. This is the
Confucian ideal. And it is also the ideal of all the great world
religions—Islam and Christianity. Confucianism, however, pre-
sumes that this ideal will be realized in due time by natural
causes, and that it can only be attained by the resolute and
united efforts of all races working for the good of mankind.

Small and weak nations therefore contrary to Bernhardi
and his school have an undoubted right to live and develope.
The Powerful nations are to assist and guide them, and not to
despoil them and reduce them to slavery. There is no greater
crime in Confucian eyes than to cause the extinction of a family
or a state. The principle of maintaining the independence and
integrity of nationalities is the first axiom of Confucian politics.
Confucianists believe in this in spite of the actual results of
history brought about by militarism because they do think that
there is a moral force shaping human destiny which will right
things in the end. Apart from the transient and shifting
relation of things and persons, there is a law of righteousness,
according to which the human soul is directed in ways often
not explicable by our present intelligence. Thus the aeroplane
appears to act in defiance of the attraction of gravitation, so
there are human deeds seemingly in contravention of the laws
of society and civilisation, will be found on closer inspection to

be in full harmony with truth, so that in complete confidence in the triumph of righteousness, the Confucianist may with equanimity watch the waves of progress and decay involving the rise and fall of nations, knowing all the time that life is ○ not all vanity, and that a glorious future awaits us after the storm. Civilization according to Confucianism is the slow but sure realization of the Divine ideals of justice of love of truth— in human society—the completing of the Kingdom of God on Earth.

WAR TIME LECTURES AND ESSAYS.

III.

THE CHARGES.

We now come to the charges which are made against Germany and her people, and the counter-charges preferred against the Allies by the Arch-enemy—the Kaiser William's own subjects.

The complaint is that the Germans have committed a series of acts that are contrary to reason, to law, to right, to morality, to religion, to dictates of humanity and to the solemn pledges of their own accredited representatives. In stating such charges in a brief and categorical manner, we may note the motives given by the Germans for their conduct since these excuses in themselves form part of the ground of accusation against them.

1. That the whole German nation had plotted the ruin of France and England without cause, and that she used means to reassure her intended victims while determined to destroy them at the first opportunity.

A charge of mendacity and hypocrisy.

2. That she had abused hospitality by taking advantage of residence and other privileges freely accorded her people through her system of espionage.

A charge of treachery.

3. That she has set up her might and her own interests as the only criterion of right and wrong to the prejudice and the hurt of the world.

A charge of egotism and wilfully causing hurt.

4. That Germany instigated Austria to send Serbia an ultimatum, which the latter could not possibly accept without loss of dignity and prestige as an independent nation.

A charge of abetment of wrongful act.

5. That Germany is responsible for the outbreak of the War by sending to Russia the instant demand for demobilisation at a time when Austria in spite of Russian warning had mobilised her troops for an aggressive act towards Serbia.

Charge for being the cause of the War.

6. That Germany invented falsehoods about the French violation of Belgian territory in order to excuse her own treachery in invading Belgium.

A charge of lying and treachery.

7. That Germany attempted to bribe Great Britain by concessions to the latter's material interests provided Great Britain would connive at her robbery, her intended crime and her infamy.

A charge of moral cowardice and of offering illegal gratification.

8. That Germany contrary to the law of nations and to her own solemn written guarantees violated Belgian neutrality by the forced entry of her troops despite the warning of the Powers, and the protests of Belgium.

A charge of criminal violence and causing hurt.

9. That the German army committed acts contrary to the Hague Conventions and to the customary practice of civilised nations in the sack of Louvain and in the war against the aged, women and children.

A charge of barbarism and vandalism.

10. That the German navy has sanctioned piracy by attacks on merchant vessels without warning causing death of innocent non-combatants irrespective of age or sex.

A charge of inhumanity and piracy, and wholesale murder.

11. That the German Government has sanctioned the bombardment of defenceless towns—the harsh treatment of prisoners of war and the deliberate neglect of the sick in Wittenberg Camp.

A charge of lawlessness and cruelty, and indiscriminate murder.

12. That the German Government—the Kaiser and the military chief—are responsible for making peace impossible and for sanctioning the criminal and lawless acts, and that the German Professors have instigated and condoned, and justified the crimes and the follies of their rulers, and that with the exception of about a dozen men, the German nation is an accessory to the detestable crimes and the hideous outrages upon humanity and civilization.

THE DEFENCE.

Let us hear with all patience and all possible impartiality the German defence, and give due weight and the benefit of doubt to anything that bears even an impress of probability or a vestige of truth.

(1.) Against the first charge, the Germans plead that the French were determined to avenge the war of 1870. That Russia a barbarous state was a source of peril to German expansion by her Pan Slavic tendencies—that the British Navy ruled the waves though the British had degenerated and had become unfit even to be shop-keepers, and that by the Divine law of Evolution, which their prophets Hæckel, Treitsche and Clauewitz had deduced from the researches initiated by Darwin, Germany had become the strongest, the wisest, the noblest of the races, as Might was the highest form of Right. Germany was obeying nature and God to take her place in the Sun, and to wrest the Sceptre of Neptune from the Mistress of the Seas.

(2.) Against the charge of treachery and abuse of hospitality by her espionage, Germany excused herself again on the plea of necessity sanctioned by the law of struggle for existence, and held that the demands of the State were supreme. The end would justify the means. Falsehood and treachery were virtues in War. Success and Victory alone counted. The Allies were free to do likewise!

(3.) The German boast of their strength, defy and challenge the world to prove the question by the ordeal of battle.

(4.) The Kaiser claimed to be the peacemaker and blamed England for declaring war and the Kaiser for not obeying his peremptory and insolent order to desist from the necessary defensive measures against the Austrian preparations.

(5.) The band of eminent German Professors in "The Truth about Germany" protest that Russia is responsible for the war. They allege that all Germans, themselves included, wanted peace. They were attacked by Russia, which had made preparations for a war of aggression.

(6.) The Berlin Government contended that if the French did not do so, that would be incredible, and as its troops had already invaded Belgium, either the Belgians had aided the French or the French had entered Belgium. In any case, Germany would indemnify Belgium for losses.

(7.) Dr. Bethmann-Hollweg could not understand Great Britain's "regard for the sanctity of a scrap of paper" and the Germans professed to be aggrieved that the British should place moral considerations above the question of kinship to the Teutonic race with the dolicocephalic index.

(8.) The Germans admitted at first that wrong had been done to Belgium by the forcible violation of her neutrality and promised to make reparations in due time. But afterwards they pleaded French violation of Belgian territory and their claim to have discovered an Anglo-Belgian convention to invade Germany through Belgium.

(9.) All prominent Germans have openly declared their belief in frightfulness as a part of the offensive in war. The Kaiser wanted his soldiers to imitate the Huns to give no quarter and to take no prisoners. Militarist leader professors and politicians believe in a cruel uncompromising war sanguinary and horrible to crush every spark of defiance to Germany. Major-General von Disfurth says: "We are and must be barbarians if by these we understand those who wage war relentlessly and to the uttermost degree."

(10.) The Germans reply that the British Blockade is starving the babies of Germany!

(11.) The answer to the charge of inhumanity and reckless murder is that in nature all acts of war are fair. Whatever hurts frightens and injures the adversary, helps the army—and is useful to the State, than which there is nothing greater.

(12.) The Germans have simply gloried in the war and in their successes but they have been anxious to lay the responsibility of bringing about the war on other shoulders. Their excuses have been dealt with in the official documents published by all the Allied Powers.

WAR TIME LECTURES AND ESSAYS.

IV.

THE VERDICT.

The whole case having been stated, it is possible to deliver the verdict of the Confucianist jury somewhat briefly. In the first place, do not mistake the opinions of Chinese for being necessarily Confucian views any more than accept the German standpoint as being necessarily Christian. The Confucianist attitude must be based on the principles that are well established on the admitted Classics and on the doctrines of the Confucian School. It is appropriate to express this judgment entirely in the phraseology, and after the manner of the Confucian ethics.

1. Everything has its cause. A tree is judged by its fruit. The origin of all the ill-feeling and the war-like preparations is the materialistic view of life. As Mencius has stated if gain is to be the criterion of success in politics as well as in private life, competition is inevitable, and the more cunning will take advantage of the honest. All the belligerents have been guilty of regarding worldly interests as the chief end of civilization, but the Germans are the most to blame for making them the supreme object of national existence.

2. Might is not everything. Ferocity does not coerce the brave. Cruelty and hate do no good to those who indulge in them. Reason and benevolence work in mysterious ways to overcome brute force, and animal passions. Persecution has always failed in history. The Germans have been under a vain delusion and have brought untold sufferings upon mankind. They have brought utter ruination to their once prosperous land. They will reap what they have sown. They have appealed to force and God will destroy them because of their unrighteousness and their reliance on Might to the disparagement of benevolence and righteousness.

3. Militarism and tyranny tend to perpetuate the rule of force and the animal conditions of life necessitating the struggle for existence. They are contrary to the dictates of Reason, which have developed chivalry, charity, benevolence, justice and altruism—the elemental qualities of civilization, just as man has conquered the wild beasts and the savages, so civiliza-

tion must triumph over the dominion of might. All the Empires created by force have crumbled away in time. The Mongol invasion of China was ultimately repulsed by a poor and illiterate monk. The Manchu Empire was brought to an end by a refugee wandering like Ulysses in strange and foreign countries, without an army and without money. The great power exercised by President Yuan Shih Kai was broken by one brave man who left Singapore at the end of 1915 and entered Yunnan alone and unarmed. The fate of Alexander, Shih-huangti, Cæsar, Attila, Genghis and Napoleon proves the futility of great conquests by means of force. The iniquities committed by these tyrants are recorded for their condemnation for all ages. The Kaiser William has been tempted to imitate Napoleon without the latter's genius, and has treated his kindest relatives on the distaff side with base ingratitude. He has relied on the strength of his military power to crush civilization. He has given ear to the voice of his tempters and has repudiated the noble principles cherished by his parents—to the eternal shame and the utter ruin of his house, his nation and his Empire. The anathema of God and man is upon him, upon his advisers and upon his hosts. The spiritual force wielded by the Inscrutable God will raise up mightier phalanges to subdue his hordes and truth and right must triumph as witness the triumphs of Christianity and Buddhism and Confucianism.

4. The breach of faith with Belgium is a crime against civilization and humanity. All neutral nations who base their constitution and law on righteousness and law should arise and exert their fullest strength to punish the criminal among the nations. The Allies represent the spiritual force of the Universe and are the Instrument of God to repress the scourge of mankind, and to bring the blood-thirsty and greedy Germans to justice.

5. For all the cruelties, murders, atrocities and barbarities committed by German soldiers, the Kaiser and his officers deserve the severest condemnation of all good men now and in the ages to come. The Allies will demand material compensation for all losses. God will also punish them in His own way to be sure. Remorse, shame, degradation, and disgrace will inflict sufferings commensurate with those which they have caused to others. God is never mocked. The disgust of mankind will repel the German from every respectable society till timely repentance shall make amends for the great wrongs done to the world on account of Teutonic ambition.

By their conduct, the Germans have shown that they are outlaws and according to the requirements of morality and religion, every man of principle should assist the Allies in every possible way to bring the culprits to condign punishment. The moral reprobation of mankind as a whole is a stigma that will cost the German nation much more injury than the loss of a hundred battles.

7. The Allies were not careful themselves to attend to the requirements of Righteousness before the Great War. When the German Emperor urged his troops to imitate the Huns in China, no protest was made by the Christian Powers, and now Nemesis has brought the same Huns to Europe.

8. Permanent Peace can only be secured by strict adhesion to the principles of justice and righteousness. The nations must consider first the claims of humanity and must put aside minor questions relating to commercial interests or territorial acquisitions. The conflict has arisen out of a struggle for a place in the sun, and in the fighting for a place, many sacred things have been trampled in the dust, the question of justice, of freedom, of law, of national liberties and of the rights of the weak, the defenceless—the minority and the defeated, can only be settled by men who understand the requirements of the physical environment, and who are inspired with the noblest ideals of civilization. Justice calls for punishment but love pleads for mercy.

Such in brief is the attitude of Confucianism towards the multifold problems presented by the greatest War in history. War is always an evil, though good may come out of it, for in nature the Sun shines upon all and by a peculiar irony of our existence, mankind learns only by realising the antithesis of things. Without darkness light is invisible—without limits, all objects fade into nothingness—without the greatest evils—the highest good is imperceptible. What is the purpose of imposing upon our intellect this tantalising antinomy ?—it is the question of religion and philosophy to solve. But this much we may be certain from the Confucianist standpoint that man's destiny is to ascend to greater spiritual heights—to leave behind the beastly struggle for existence and the vain competition for worldly possessions and to attain the perfect peace of the Soul in the kingdom of light and righteousness.

WAR TIME LECTURES AND ESSAYS.

V.

The Peace of the World.

The history and culture of a people are often reflected upon the words of its language. Thus the English word Peace reminds us of the Feudalism introduced by the Normans, while both the English and the French words have their root in the Latin Pax, which in turn was derived from another word meaning to agree or to bind, peace among the Romans being the fruit of wars and resulting from solemn engagements, breach of which immediately and surely called forth the mobilisation of the whole might of Rome.

Among the ancient Teutonic races the idea of peace is expressed by words meaning rest or freedom, but reflecting also no doubt the ruthless campaigns of the ubiquitous Romans. Peace meant to these wild savages freedom from the encroachment of the Romans and liberty to live free from the entanglements of restraints, imposed by the conquerors from the South.

The Chinese have a word for peace akin to the Latin *quies* meaning tranquility or repose, but the proper term for peace equivalent to the Latin Pax is the dissyllabic word Taipeng. All of us of course know of the prosperous mining town of that name in Perak, and may also remember of the great Chinese Civil War which Gordon helped to suppress and which is known as the Taipeng rebellion. It may not be generally known, however, that Taipeng means universal Peace, and that the founder of that ephemeral celestial dynasty claims to be the messenger of God to bring peace to a suffering world.

At any rate the word Taipeng literally *equalitas* is taken from the Confucian Classics, and there we find that Taipeng means the equilibrium of the Golden Mean by which the nations continue to live in happiness and prosperity when justice and rectitude will guide every individual action ; and when social order and human law will become unnecessary as man will have overcome selfishness with the whole world united for the promotion of the welfare of mankind and for the furtherance of

knowledge and civilization. Thus the Confucianist and the
Christian alike await for the dawn of the Millennium—

> "Till the war drum throbbed no longer, and the battle
>   flags were furl'd
> "In the Parliament of men, the Federation of the world."

So much then do history and culture throw light upon the
meanings of even such a familiar word.

WHAT NATURE TEACHES.

When we examine the world around us to discover what
phenomena have given rise to the notion of peace—we find that
nature outside the pale of humanity has little or nothing to
show about peace but on the contrary appears to be the arena
of ceaseless wars. We search in vain throughout the organic
world for peace anywhere, save the awful suspense in the
absence of life itself. Among inanimate things however there
reigns only an apparent tranquility for even with them the
physical, and chemical forces—terrestrial and cosmic are contending for eventual mastery and the apparent immobility is
the only prelude to the explosion—the proverbial lull before
the storm.

It is now universally recognised that there exists a struggle
for existence among plants and animals. The strife is keener
and fiercer the higher we ascend in the scale of living
organisms. Thanks to the patient observations of Darwin and
Wallace, the great biologic law of the survival of the fittest is
found to be the explanation of the apparent chaos of conflct in
which every individual and every race seem to fight for
supremacy, and on this account the conclusion that "the
weakest goes to the wall" seems to be justified by the data of
science. The Nietzchian philosophy, which has captivated the
imagination of Bernard Shaw, is founded on a misconception
and misconstruction of this law of nature. How far the
doctrine of the Superman is from the truth can be seen at a
glance when we realise that the survival of the fittest explains
the existence of the defenceless dove as well as of the incon-
venient appendix of man. On the other hand, the fiercest and
most blood thirsty as well as the most powerful beasts have
been disappearing throughout geological time, and out of this
ceaseless welter of force arises man without fangs, without
claws and without talons—but with intellect, reason and a

capacity for altruism, and this apparently defenceless man of flesh has dominated the beasts of the field and has conquered and vanquished the dragon, and all the life-destroying beasts of the world.

MAN ONLY CAPABLE OF PEACE.

Although the study of evolution reveals a state of perpetual war in nature, it also indicates the developement of reason and love and proves unmistakeably the existence of other forces than those of destruction. As the Russian Prince and Socialist Peter Krapotkin has abundantly demonstrated the science of evolution illustrates the operation of mutual aid and social co-operation no less than that of the fierce struggles for existence. Man however is threatened with extinction by perils all around. He has had to defend himself against the forces of nature, against the attacks of wild beasts and against the machinations of his fellow men. Owing to the difficulty of procuring food, savages are not even safe from their own kinsmen who sometimes resort to killing off their old folks. According to Grimm, the ancient Germans put to death their sick and aged or even often buried them alive. and to-day the world is aghast at the atavistic appearance of Teutonic brutality and ferocity. However as the late Professor Henry Drummond has poetically said "Evolution is not progress in matter— it is a progress in Spirit in that which is limitless, in that which is at once most human, most rational and most divine."

Slowly in the course of untold ages, love and reason find the means of overcoming the stern realities of War. Instead of fighting one another to mutual extinction, man made compromises and concluded peace which enabled the vanquished to live in tranquility upon condition that the wishes or requirements of the conquerors were met by personal service by money or other tribute and by concessions of land and other rights.

History records the ceaseless struggles between might and right—the conclusion of peace as merely a preparation for further war and the lamentable failure of Buddhism, Confucianism and Christianity to cement mankind in one great brotherhood upon the common basis of Love and humanity. Despotism cannot extinguish the burning embers of human liberty which is ever ready to burst into flame at the first opportunity till peace which guarantees freedom instead of slavery, enables the human spirit to develop in a more congenial sphere.

The annals of all Empires and Kingdoms and Republics confirm the fact that permanent peace, however desirable, is only
possible when the people enjoy freedom and contentment as
the result of the operation of just laws under a benign and
righteous government.

CHIVALRY OR BUSHIDO.

In course of time, the sword became transformed into a
mighty weapon of defence. Throughout feudal times the
knight though often brutal and heartless to his retainers—
cultivated noble qualities towards his equal and towards women,
so that the institution of chivalry became a bulwark of honour
and of religion. From the earliest ages in China, the knights
were inspired by the teaching of the sages that it was nobler
to die rather than to do wrong or to suffer ignominy and dishonour, and that it was the inherent obligation of every
Confucianist to defend the weak and to punish wrong.
Professor Nitobe of Kyoto tells us that in Japan the knights
and Samurai under the influence of Bushido practised the ethics
of Confucius, and wielded their swords in defence of righteousness, and in the interests of peace.

GOODWILL AMONG MEN.

But Confucianism tells us further that there will be no
peace on earth till every man and woman are taught to realise
what human life is—how sacred is duty to others and how
glorious is the destiny of the race. The individual must become
conscious of the claim of altruism. He must cultivate love as
a living force and he must show it in his life—from the cradle
to the grave treasuring the love of his parents as a perpetual
example in order to extend its beneficent influence of goodwill
to all men. In this way only can there be contentment and
harmony in the family—tranquility and order in the State, and
peace and happiness in the world. Greed and egotism must
be up-rooted, and in their place must be installed righteousness
and love and then sincerity will be a powerful impulse to
transform and elevate mankind, making the ideal of peace no
longer a vision but a real force in civilization.

By gradual degrees, civilised men are finding out means of
mutual aid and co-operation, and of solving factors that make
for conflict and disagreement. Charles Darwin pointed out
in the "Descent of Man" that man's "social qualities" had to a

great extent counteracted his "want of natural weapons". As civilization developes the competition for profit between capital and labour in the exploitation of industries has necessitated schemes for maintaining industrial peace. In the United Kingdom confidence is laid on mutual understanding as the outcome of discussion, and the object of negotiation is to prevent a premature rupture of friendly discussion of terms by strikes and lock-outs. On the other hand, the organization of workers tends to extend beyond the spheres of political limits and become international. It aims at a universal federation of labour and its extreme parties like the syndicalists and anarchistic socialists declare war *a outrance* against all established institutions and even against Reason itself!

The existence of irreconcilable differences and bitter antipathies among the classes in all free countries was well known to the Germans in 1914. They had hoped to benefit by internecine struggles in England and in France. How deplorable and how disastrous these industrial grievances of a discontented proletariat may be, we can judge by the serious obstacles they have thrown in the way of the effective prosecution of the war. But even in Germany herself and in America, there are the forces engendered by class ambition and by heartless commercialism, ready at the psychological moment to rend society to pieces. There is indeed something rotten in the civilization of the world because under the cloak of high-sounding shibboleths man exploits his fellow man mercilessly and the rivalry for wealth and power among individuals and classes is not a whit less demoralising than the international race in armaments.

The only possible conclusion of such military and naval competition as the Great Powers had been engaged in, is the terrible war, which is scourging civilization. But horrible as this war has proved itself to be mainly through the folly and the madness of the German leaders, the class war of the future, in which capital and labour will struggle for mastery will probably be infinitely more harrowing and more frightful on account of the long pent up fury of the discontented and of the develish doctrines which deny at once the practical sanctions of morality and the solemn dictates of religion. If popularization of German pseudo philosophy like that of Max Stirner and of Nietzche is to lead the socialists and working men to creating new standards of life and ideals then the outlook of the future is gloomy indeed.   This greater fratricidal war of the classes looms like a lurid spectre behind the smoke and cloud of the present Armageddon and unless the state and the church take warning from the writings on the Wall, there will be no peace in the West, and the efforts of those who labour for peace and righteousness will be wasted on a sisyphean task without any prospects of success.

THE CAUSES OF WAR.

However there is every hope that this great war may bring home to many some wholesome truths and may lead the peoples of all countries to meditate on the merits of a lasting peace founded not upon some temporary advantage of the conquerors over the vanquished but upon the everlasting merits of justice and right.   War is the result of the conflict of forces, and is dependant upon causes which can be studied and analysed with the same precision as that employed in depicting the cause and estimating the force of a typhoon.   From of old, the ambition of great military leaders maddened with successes, and goaded to greater exertions by the flattery of their tools, has been a great menace to the peace of the world.   Alexander of Macedon, Hannibal Julius Cæsar, Napoleon, Shih-huangti and many others have utilised their military power to give effect to their grandiose ambitions.

Every country has suffered from barbarian invasion and perhaps no country more than poor Belgium or unfortunate China.   The Teutonic races have been the scourge of Europe, and have inflicted incalculable losses upon humanity and civilization.   From the pirates that settled in the British Isles the Goths and Vandals, the Franks, the Longbeards—down to the Germans that effect the present invasion of Belgium, France and Poland, the Teutonic races have manifested the same spirit of brutality and arrogance.   Everywhere however, the Teutons could not long maintain their original character, and as soon as the horrors of war had been forgotten, the Germans began to imitate the habits and the cries of their victims, and during the ensuing Peace, the Teutons in the lands they had conquered were punished by absorption in the races they had robbed and wronged.   Down to our day this de-germanisation of the Teutons has been steadily going on.   The Wars that resulted from German invasions caused in the end greater loss in manhood to the Vaterland.   This is the irony of fate, which the Germans do realise, but with characteristic stolidity, they failed to discover the true cause of this denationalisation, and employed the full force of their ponderous intellects to devise the Pan Germanic league for the domination of the world after the destruction of France and Britain.

Then again many wars have been caused by religious fanaticism such as the invasions of the Saracens and the Turks and the mediæval crusades of Christendom against the Moslems. Racial antipathies emphasizing psychological and social antagonism like those existing among Chinese and Tartars, the Celts and the Saxons, the Teutons and the Slavs will long remain as the predisposing causes of war.

THE SIN OF PRUSSIA.

Political considerations also in the eyes of war-like nations justify the practice of machiavellian principles at the expense of weak neighbours, without regard for justice and in defiance of solemn agreements. No country in the whole history of the world has sinned more in this respect than Prussia under the Hohenzollerns—from the time of Frederick, the Robber, otherwise known as the Great, down to the present time. William II is as bad as any of his knavish ancestors if not worse for, despite his vulgar protestations of piety, facts are revealing his true character as a real modern Tartuffe.

Then there are wars that arise from disputes connected with trade and economic interests. The European wars of the last couple of centuries—the devastation of Asia, the partition of Africa, the colonial expansion of European nations, the modern wars waged by Japan, all belong to this category. The most interesting and the most awful war in ancient times arising from economic pressure and contest is the titanic struggle between Rome and Carthage, which only ended after the exhaustion of Rome and the annihilation of the Punic state.

Lastly let us not forget the righteous Wars fought in the cause of justice and freedom—to destroy tyranny, to repel invasion, or to defend the weak or the innocent. The American Civil War will always redound to the glory of the United States for it was fought in the highest interests of religion, and of humanity. The Great War now before us is so far as the Allies are concerned a religious war for the maintenance of national ideals and for liberty.   To Great Britain, it is more than that also inasmuch as she may justly claim that she is fighting as a champion of civilization in upholding the sanctity of treaties, and in defending the righteous cause of a small nation but a brave and heroic Ally.

A PANACEA.

Such then briefly are the varied causes of War.   From the earliest times, mankind has turned away from the horrors of war, the poets have sung of the blessings of peace, and the prophets have held forth the olive branch and have spoken of the blessed time when war shall cease and the nations shall weep no more.

Many remedies have been suggested to curb the fiery spirit of the race, but so far there is no specific, and war, like the plague, must be suffered till man will awaken from his spiritual slumber, and enter upon his heritage of the Kingdom of Heaven upon earth !

THE FIRST PEACE CONGRESS IN CHINA, 546 B.C.

The quarrelsome States of ancient Greece guided by some of the wisest and the greatest men that ever lived endeavoured to prevent War by submitting their secular disputes—their religious dissensions and their diplomatic differences to the judgment of the Amphyctionic Council which consisted of representatives of the States, and which enforced its decisions by calling upon the States to declare a Sacred War against the delinquent, but unfortunately as the necessity for the sacred wars plainly shewed, neither the wisdom of the Greeks nor the authority of the Amphyctiony could give peace to the Hellenic nations.

But perhaps the earliest attempt in history to bring about disarmament by means of a peace congress,—was made in China as far back as 546 B.C. in the feudal state of Sung in what is now the province of Ho-Nan.   It is rather curious and humiliating to the modern politicians of Europe to contemplate that the Statesmen of ancient China actually anticipated the views that the disarmament question has called forth in our day in all countries.

In those days, China was split up into many fighting states. Ceaseless wars were the curse of the age.   Men were weary of fighting.   The fertile fields had often been turned into shambles. The fairest cities had been laid waste.   Avarice, ambition and self-interest dictated schemes of aggrandisement, and the military ardour of the fighting men availed itself to the fullest extent of the feudal code of honour that was so hysterically sensitive of whatever concerned the *amour propre* of the nobles. The time seemed ripe for calling attention to the wastefulness and the wickedness of war.

Hiang Hu was an officer of the State of Sung. He pursuaded the feudal chief of the State to summon a conference of the principal States to discuss the question of disarmament. In the abstract the problem appears so easy and so simple that it seems only yesterday the politicians and Statesmen of Europe—like their predecessors in ancient China, were striving in vain to realise a beautiful but tantalising chimera. The meeting was actually held. For a time the founder of the movement began to think of himself as the greatest benefactor of mankind and to claim that his scheme would prevent destruction of life and property. He then demanded that the ruler of Sung should reward him richly for his great services to the nations. The chief of Sung was rather weak-minded if we may judge from the way he yielded to the promptings of the Pacifist. However he referred the question of his proposed bestowal of land to his minister of works, who protested against the rewards and honour to be showered upon the dreamer of universal peace. Tzu-Han the courageous minister of works criticised the proposed recognition of services rendered by the mad man who in his opinion should be denounced for preaching a foolish and dangerous doctrine, as disarmament would make peace precarious, and would tempt the ambitious and the lawless to make a bold bid for power. Hiang Hu confessed at last that he had been misled by the glorious possibilities without thinking of the ultimate consequences. Thus the first Congress ended in a *fiasco*. In any case none of the signatories would act and each state waited for the other to begin the dangerous expedient.

No more successful have been the peace endeavours of the Tsar Nicholas II whose efforts, in promoting the Hague Conferences, have been quite futile of results. Since 1908 wars have cropped up like mushrooms, and despite Mr. Andrew Carnegie's colossal Peace Palace the greatest War in history is being fought almost at its doors, and the barbarism of the Germans has thrown the world back many centuries and made war as hideous as if the fighters were men of the dark ages.

It is now quite needless to enumerate all the studied details of the civilised code of war and of honour, which the representatives of the nations—divided into classes according to their military strength—solemnly coded for the edification of the world. Alas the Hague Conventions are at present just "scraps of paper," and the Minister of Works of Sung was right in condemning disarmament as the bait to catch the unwary and as the inevitable temptation to an unscrupulous people such as the German nation of to-day.

THE CHRISTIAN DOCTRINE OF NON-RESISTANCE.

There is the great and mystical doctrine of non-resistance and non-action. Lao-tzu the recluse says "By gentleness, the hardest heart may be softened. But try to cut and polish it—'twill glow like fire or freeze like ice . . . . Abandon wisdom and discard knowledge and the Empire will be at peace." (Chuang Tzu XI Cap.).

The teaching of Buddha and Christ may be summed up in the words of St. Matthew "whosoever shall smite thee on thy right cheek, turn to him the other also." Love your enemies, bless them that curse you, do good to them that hate you, and pray for them which despitefully use you and persecute you."

These be deep truths which dazzle our weak faith and blind us altogether with the result that we go about as hypocrites "seeing and approving the better but yet pursuing the worse." Surely though we cannot realise the whole mystery which goes to the very abyss of human nature, far be it from us to shut our eyes to its beacon light, however distant it may seem to appear.

A PRACTICAL REMEDY.

However, Confucianism it seems to me suggests a practical way of dealing with an enemy that does one a grievous wrong.

Confucius says—"Do justice to your enemy."

So that from the Confucian standpoint peace must be based on justice, and just punishment must be meted out to those who have done wrong and caused suffering to others.

Moreover Confucianism insists that military preparation and exercise should be part of ordinary education. The Japanese Bushido is simply a code of Confucian Ethics for the use of military men that is to say all men fit to fight for their country and that all States should be prepared for self-defence and for punitive expeditions in the cause of justice.

Peace that is patched up as a compromise with any wrong and injustice is a crime to civilization. Whatever the cost, civilized men must resist the powers of evil and wickedness in high places. Death is preferable to dishonour. Such in brief is the practical but emphatic teaching of Confucianism.

Finally lasting peace should be the object of every War. As long ago as 597 B.C. Prince Chuang of the Chu State when advised to build a monument to commemorate a victory gained by him reproved his officer in these memorable words : " Prowess in writing is represented by two characters which mean to stop War. The use of military art is to repress cruelty—to call in weapons, to preserve the ordinances of Heaven, to establish merit, to give peace to the masses, to unite all states in harmony and to increase the wealth of mankind." (Tso Chuan).

THE APPLICATION.

Applying the principles just set forth to the great European War, we must come to the conclusion that on no consideration whatever should any suggestion of peace be entertained, till Germany and her tools are either beaten or are prepared to admit their error and to submit unconditionally to the Allied Powers.

As Price Collier, an American writer has said : " From an American point of view, any sacrifice, any war were better than the domination of the Prussian methods of nation-making. They must be punished in such a way that they cannot utilise the ensuing peace for preparing for a greater war.

Justice and reparation must be given to those who have suffered.

THE FUTURE.

The Allies have already formed themselves into a league for the defence of liberty and the rights of all nations. They should retain this self-imposed status and would be the nucleus of the International Police, to vindicate the law of nations.

One blessing that may be expected out of the horrible evil is the dawn of a new era, let us hope, of growing reasonableness among the nations, and of greater regard for truth and righteousness and of a better appreciation of the essential unity of the races of mankind.   Then only may the world be blessed with peace.

> " Yes peace ! for War is needless,—
>   Yes calm ! for storm is past,—
> And goal for finished labour,
>   And anchorage at last."
> That peace—but who may claim it ?
>   The guileless in their way,
> Who keep the ranks of battle,
>   Who mean the thing they say :
> The Peace that is for Heaven,
>   And shall be for the Earth ;
> The Palace that re-echoes
>   With festal song and mirth.

" Rythm of St. Bernard "

By J. M. NEALE.

WAR TIME LECTURES AND ESSAYS.

VI.

THE INFLUENCE OF ART ON CIVILIZATION.

(An Address before the Amateur Drawing Association.)

There is nothing in human life more characteristic of the divine spirit within man than the innate love of the beautiful and the artistic in all that are comprehensible to the senses. It seems that the system the order and the beauty of nature may be, as philosophers suppose, the reflection of the Divine mind but there is no doubt whatever there is within the human consciousness a subtle and unaccountable sense of the sublime and the beautiful. There is a faculty in the brain concerned with the perception of harmony, and of beauty. It creates also the ideals which are translated into poetry, into sculptures, into painting, into music, and into architectural forms. Dr. Russell Wallace has found it difficult to explain the origin of this æsthetic faculty as a result of evolution. The origin of such a delicate function of an obscure part of the brain must be difficult to trace. The practical thing is to recognize that man has the faculty of appreciating what is beautiful in form, in colour, and in sound. If the possession of an intelligent language is the criterion which distinguishes man from all other animals, the æsthetic sense gives him the claim of relationship to the gods. A world deprived of beauty—of harmony and of sweetness would be a miserable chaos absolutely unsuited for the development of the human spirit. The truth is that the outside world is the perpetual source of stimulus upon the human mind. And art is something beautiful or sublime that is produced by the skill or ingenuity of man. Like poetry and music, it is the outpouring of the innermost spirit of what is truly human, and may be said to arouse the most subtle susceptibilities of the æsthetic sense. That man will readily respond to the stimulation of the beautiful, is one of the most marvellous things of nature, and is a fact of far reaching consequences to science, politics and religion.

The creations of genius, which one calls works of art, are more or less the faithful incarnation of the authors' ideals. When expressed in words so as to conjure up beautiful or sublime thought in a pleasing and rythmic form—it is poetry. More wonderful still is music with its harmony of infinite sound variations and its combination of tonal and other elements of sound, to produce a soul-stirring effect upon man. Music speaks a heavenly language understanded of the soul ; no religion therefore worthy of the name has been able to progress without the aid of music and poetry. The sacred anthems of all nations form the most emphatic proof of the essential unity of mankind. Amidst all the diversity of tongues, customs, and habits, in the things of the spirit, the solidarity of the human family stands out prominently to-day more than ever before. If music and poetry have a powerful effect on the religious instinct, formal religion has in turn exercised a greater influence on music and poetry. In Europe, the grandest musical compositions have been dedicated to the service of God. In every civilized country, where art has not been killed by a wrong view of religion, there is no religious ceremony without song and music. In ancient China, as you are no doubt aware, music and song were carefully taught and regulated under the careful supervision of a special state department. The cultivation of both was considered by Confucius as one of the most important duties of a man. Even to-day the worship at the Temples is accompanied with music, especially in the Temple of Heaven, and in the Temple of Confucius.

Leaving the influence of music, and poetry, which appeal to the ear, we have the other branches of the fine arts, which are appreciated for their beauty in form and colour. We cannot linger over the claims of architecture, ceramics, sculptures and modelling. All these play a very large part in promoting the happiness of mankind, and in aiding man to realise his higher destiny by means of the senses. In every land and throughout all time, religion has exerted the most potent influence upon their production, and they on their part, have helped to promote the interests of religion.

As your Society is specially interested in the pictorial art, we shall devote special attention to it, and although you have chosen a very modest name for your society, some of you have attempted painting in oil and have done quite creditable work on very difficult subjects.

Naturally you will expect me to confine myself to the subject of Chinese Art, as you must be aware I am a greater ignoramus than any of you on the great topic of European Art. If a visit to the great picture galleries of Europe affords an excellent opportunity of seeing the works of the great European masters, one certainly goes away with a painfully bewildered impression, because too much light has actually blinded vision by its excessive glare. Nevertheless one thing stands out most prominently and cannot be missed by the dullest. Everywhere one sees the most intimate connection between the pictorial art and religion. As far back in civilization as we may wish to go—back to the awe-inspiring temples of Egypt and their weird representation of Osiris and the other gods, or to the noble places of worship of Assyria and Babylon, we shall discover that man has utilized graphic representation to convey unspeakable ideas to others, by form and colour. In pre-confucian days, the ancestral temples of the kings and nobles had their walls decorated by mural paintings or bas reliefs, illustrating ancient legends, or important historical events with the view always of imparting some moral or religious lesson. Down to the Han dynasty, this practice seems to have continued, for at the beginning of the Manchu regime, discoveries of important temple bas reliefs were made and have been preserved. Representation of these have been published and Prof. Chavannes of Paris has published an important and valuable monograph on them. These pictures suggest that the ancient Chinese were somewhat related to the Egyptians and Assyrians because the scenes depicted are very suggestive of the silhouettes, with which one is familiar in connection with Egyptian art. Moreover the form of the sacred tree reminds us of the Assyrian emblem, and the sacred Tree of Eden of the Old Testament. Then the warriors in chariots, the occurrence of birds and animals to fill up gaps in the picture, and pictures of winged beings in human form, are all very striking. Similar bas-reliefs or paintings occur in the ruins of Egypt and Assyria.

The pictorial art had then grown up very early in China. The principles of the Chinese pictorial art had been laid down for all time by the artist Hsieh-ho in the Southern Sui dynasty at the end of the Fourth Century, and it is admitted on all hands, that these are more akin to those of modern European art, than are those of the painters in Europe during the middle ages.

The philosophic religion of the Literati is clearly responsible for the form that Chinese art has assumed. Without some knowledge of the emotional and intellectual elements of the national life, no one can understand why the Chinese pictorial art should differ so widely from that of Europe for so long. From the time of the Greeks, there has been in Europe, a glowing desire to elevate man out of nature, and consequently in religion as well as in art—the lord of the creation has been the subject of art, poetry and philosophy. The fall and the apotheosis of man constitute the most serious problems that have stirred the imagination of Europeans for ages. Consequently in European art, man figures prominently, the rude anatomical figures, human undertakings, historical episodes, the crucifixion and man's ascent to spritual heights, one and all form the recurring theme of painting, sculpture and poetry.

But in China, the influence of the I-King-or Canon of Evolution had given religion and philosophy a special leaning towards transcendental and dynamic idealism. The whole cosmos has always been conceived as a living unity, and the life of man is only a wavelet in the immeasurable and infinite ripples of the universe. In such a view of the world, philosophers tend to minimise rather than exaggerate the importance of man. The great factor of rythmic motion in this world's life, is recognised in the constitution of the mind, and Hsieh-ho rightly demands that all works of art, should show what he calls rythm and life. Fidelity of form must follow the first. The other canons are necessary corollaries to the first axiom viz., the pictures must be true to nature and the colouring must be harmonious. The gift and genius of the painter decide the composition, and give it the necessary finish. The art critics of Europe have in recent years given due credit to the Chinese for the high standard they had elaborated, and have justly considered that in the department of landscape painting, the best Chinese works are still unsurpassed.

There is in Chinese pictorial art always evident the ideal to present the painter's impression of the life in nature. Chinese artists endeavour to suggest thought rather than picture details so that sometimes without the great help of chiaroscuro, they give in a few bold but significant lines, a true representation of nature, which recalls in the memory light vibrations as effectually as the lines and grooves on the gramaphone plate can reproduce sound waves in the ether. The influence of a dynamic religion is seen in the subjects preferred by the artists. Nearly every Chinese painter or artist during the great periods of Tang and Sung were also the most noted thinkers of the day. Caligraphy and drawing were then a gentleman's necessary accomplishment. We need not wonder therefore that the great painters of the Tang like Ku Kai-chih and of the Sung like Li Lung-mien, should reflect the philosophical and religious views of the Confucian School. The landscape pictures of these periods are so grand and so unique because they attempt to do what the great invention called Cinematograph has at last accomplished. Chinese artists have always a penchant for nature in motion. The sea with its ceaseless movement, the wind—the shower of rain, the mist, the falling of snow—the bamboo and the willow with infinite vibrations of innumerable leaves, animals in motion, horses gambolling in packs or fish moving in water—these and kindred themes show nature as a living organism. The pictorial art of China is the highest achievement of human genius in Asia, and is the standard upon which that of the surrounding states of the Orient has been formed.

Religion makes the soul of man move in unison with the spiritual rythm of the universe. In the spirit of ecstasy and devotion, the mind of man transcends the limitations of the flesh, and catches a glimpse of the eternal. Under the inspiration of faith and piety, mental images are transformed accurately into muscular motion, which in turn give us the lines, and these in turn, reform the ethereal vibrations, which had at first formed the images. In this mysterious way, through the human spirit, mental images are capable of being conveyed from one mind to another. The first impulse to create concrete forms out of images of the mind, may be seen in the primitive sculpturing or etching of the savages of the palœolithic period. The wonderful figures of the mammoth and other animals already indicate the existence of a new power of expression, which in the future age, is to add so much to man's happiness and satisfaction. The archæology of China is still unborn, but we may predict a huge progeny in the immediate future. Then it will be found that relics of the past will bear out the claims of Chinese tradition that man has slowly groped his way from darkness into light. In this onward march, nothing has helped him so much as calligraphy and its sister, the art of drawing. Pictorial representation is in fact the precursor of writing as the hieroglyphics in Egypt and in Chinese "characters" abundantly testify.

The Chinese have paid the greatest veneration to writing, and have from time immemorial treasured works of art. They honour painters and calligraphists, and show respect to pictures of heroes, saints and gods. This seems a very natural consequence of that belief in nature as a great organic unity. It is surely a reminiscence of this primeval animism, which flourished in China for thousands of ages.

In the belief in immortality and in the continued existence of the soul, after death, the Chinese retain the most primitive ideas of humanity. Under the influence of this faith, much thought has been lavished upon biographies, poems and monu- ments. To record the deeds of heroes or of beloved ones, the artist is called upon to preserve in pictures the scenes which a grateful posterity wishes to commemorate. This practice is so universal that we may say it is characteristic of civilised man. To this habit, we are indebted for the great art works of antiquity, the temples of ancient Europe, the monuments of the modern States, the bas reliefs in China, India, Cambodia and Java, not to speak of the great relics of ancient Mexico and Peru. Unfortunately in China, after the terrible holocausts of the internecine wars of the Han, religion and civilization began to decline and in spite of a temporary period of revival under the Tang, Chinese civilization became stagnant.

The entry of foreign religions coincided with the arrest and stagnation of the national faith. Nestorian Christianity and Buddhism found numerous votaries. They gave rise to a sort of art but never produced the same influence as the more primitive philosophy of China. Buddhism was the means of introducing a taste for Indian art. The grouping of figures, the dress of the Buddhas and Bodhisatvas, and the pagodas and stupas show the influence of the Indian missionaries, but instead of improving the native art, the influence of India has been on the whole harmful, because the Indians' love of tinsel and gaudy colours, and the conventionalised forms necessitated by the priestly ritual, have steadily exerted a pernicious influence on the native taste.

With the decline of the true Chinese religion and civiliza- tion, Buddhism flourished for a time, and under its influence, painters and sculptors have been produced in abundance, and much of what we call artistic work has been done in connection with the Buddhistic religion.   Curiously, European art work is being introduced into China under the auspices of the Roman Catholic Mission.   Large numbers of young people are trained by European artists to paint, and to do modelling and carving. These boys are generally orphans.   They copy the classical pictures of the crucifixion, the Madonna and child, and other decorative work, peculiar to the Roman Catholic Church.   The "sacred" pictures sold and distributed through the agency of the Church, can only tend to degrade artistic sense and artistic spirit.

Under the influence of the Buddhistic religion, great painters have arisen to paint scenes in the life of Buddha and portraits of saints.   Figures of Amitaba or Omitofu are among the most famous subjects chosen by artists in China and Japan. Perhaps the most popular deity is Kwan-Yin—the Indian Avolokeshtara who in the Chinese tradition is the Goddess of Mercy, and in the conventional type is the exact analogue of the Madonna.

Tourists philosophers have vied with Buddhist pundits in works of creative imagination, and believing in everything that is alleged to be mysterious, they have absorbed wholesale the Buddhistic ritual, and have added largely to the realms above and below *terra firma*.   Modern Taoism has therefore also given rise to art production and among these, the Garden of Immortality (*Wan Shou Shan*) the images of Laotzu, the figure of the Taoist Pope riding a tiger and genii of all shapes and in all sorts of combinations, are the best known.

As a result of the prevailing hero-worship and of the survival of the ancient worship of nature and ancestors—we have a whole class of artists devoting their best attention to portrait painting.   Figures of the Lares and Penates may be bought everywhere.   Noble pictures of Kwan-ti—the God of War were formerly greatly in favour because Kwan-ti—the famous general of the Three Kingdoms period, was selected by the Manchus as the Patron Saint of the Dynasty.   The Chinese of Manila solemnly affirm that according to the tradition of the city, Kwanti appeared in that citadel of cruelty and corruption to defend the Chinese when the Spaniards persecuted them in the eighteenth century.

As a matter of fact, all the important works of art appreciated by the general mass of the people, are devotional or religious in character.

Now that there is a great religious revival, and also a great upheaval of materialism and commercialism there will be correspondingly great changes in art, conception and production. Moreover the influence of European ideas is making itself felt, and already the science of perspective is studied by all serious artists in China.

Is art necessary to culture? Is its cultivation and encouragement a duty of a democratic government? The answer is emphatically in the affirmative. Like music, poetry, and æsthetic pursuits generally, fine arts are most democratic, because they are pre-eminently human. Chinese pictorial art especially has attempted every variety of work, and has elevated the most bourgoise *genre* to the level of the most classical and historical topics. The Chinese will find that in the general dissemination of an intelligent taste for music and fine arts they will be helping to lay down an abiding foundation of a true democracy.

It is time that I must conclude, and before closing may I express a hope that these long and desultory remarks, may awaken in you an interest in the art productions of China, and that in your search for models and for inspiration, you may seek for guidance as your fore-fathers have done, at the fountainhead of true wisdom and insight. Although you are amateurs, you should realise that all artists worthy of the name, work because they love nature, truth and beauty; and therefore if you think because you are not *professional* artists you need not have the inspiration and the assiduous application essential to art, then you had better spend your time in out-door sports, and benefit your health, than "killing time" by making worthless copies.

WAR TIME LECTURES AND ESSAYS.

National Stagnation and its Remedy.

I GENERAL OBSERVATIONS.

Wherever we turn, we are confronted with ceaseless motion. There is no dead pause anywhere. Stagnation therefore with reference to any thing we can know of is only comparative slackening of speed. This is a fundamental fact of nature which reaches to the root of things, and which helps to explain the character of cosmic processes that permeate all mundane affairs.

With reference to this universal motion, another fact of paramount importance is that its rate is never uniform and that wherever observed it invariably exhibits a periodicity which varies in response to the influences of varying and multifarious concomitants which determine the form and the duration of each phase of the motion.

In the study of the dynamics of civilization the rise and fall of dynasties, of human schools of thought—of systems of religion and what not, illustrate clearly enough movement in waves which can be represented in diagrammatic form if we care to reduce human achievements to terms of numeric values. In the gross we apply general terms such as progress, stagnation and decay to human society, and generally such borrowed terms are unsatisfactory as they are liable to be misunderstood.

The fact that human evolution marches onward not in a straight line nor at a uniform rate but in periodic waves shows conclusively that whether there be a *premum mobile* or not, the forces that move our being correspond in principle in a remarkable manner with those permeating the universe.

It is the province of philosophy to trace the origin of these forces—to explain their operations and to predict their destiny, and if possible to postulate the characteristics, which distinguish them. History deals only with phenomena and deduces lessons of a practical nature from purely empirical data.

The laws of motion are of universal application. Stagnation implies retardation of motion. Is the loss of speed due to external obstacles and friction or to some inherent defect which diminishes the internal energy ? Regarded purely as a physical and natural phenomenon, the stagnation of human society results from interaction of many forces, and it is necessary to really understand the very nature of social and national stagnation in order to comprehend what remedy is in a given case the best anti-dote to degeneration and decay.

The analysis of all the factors which constitute this motion as affecting the course of human evolution—shows that one must distinguish besides the purely physical cosmic forces—and others of a more subtle character which for want of a more definite term may be called spiritual. In this mælstrom of forces—there stands out the play of the human ego—as a powerful impulse which shapes human destiny, and which sheds a new light upon the nature of cosmic movement, revealing a definite order in the midst of chaos, and pointing to a harmony of simultaneous vibrations, that give rise to the sense of the unity of the universe, and to the human perception of the purposiveness of the majestic operations of nature.

It is not possible to state exactly the rôle played by the physical, spiritual and human factors of these cosmic forces in human evolution. To recognize their existence is surely a stepping stone to a deeper knowledge of the dynamics of human action. Facts and human experience demonstrate that the doctrine of determinism is not entirely devoid of truth, but they also prove that there is room for the exercise of Freedom, and for the play of the human spirit in the world. As the old Chinese classics teach us, man finds himself between the material universe and God, and gropes for his salvation through mazes of conflicting impulses, rising and falling, until at length he discovers a concord in the ceaseless movement and interplay of the momentum of matter—of the self-consciousness of the ego—and of the creating energy of the spirit.

The discovery of the antinomies of existence need not lead us to pessimism nor need the occurrence of stagnation in human history occasion despair. The history of mankind has been a perpetual revelation of continual growth, and though individuals may perish or tribes and races may pass out of memory, the human family continues to rise in the scale of civilization, the phases of stagnation being merely secondary depressinos in successive waves, which advance higher and higher, till the human imagination refuses to recognize the limitations imposed by the intellect and the reason, and till the Divine intuition lays the foundation for the apotheosis of man.

II. CHARACTERISTICS OF STAGNATION.

(a). Unprogressiveness.

Throughout all history, the arrest of progress is the most obvious symptom of natural stagnation. This may happen at any stage of human culture. Some races remained stationary for ages and then showed a remarkable activity for a time, only to relapse into a state of lethargy. The Chinese who have survived as a community through four thousand years at least, passed through alternate cycles of progress and decay but all the time the race was advancing towards higher ideals.

The Germans remained savages till about a thousand years ago and the Slavs on the whole became civilized and progressive at a much later period. Modern savages must have remained stationary for untold ages, and though many show skill in making stone and bone weapons such as the Maoris and others, they do not seem superior to the paleolithic men who fashioned remarkable arrow heads and executed striking figures of the Mammoth and other extinct creatures.

Primitive men seem to have made an advance in their handicraft at long intervals—each step being heralded by some momentous discovery that enabled man to overcome the influence of environment. Thus the stone age must have lasted untold ages. Then came the discovery of the production of fire—recorded by the Chinese Chronicles as an invention of a sage who produced fire by means of friction between two pieces of wood. The Greeks gave us the legend of Prometheus and so great indeed has been the influence that fire had exercised on human civilization that it could readily be understood why the ancients thought so highly of the discovery. The use of fire led to the production of pottery—the use of bronze and iron—these marking successive steps in human progress.

The domestication of the household companions—the dog and the cat, and of the sheep, the cow, the pig, and the poultry stocks considerably altered the habits of primitive men. Then came agriculture which prepared the conditions for a settled life in villages. History confirms the findings of archæology and show how the pastoral peoples, like the Arabs and Mongols, are still nomads, while all agricultural populations in Egypt, Chaldea and China had ages ago become attached to the soil.

In our day we have seen how the nations of the Earth have remained stationary for hundreds of years till all at once the application of Steam as a motor power has given a new impetus to civilization, and in one century has completely revolutionised the industries of the world. The age of Coal is in every way more marvellous than any former epoch in the history of man. It is likely to be eclipsed in the future by the period when man acquires greater knowledge of radio-active matter, and can utilise electricity, light and radium, or their substitutes in a sure and efficient manner.

Many people remain satisfied with what had been known for ages, they will remain stationary—and no progress can possibly be made. A new idea starts a whole train of new views, and new conjectures as to possible combinations and applications of principles and methods so that when left untrammelled, discovery follows upon discovery till Science has become the indispensable handmaid of civilization.

(b). Ignorance and Superstition.

The most important consequences of stagnation are seen in the prevailing ignorance and superstitions. Thus the illiterate natives of India, China and Persia, and of Ireland, Russia and Turkey may be profoundly ignorant of all that have taken place in the world in the last century. They still hold beliefs that were current two or three hundred years ago, and are therefore said to be superstitious.

Education is either neglected or entirely defective and unsatisfactory. Thus in India, China and old Japan—the people have been very keen for centuries to have a good education. Yet in spite of their mental training—they could not make any progress because the knowledge imparted was so tainted with error and fable that all enquiries into nature were futile in as much the methods were defective and no systematic control of experiments was devised. Opinions and conjectures filled the literature of the past, but no new light was shed. The only result of dogmatic science and philosophy was to set up insuperable barriers that were to hamper and to delay the growth of true science by the cobwebs of pedantic sophistry and charlatanism. During the middle ages, Europe suffered very severely from the consequences of this sort of learned ignorance and of the false systems of science and philosophy which frequently made simple truth often worse confounded as Bacon proved, by elaborate arguments in a circle. In such a condition there is much labour lost. When, however, religion had as in the past in Europe usurped and abused the functions of the state and attempted to establish an orthodox conformity not only in matters spiritual but also in all the domains of thought and action, the most pernicious consequences were inevitable and until the dawn of the nineteenth century, the evil genius of hierophants had dodged the footsteps of science ever ready to compromise issues which were not understood, and to oppose the far-reaching conclusions of inductive researches by antiquated *a priori* notions. Thus every Church consistently opposed in turn each scientific discovery which exploded the false doctrines of nature which its schools had adopted. From Galileo to Darwin, the conflict between science and religion in Europe had been a ceaseless duel—without truce, but fortunately it has resulted in the complete victory of science and reason, and in the reconciliation of faith with established truth.

The appalling ignorance and the consequent superstitions of all peoples unenlightened by the living knowledge which science only can bestow may be gauged by comparing the state of culture in Europe in the 16th century with what it is to-day. Japan before the Meiji period is also a good illustration and at the present moment, the transformation of China is going on with astonishing rapidity.

Superstition exerts a pernicious influence. It has its roots deep down in the depths of human nature. The human mind desires certainty and abhors doubt and superstition provides the working theory all complete. Hence we have the fairy tales, epics, sagas and myths which tell of the wonders achieved by impossible beings so beloved of primitive peoples and still so full of interest to the young all the world over. Every known

phenomenon has been explained, and before the dawn of
science, superstition provided the means of satisfying curiosity
and inquisitiveness without the need of furnishing evidence or
proof, and the plausible explanations it gives fit in well
with popular ideas. That a spirit could do wonderful things
is readily acceptable, but it is not easy to comprehend an
abstract law of nature. Thus children and mentally undeveloped people find no difficulty in understanding *e.g.*, that
a spirit makes the wind blow but will not appreciate a
scientific account of the origin of winds. The story of the
creation is familiar in all countries, but it will be a severe test
of a teacher's powers to request an ordinary school master to
explain the scientific cosmogony of our day. Should the teacher
succeed, the pupils would probably find the lessons were beyond
their depths altogether. But the first sign of national awakening has always been indicated by the loss of faith in superstitions and by the reformation of true religion.

(c). Sterility of Thought.

The most important result of the preceding conditions is
the barrenness of thought. Whenever and wherever the people
have lapsed into a stagnant condition, their thinking has
ceased to be an important object in life, except in reference
to routine business and occupations.

The curious thing about human degeneration and social
stagnation is that the people effected of course remain uncon-
scious of their fate. They usually feel quite satisfied. To them
there are no unsolved problems, everything is in its right place,
and everybody knows all about everything. Hence there is no
curiosity to learn and no ambition to do anything. Than this
hopeless mental attitude nothing in the world can be more
paralyzing. The majority of very backward semi-barbarous
peoples remain in this state.

The Chinese and Indians have so many oriental superstitions to account for the varied things happening around them
that though they readily express appreciation of any new discovery they immediately proceed to explain these in terms of
their old fables. They seem incapable of surprise! Therefore
they do not trouble themselves to make any inquiry. Everything is readily explained when reduced to myth and analogy.

The Chinese *e.g.*, are satisfied if they call any complicated motors electric. In the middle ages, a miracle is a good explanation of anything not understood.

(d).   *Apathy and indifference.*

Life among a stagnant population is a monotonous hum drum of endless routine. The educated continue to burrow deeply in the musty volumes of the past. The ignorant toils without hope. Usually despotism and oppression keep the country illiterate, and encourage the people to go on uninfluenced by the agencies that are moving the world.

The people themselves are resigned to their fate. They have time to think only of their livelihood. They can care for naught at any moment, in many parts of Asia where the virus of progress has not found its way, human beings may be seen working like machines for the merest pittance. There is no time for anything except to eat and sleep. Everything else that is necessary is done during a temporary stoppage of work. Toil, toil, ceaseless toil—day and night till the brain fags— the human spirit is chained to the flesh, and the man or woman becomes only a machine. Specialisation of work, undue competition, the work of new occupations, and the general poverty all help to produce this horrible levelling down of human beings to a state of apathy and dullness.

Among the easy-going Malays, who still enjoy life in their villages, stagnation reigns supreme also. There we find apathy of another kind. It arises from the contentment of ease—the result of non-development from want of stimulus.

Wealth and success in life are dangerous to individuals and nations alike. If they do not give rise to arrogance and carelessness they are prolific causes of national decay. Very few people can bear great wealth with equanimity. Some become misers, some give way to extravagance while others fall into a state of indifference being well contented to enjoy all the good things of life. There is to them no necessity for work—for thought or for exertion, and the general result is that the mind becomes in time incapable of continued effort. Unless this tendency has been combated by proper education, experience has shown that the children of the wealthy in young countries such as the Straits, invariably succumb to the benumbing apathy of surplus wealth. Constant activity is the condition of life and vigour. Accumulated wealth tends to indolence among those who can live an easy life without work.

To be spoon-fed is to have all stimulus removed from the mind. A habit is at once formed. The mind at rest means vacuity and apathy. When it has become accustomed to remain vacant—it will not be easily roused. Hence it is most difficult to interest the adults of this community who have allowed themselves to drift on in life without more exertions than are necessary to carry on their simple business operations. To such "sufficient unto the day" is more than evil enough. The hideous egotism that glares to the obliteration of all else is the result of such a life. The community is dull and uninteresting except in the cultivation of selfish pleasures. Gratification of the senses and the appetites form the sole happiness. All other considerations find no place. Nothing in heaven or on earth outside the blaze of egotism is of any consequence—outside of the pettiness of self and its sordid pleasures—the universe is a gloomy night with the stillness of death.

(e) Effeminacy.

The hatred of strenuous activity leads to a love of repose. Habitual repose creates repugnance to exertion. Peace at any price seems then much wiser than fighting to the death for the sake of honour or anything else. A new valuation of ideals has become necessary.

Stagnation has a calming soporific effect on the multitude Like a kind of sleeping sickness, it causes an unwillingness to make great efforts. Nothing stirs the emotions. Everything is reduced to a cold blooded calculation of gain or loss. It is crass materialism.

The greatest evil is disturbance of the peace—the worst calamity is injury to one's person. Let there be quiet. Pay anything—sacrifice all for peace!

Such people naturally become unwarlike. Being incapable of self-defence, they have to submit to all sorts of humiliation. The Javanese people to-day are in this unfortunate position. The Chinese and Hindus until quite recently were not much better.

They shrink from suffering of any kind and endeavour to evade it at all costs. They tolerate slow oppression and serfdom. They have lost every spark of nature and have forgotten even the innate instinct of self-defence. The Hindus generally are thus afraid even to retaliate the most brutal attack unless they have an opportunity to stab in the dark.

To a large extent Asiatics have been influenced by the doctrines of non-resistance and altriusm. Just as Christianity is said to have caused the wild Teutons to become milder and to lose their prestine savagery—so in like manner, Buddhism must be held responsible for the effeminacy of all peoples that had come under the sway of the Great Love of the Buddha—love that is aggressive and that knows no bound, friend and foe alike being regarded as the same, and that places no limit to non-resistance however cruel and however unjust.

Of course practical Buddhists and Christians who meekly suffer injustice and persecution, do so because they really believe their enemies will get a worse punishment than they themselves could give them. But nevertheless nature favours the principle of struggle and competition. The people that will not prepare to fight for its rights must submit to invasion, oppression and slavery. Effeminacy is a constant feature of a state of stagnation arising from whatever cause. It was apparent among the Greeks after the Roman conquest. It has been the cause of the weakness among many races for long periods.

(f) Moral Deterioration.

As an invariable consequence of the preceding conditions operating for a long period, there is a general deterioration of morals. There is a slackening of moral fibre. The national effeminacy is reflected by the prevailing laxity in all efforts to control anti-social tendencies and to enforce the requirements of justice and right.

Compromises are tolerated. Expediency is accepted as an excuse for turpitude. Social life is on a level with the national apathy.

Men in such a Society will make no sacrifices. They behold appalling wickedness, baseness and injustice quite unmoved. Careful only of preserving intact their worldly possessions, they will condone wrong in the powerful and submit to the most shameful humiliation. Such a people can expect no liberty and indeed are incapable of comprehending its benefits.

III. CAUSES OF NATIONAL STAGNATION.

It is only possible to indicate very briefly the many causes that combine to produce national decay.

(i.) *Exhaustion.* By numerous agencies such as war, pestilence, tyranny, misgovernment and so forth, a country is bled of its manhood through death or emigration. National exhaustion is synonymous with poverty. The worst form of stagnation is generally the result.

(ii.) *Isolation.* Geographical situation sometimes explains the want of progress of a nation. This is so obvious that it is unnecessary to enlarge upon it.

(iii.) *Arrogance.* Prolonged peace and prosperity have been observed from the remotest ages to have been followed by degeneration and decay. Either from self-sufficiency the people begin to neglect what is needful to maintain their prestige or from excess of pride, as in the case of the Germans, they essay too much, and to borrow an apt colloquialism " bite off more than they can chew." In the one case, they will degenerate from internal corruption which in the other, they will be disrupt by forces from without.

(iv.) *Language barrier.* There is no doubt that a difficult and outlandish language is a great barrier to progress, unless the people create new centres of learning and science.

The Chinese, Russian, Japanese and Indian peoples are at a great disadvantage in following the great progress of western civilisation. Whereas in the West, interchange of views is simple and rapid, these oriental populations find it almost an insuperable obstacle to render technical terms into intelligible colloquial. The Russians have been obliged to use French and German freely in their scientific enquiries till they have established the sciences among themselves. The Japanese have also done likewise. The Chinese and the Indians are rapidly adopting English as a second literary language. In this way the barrier is overcome, but until science is cultivated as an indigenous element of culture, there can be no true progress for any great population.

(v.) *Internecine strife.* The effect of continued civil struggle is of course exhaustion. Hence this cause may properly enough be included under that heading; but history shows how dissensions in a country have so frequently resulted in paralysis of national progress and in foreign invasions that there is every justification in regarding disunion among the leaders of a people as a potent cause of stagnation. It can be seen at a glance how it is possible at a national crisis for mere civil war to be dangerous *e.g.* in the present position of the British Empire vis a vis the Great War—how fatal must be the outbreak of domestic disputes, although the British Empire may be said to be in the very acme of strength and fitness. The fratricide wars of the Greeks destroyed the Hellenic states. Civil struggles in China paved the way to conquests by foreign foes time and again.

Perhaps the most useful lesson is that afforded by the history of the Teutonic peoples. For ages, they fought against one another—and became hirelings to decimate their own kinsmen. Almost up to the period of the Napoleonic wars, Germany was the most backward country in Europe barring Russia and Turkey. Once unity was achieved especially after 1871, the Germanic states have severally and collectively made the most colossal progress the world has ever seen.

(vi.) *Defective education and the absence of proper scientific training.* Throughout every age, defective education is a sure cause of stagnation. The middle ages of Europe afford the most striking illustration. The meteoric rise of Japan upon the basis of an obsolete feudalism and through the vehicle of the most difficult and uncompromising language is due solely to the introduction of modern sciences. The formidable position of Germany to-day in every respect in peace as well as in war has been brought about entirely by the national cultivation and organization of science as the means to national power and national greatness.

(vii.) *Influence of religion.* Religion has played a no mean part in the advancement of mankind. But alas in its decay, it has also caused retardation of progress. The history of the world is a painful commentary on this great theme. But religion is quite indispensable to the progress of humanity.

(viii.) *Ethnological factors.* Social customs and national habits may so stereotype the mind and the ideals that no progress is possible without frightful upheavals. The French Revolution was the thunderclap that prepared the way for democracy in Europe.

In India, China and old countries castes, tradition and fixed ideas have held great communities hide bound in spite of all the evidences of great European progress and superiority before the eyes of those who can see !

These ethnological factors are even more important than mere language troubles because they penetrate to the inmost recesses of thought and emotion.

(ix.) *A vicious Cycle.* The very conditions which constitute national decay tend to aggravate all the circumstances which give rise to the psychological, ethnic and political features of stagnation. Once started the processes of devolution proceed apace. Out of the ignorance, weakness and poverty of the masses, develop the ugly social and insanitary evils which prey on the vitals of the nation. When the whole people are further oppressed by tyranny and a foreign yoke, they may be reduced to the most abject misery.

(x.) *Immorality.* The neglect of the restraints of morals have been very significant during all epochs of national decadence. It was seen in ancient times in Babylon and in Rome. The same observation applies to modern states and people.

The people in a society undergoing moral decay are not necessarily more vicious but they become careless of the requirements of ethics, and parade their weaknesses. This laxity creates an atmosphere conducive to the greatest excesses and the wildest orgies that sap the power of any nation. Indifference to the opinions of one's neighbours can be carried to a pitch that savours of contempt for decency, without any restraint of any kind ; mankind usually falls into the slough of egotism, and sinks in the mire of sloth and inefficiency, being dead to all impulses that quicken the spirit, and living only for the pleasures that narcotise the noblest sensibilities of the race.

There is no dubiety that the greatest progress in the world among any race at any period has always been made by people inspired by the highest moral impulses and sustained by lofty religious motives. On the contrary, neglect of morals is a certain prelude to ruin and disaster. On this question, all religions are agreed, and upon this solid foundation, all the conflcting faiths of man might well base their propaganda for the Kingdom of Heaven.

That righteousness exalts a nation is a truism that is often forgotten in the glamour of mere material achievements especially when coupled with the glory and triumph of a successful war. Such is the case with Germany. Though the Belgians are temporarily driven out of their homes, we need not hesitate to believe that the evil deeds of the invaders will sooner or later recoil upon their own heads. There is a moral conscience in the world. Remorse will one day paralyse the strong arms even of the Teutons. In any case, the righteous indignation of the outraged nations, will be the invincible Arm of the Lord to fulfil the law of justice and righteousness—in order that brute force shall not enslave the meek. Thus as of old vaulting ambition overleaps itself and the once proud and mighty Teutons will be crushed by forces attracted by their crimes, and they will assuredly suffer from the effects of stagnation after the War, on account of all the physical, moral and psychological reasons already adduced unless thir leaders turn away from the evil ideas that are driving them to perdition.

IV. THE REMEDY.

The whole problem is a question of the dynamics of civilization. To apply the simile now to its solution, we may say that religion, philosophy and science have to discover what counteracting forces can be applied so that the diverse and manifold impulses may be so influenced as to operate in the resultant direction that is most beneficial to mankind.

The main difficulty is that man is not a mere machine. Every people labours under the inertia imposed by heredity, tradition and environment. The human mind is confined within entanglements fraught with more deadly perils than those on the battlefield.

Tolerance of wrong, of poison, and of pain is a merciful gift of Heaven. Otherwise this world will be to many worse than a hell. Unfortunately this very quality which habit so quickly engenders, offers often an effectual resistance to the operation of any remedy.

A people that is sunk deep in ignorance and that is narcotised by moral indifference can only be aroused by constant endeavour to instil a new spirit into the young by means of education and religion. The work of centuries cannot be counteracted in a few months or even years. "Rome indeed, was not built in a day."

To arouse a people from centuries of stagnation, and to cure all the evil effects that have been produced upon Society and upon human thought itself cannot be achieved by a mere revolution however terrible and however bloody. An upheaval of this nature is only comparable to the forest clearing undertaken by the planter. The trees have to be felled, the whole debris has to be set on fire, and after all, the work of planting is scarcely begun. A revolution does not achieve much more. The history of France from the storming of the Bastille till to-day testifies to this, and the Chinese revolution is strangely enough going to repeat before our eyes the same ironies and the same tragedies of inexorable destiny.

Every religion and every system of philosophy have professed the means of salvation. But it seems man has remained obdurate and is difficult to be moved.

Practically we must deal with the young. A clean sweep must be made of the jungle or forest in the shape of all hindrances. A new culture must be grown on a *terrian* made sterile. This law applies apparently to the spiritual as well as to the material world.

If any one attempts to grow anything and neglects to keep out the weeds and the undesirable remnants of the forest that survive, the result is in most cases irreparable loss for there will be no plantation but a secondary jungle in the end.

Education therefore must be thorough. It must be carried through consistently to the bitter end. Nothing of the past must interfere with its growth. This has been achieved in Japan to a marvellous extent.

It does not matter what religion one adopts. Under the influence of every religion sincerely practised, human progress has been achieved, and unfortunately when religion is only a cloak without the substance, stagnation has not been avoided no matter what the religion is. Let those who preach a religion live up to its teaching and ideals, and they will earn the respect of honest men, and will surely do good to the community.

The peope who require an awakening must be prepared for the treatment.

The creation of a new spirit is essential. It is this that gives coherance and ensures success. The Government must direct this new force and carefully cultivate it by means of education. The character of the people must be such that it is compatible with the frequent changes, necessitated by altered circumstances, or in other words the people are willing to change their habits and customs and adapt themselves to new conditions of life. Thus we have the contrast between the Chinese and the Japanese, two cognate races reacting differently to the influences of Western civilization. In China, until a new spirit of nationality and a new temperament were generated by unprecedented events that roused the nation, the population remained like a sphinx and the assaults of the occident in every direction spiritual or intellectual recoiled fruitlessly like the waves from a rock-bound shore.

Nations like individuals must have an object to live for. They cherish certain ideals towards which they will aspire, at any cost. Sometimes they are led by visionaries. At other times they are driven by military leaders like Alexander of Macedon and Napoleon the Great. All the same, the people pursuade themselves that they are achieving something for their vain glory. Hero-worship is a very potent element in human psychology. Hence every wave of progress is named after the chief who initiates it. Therefore reformers and leaders are necessary to transform a stagnant people, and in order to combat all the evil influences they can only expect martyrdom as their reward. Not till altruism has produced men ready to lay down their lives for the betterment of their fellow men is there hope that national stagnation will give place to progress and to activity.

These general principles will be more readily understood if they are applied to a concrete case.

No one can deny that in more than one community in our midst there are symptoms of stagnation and degeneration. Do we not see how people are drifting in life without hope and without ambition? The influence of religion is either wanting or only skin deep! Education helps only to make the enveloping darkness more evident. There is a want of energy. The spirit is paralysed if not dead. What are the ideals of the masses?

Is this torpid condition due entirely to the climate?

Well such communities require a good education for the young—Education must make men of them not mere pedants. The heart the head as well as the hand—the three H's if you like, must be trained until the Soul is attuned to what is right to what is beautiful and to what is pure and to what is noble.

Science must give a true view of nature and show the relations of all things in their true perspective.

Then the young will be filled with the joy of living and will strive to advance the interests of humanity as a paramount duty. Sober optimism shall disperse the darkness of ignorance. Faith in the future will give rise to contentment. Piety and patriotism will impel the youth forwards on the path of duty— making self-sacrifice the highest honour to be sought after. Religion will become a real bond to draw man up to Heaven. Then the mind will be on the alert. There will be a ceaseless striving for change for improvement and for progress.

The awakening of a people if real, will be accompanied by the moral quickening and the intellectual keenness of the young. The whole community will act for the public welfare and the schools of learning will add to knowledge and attract men from all parts of the world.

What do sleeping communities require in order to wake up? Three things—1 religion, 2 knowledge, 3 energy or will-power. These must be of the right sort; but without these there can be no general progress for a whole people.

In British Malaya there is growing up a mighty stalagmite of stagnation among the people despite the irridescence of wealth and material prosperity reflected from the surface. Have we not here conglomerations of men, no matter of what

race, eager to get rich and to enjoy themselves but how few
amongst such also think and work for the good and the happiness of the land on which they have made their money. The
leaven of progress must be inoculated. The Government can
do it through the schools and in other ways. At any rate every
patriotic son of the soil has the inherent obligation to contribute
his share however humble, of stirring the stagnant waters to
give them life. Are the children of the pioneers better or even
as good as their progenitors in the stirling qualities of the
races? Let us admit they have as good an acquaintance with
the rudiments of English as the wisdom of our Code could
confer. But what about other more vital qualities :—stamina,
character, skill, perseverence, thrift, constancy and so forth.
Alas, it must be confessed with sadness that those who ought
in every way to be better than their fathers on account of the
betterment of social position and of the increase of wealth of
the family are in the vast majority of cases scarcely equal to
their fore-fathers. They are richer and have had a better
schooling: they are gourmets and they are great connoisseurs of
all things that delight the heart of an epicure. But they are losing the indomitable spirit that conquers the jungle, and that
gains victory against a world in arms. They have drunk deep
of the Circean potion in what passes current as civilization.
They are the crystals that our years of prosperity in material
wealth are throwing down to augment the mass of the stalagmite
which will eventually obstruct the way to real progress and to
true happiness.

The descendants of all the races are in the same boat. They
have breathed the same mephetic atmosphere and drunk the
same bewitched nectar, and until the air is cleared, and the
antidote is administered, there will be no deliverance, and the
children of the English, the Dutch, the Portuguese, the Chinese,
the Arabs, the Malays, the Indians or the Jews will only escape
enchantment by temporary refuge, and asylums in more
hospitable lands! Knowing the pendulum swing of the forces
behind civilization, we should naturally adopt such necessary
prophylactic measures as the national or other conditions might
necessitate. In a time of great material prosperity, the teachers
and philosophers must warn the masses against the enervating
influence of ease and wealth; while during the period of
depression, decay or stagnation, the people must be continually
roused by constant appeal to the primal instincts and to the

intellect and the reason. The Government should conduct and control the national education in such a manner that every one is trained for citizenship of a progressing State. The sense of duty and the love of knowledge will be adequately and strongly aroused both in the home and at school.

Let parents who are obliged to bring up their children in our environment see to it that they do surround their young with all those influences, that help to build up nobility of character—that sustain the spirit of liberty duty and loyalty—and that generate the manly impulse to stand up for the right and to strive for the best not only for one self but also for the world. Religion, education and public spirit let me repeat are the forces which create civilization. The great war has put our modern civilization into the crucible. Even in far off Malaya, we must feel reverberations of the titanic conflict, and we must be morally and spiritually dead—if those tortures of the flesh and those convulsions of the Soul, do not arouse all of us to do our duty to God and to man.

WAR TIME LECTURES AND ESSAYS.

VII.

SELF-SACRIFICE.

Being the substance of a lecture delivered to the Students of the King Edward VII. Medical School.

Gentlemen,

When requested to address your Society I felt it my duty to contribute my share to your proceedings, although I fully realised that I could hardly have time to present your Society with a full discussion of a topic which might not only be interesting in itself but also useful in these awful times. The subject which I have chosen has special significance at this critical moment in the world's history, but to those who are preparing to enter the medical profession, it may serve also as an elementary introduction to that much talked of but often misunderstood subject of medical ethics. To be sure there is no extraordinary rule of conduct involved in the Code of Ethics recognised by the medical profession. The golden rule is the basis of the medical as well as of any other code of morals. To live according to the highest ideal of the medical profession, the medical man must have clear ideas of the meaning of self-sacrifice and must have the resolution to do his plain duty without hesitation and without murmur. But self-sacrifice is not only a question of interest to Medical Students. It is in fact indispensable in civilised society. The soldier's life is simply the glorification of this virtue, for the soldier is laying down his life for the good of his country. Do not think for a moment, therefore, that self-sacrifice is a moral topic fit only to be preached from the pulpit. At every turn in life, questions crop up to be decided between self and others. Here is in miniature a rivalry of interests. Is it self or others? All at once, you will think of that great law of organic nature—that of the struggle for existence. What does nature teach us? Malthus

long ago suggested that food problems would furnish the key
to the visible competitions among living things. Darwin's
studies of evolution have shown that the fiercest struggles were
not in vain, countless individuals are sacrificed but in the end
the race, the tribe, or the species is saved. Hence arises,
by misconstruing the meaning of this, the philosophy of the
superman. The real German is he who casts away the
obsolete moral code of civilization with its golden rule, and
its law of chastity and charity and its insistence on self-
sacrifice. The superman is to survive the contest with moral
weaklings and physical degenerates. Pity, humanity and
charity are attributes of degeneration. Yet even in the severe
code of German discipline, self-sacrifice is enjoined upon
the men in order to achieve victory. Just think of the masses
of men that have strewn themselves upon the impregnable
fortresses of Verdun, since 1914, and of the sacrifices made by
the defenders and you will realise the importance and the
absorbing interest of the subject I am asking you to consider.

In that battle-scarred Verdun, you can study the whole
problems of the philosophy and ethics of self-sacrifice. There
we have a complete picture of Nature. The immense hordes
of fierce Germans with all their engines of destruction represent the animal world which has been so minutely studied by
zoologists, and which has given us all the current notions of
evolution with its corollary—the doctrine of the survival of
the fittest. But within the forts are operating the agencies of
the spirit, which are mightier than the brute force of the
mailed fist. Within, the French sacrificed themselves for
country, for civilization, and for mankind. Without, the
Germans are virtually seeking the bubble of ambition at the
cannon's mouth. So Verdun may represent in miniature the
epitome of the great world struggles, and these, after all, are
in themselves the outcome of that conflict between two
forces—the Old and the New—the animal and the spiritual,
which will dominate human existence to the end of the world.
In a vision of the history of the world the cosmogonist beholds
the coming out of worlds from chaos. Then passes the
panorama of endless cycles of living forms with the most
awful carnage in the extermination of the unfit. At last man
comes on the stage and slowly he eliminates the rule of
Force and modifies it by his reason, his sympathy, and his
love. He helps the weak and sickly of his race. He shows

mercy to his enemy. He builds up families, cities and states, by the same social impulse. Until man appears on the scene, the fit and the strong crush the weak, and mercilessly deprive these of their food. In human society a new force manifests itself. Altruistic ideals slowly acquire driving power over the minds, and very early the first trait of development is seen in the readiness of man to sacrifice himself —his time and his desires—for the sake of family peace, or social progress. The observer, it is true, may trace this altruistic impulse right beyond man to the animal world in the maternal instincts of all animals with helpless offsprings, and to the social habits of ants, bees and gregarious mammals.

Thus this power of repressing personal appetite or desire or foregoing something on behalf of another can also be shown to have grown up in the world as the result of evolution. Among human beings the ethical training and general education determine in what manner self-sacrifice is practised. The love of parents for their children is instinctive and is the most common cause of self-sacrifice. The love of the other sex stands next to this in point of importance, and is in some obscure way related to parental love, for the whole phenomena of sex relate solely to the propagation and preservation of the race. The human family cannot exist if the parents are not prepared to make sacrifices for their children. It is not customary to regard this as a virtue, for it is surely a simple duty, but in essence it is really self-sacrifice in all essential particulars. The influence and example of parents will determine the character of the children. Will the brothers and sisters be unselfish to one another? It is in the family that love has the best chance of operating, and if it fails now in the nursery—it has no chance at all in the market place. Thus the Confucian family stands together because every one is taught to make self-sacrifices for the common good. The moment the idea that a man should first look after his own interests prevails, it becomes quite impossible to remain together. But a certain degree of self-sacrifice is quite necessary to keep human society together. The natural instinct is self-assertion. Every untrained child like the beast or the Hun is a bully. This aggressiveness must be tempered by a spiritual force. Directed by reason, sympathy and love, it reveals its true character. At the present moment the war has made all think deeply of King and Country; but this love of country or patriotism is only an extended form of that brotherly affection of the family. Patriotism is meaningless without self-sacrifice. The intellectual advancement of mankind is accompanied by an extension of the altruistic impulse that is to say by the suppression of the Ego. If family duties pass into civic virtues, these latter are enlarged into patriotic endeavours, which, in turn, may develop into a zeal for the good of mankind.

At every step of this spiritual ascent of man, self-sacrifice in increasing intensity is required. At first you make self-sacrifice for your parents and for kith and kin. This helps you to understand why you must if necessary deny yourselves on behalf of your neighbours. Then comes the claim of the country at large. Lastly the impulse will be irresistible, and the injunction to love all men and all things will be realised. In these considerations, we have not considered the rewards which self-sacrifice may earn because as a rule these do not enter at all into the calculation. When a man reckons up what a certain act of self-sacrifice will cost and then totals up the rewards which it will bring back—then will probably nothing or little be done. Mankind—the majority that is of human beings— has a short memory and seldom rewards a man's good acts till the man himself has been buried for a hundred years. But this instinct of the spirit to emancipate itself is irrepressible. Stirred up by wrongs or by injustice, the spirit of humanity leaps up and urges the heroes to defend the helpless and the weak. Thus this great European war is the outcome of the struggle of the spirit for liberty. Great Britain and the Allies represent the spiritual force, and hence have been making the sacrifices for the sake of poor Belgium and Serbia. Had Great Britain stood aloof would the Britons be better off in the future for the Germans would have crushed their enemies and the progress of the world would have been greatly retarded? This subject of self-sacrifice requires to be constantly brought to the attention of the young. In the island Empire of our Eastern Ally the most patriotic country in the world, there is the cult of Bushido which is a form of Confucianism applied to the feudal requirements of medieval Japan. Under its teaching the young are constantly taught to meditate upon the requirements of love, justice and honour, and to practice in solemn assemblies of the family a rehearsal of that awful act of *hara-kiri* or suicide by disembowelling. This is now a thing of the past, but its memory burns incandescent in the life of modern Japan, and ever spurs the nation to the sublimest heights of valour and self-sacrifice. So it seems that it will greatly benefit us that during these terrible times of storm and stress, all of us strive to put into practice little sacrifices day by day until the power of self denial becomes a potent force and the individual is ready to lay down his or her life for the good of the country, or of mankind.

Before I conclude, allow me to show how this spirit of self-sacrifice is essential to make a good physician. In no other profession, except that of medicine, is the expert expected to expose his life to danger without special remuneration, nor is he called up to attend to any one at all hours, without first arranging as to the cost. Perhaps after a day's hard work, you are just settling down to prepare for your dinner. Suddenly the telephone rings violently and summons you to a patient six miles away. Perhaps you have made an arrangement to take your family to the opera. The physician smiles and hurries through the dinner probably leaving it unfinished to rush off to the ailing creature far away, leaving the family to find its own way. In epidemics of plague, cholera, and typhus, the doctor runs enormous risks of infection and no one who is not prepared to run risks and make sacrifices should adopt the medical profession. Of course all precautions should be taken against infections but all the same, the medical man must be ready for some sort of self-sacrifice every day of his life. Your patients will require you to give up your time, your pleasures, your leisure, your sleep, your meals, and unless you have the *patience* to continue making these continual sacrifices you will probably lose your patients. Therefore to the medical practitioner, the ethics of self-sacrifices must be learnt and put into practice. Then there are other medical practitioners to deal with. Some foolish patients may be recommended to you, and leave his own doctor. If you know the fact, you will be well advised to refuse to accept his empty compliments, and pursuade him to stick to his own advisor. The temptation to show off one's own skill is very great especially in a young man, but to one accustomed to make sacrifices it would be a simple duty not to take advantage of one's neighbour in his absence. Thus in dealings with your professional brethren, you will also be ready to make sacrifices for the good of comradeship for the glory of the profession.

Now at the present time what do we call the man who is not prepared to make self-sacrifice of some sort? He is the drinking sot, the miser, the misanthrope, the traitor, and the shirker.

In conclusion we find that religion, culture, and love of freedom alike teach that self-sacrifice is required at every step in the moral progress of mankind.

VIII.

Why China must declare War against Germany ?

An open letter to President Li Yuan Hung.

The Chung-Hua Republic stands for peace and democracy, hoping to foster friendly relations with all nations. Its ideals of liberty and civilisation are founded on the established truths of a social morality which has been tested by a history dating back thousands of years. It has been established to uphold the rights of race, and religion for equal opportunity and free development untrammelled by oppression and tyranny. It maintains the sacred rights of humanity to justice and freedom within the limits of righteousness. It proclaims the universality of the moral law, and professes to base all its political and diplomatic actions on the principles of the Golden Rule. It acknowledges the sovereignty of the Almighty Ruler over all human actions and therefore vouchsafes religious freedom to all mankind.

In these claims and professions, the aims of the Chung Hua Republic are in fact identical with the hopes and ideals of Great Britain, France, the United States and their Allies in undertaking the onus of fighting Germany and members of her league. Great Britain and France represent the democracies of the world ; Germany and Austria fight for the supremacy of might and despotism. The contest between the powers is really a struggle between democratic liberty and militarist autocracy. The rights of weak and small nations to free development and independent political existence will be guaranteed by the victory of the Allies whereas German triumph means the subjugation of all conquered nations to the military necessities of a universal German Empire. If we may judge of the spirit of German Imperialism from the past acts of the Germans in their colonies and especially of their behaviour to coloured and undeveloped races, one may safely say that German victory will entail serfdom upon all non-European races and tribes that will come under their austere military rule. The fate of the Hereros and of the unhappy Moslems in East Africa should serve as a warning to those Asiatics who may have listened to the wiles of German propagandists.

The Chinese people have the words of their sages from Yao and Shun down to Confucius and Mencius to guide them as to the attitude which the nation must assume in this world war. Confucius says that "it is cowardice to abstain from doing that which is right." Chinese ethics recognises the unity of civilisation and human society, and Chinese history affords innumerable examples of nations entering into war for the cause of right and freedom in order to vindicate the just cause of weak and oppressed nations. The British Empire and the Uuited States have no selfish interests to seek in joining in the fray. These have been forced by moral and spiritual considerations to make the necessary sacrifices for the sake of humanity. The same considerations appeal to the Chinese nation. According to the moral and political ideals of the Chung Hua Republic, no State can exist for itself nor stand alone. It must co-operate with its neighbours for the maintenance of civilisation and for the advancement of mankind. Civilisation itself is now threatened by German militarism. Lawlessness is rampant in the world, and the Central Powers under the leadership of Germany, disregard all laws and conventions, presuming to impose their cruel and arbitrary rule upon all nations, regardless of the lives and properties of man, woman or child. Appealing to the urgency of necessity, and to the law of animal existence, the Germans claim to be supermen in virtue of their military machine and their preparedness for war. They have the temerity to despise all rules of chivalry and have no pity nor compunction in their cruel and insensate outrages against the aged, the helpless, the sick or the wounded. Nor have they shown any regard for the modesty of women. By one fell swoop, the mighty and fierce German races and their lawless allies have descended to the depths of mediæval barbarism and have even surpassed the ancient barbarians in their wanton cruelty and devastation without the excuse or the justification which the savage hordes of Goths, Vandals, Huns, Turks or Mongols could plead in extenuation of their ferocity and excesses. The hopelessness of bringing the German Government to its senses in its cruel and insensate attacks upon neutral nations has compelled the United States of America to sever diplomatic relations, and at last to declare war against the faithless Teutons. The Chung-hua Republic also has been inspired by the noble example of America and has lost no time in breaking off diplomatic relations with a nation who has lost caste among the civilised peoples of the Earth. If the diplomatic political and moral reasons which justify the President in sanctioning the national desire to sever diplomatic intercourse with Germany, are at all sound, then there is no other cause left for the Chung-hua nation but to declare war, and to give the Democracies of the West all the assistance which may lie in the power of the Flowery land. The struggles in the West must continue long and bitter. They are not to be decided by the victories over territories. They are to end only with the utter exhaustion of one or the other or of both parties. It is therefore very important for the Chung-hua Republic in the great interests of humanity, justice and freedom to throw in her lot with those civilised peoples who are sacrificing all material interests on behalf of weak and small nations in order that civilisation may prevail throughout the world. The Chung-hua Republic has done the best political action the nation has attempted for a century by cutting off all diplomatic association with the intriguing Huns. The Government has now no alternative but to proceed to the natural conclusion of the movement that has been started. Is China too weak? Surely the Chung-hua nation realises too well from the teaching of its best thinkers since many thousand years that the real strength of a people depends not merely upon its military preparations, but mainly upon the unity and patriotism of its people. As the Chung-hua nation has cast aside the traditions of the past and has established a democratic Government upon a foundation of the most ancient despotism, the people throughout the length and breadth of the country await with anxiety for the fateful decision to know whether the President will decide to march with the democracies of the world and to make what sacrifices that might be necessary for the cause of freedom and right. Hesitancy will be highly injurious to the State and the Nation. The Chung-hua Republic cannot afford to stand isolated from the democracies of the world. Her interests, ideals and aspirations are identical with those of the United States, France and England. She must join them or else she must perish through internecine disputes and foreign complications and intrigues. There are still dormant elements of the autocratic regime smouldering away but ready to burst into flame at any moment.

The great masses of the people are still very backward in education and knowledge. Superstition is still the great curse of the country. For the sake of consistency therefore the Government of the Republic must without delay proclaim its abhorence of German crimes, and must throw in its lot with the governments of the great democracies of the West.

There is great danger in remaining in the present position of a very equivocal character. What is to be gained in severing diplomatic relations? The German Government has treated the action of the Chung-hua Government with ridicule and contempt. The only thing which the President of the Republic can do to save the national honour is to ask the Senate to approve of a declaration of War. The people of Chung-hua can do much to help in bringing the Germans more speedily to their knees. There are millions of men physically fit to fight in any battlefield. In a few months a million men could be trained. But China could assist immediately by sending artizans and agricultural workers who could no doubt solve the food problem in England for example. Fifty thousand agricultural workers in France and the same number in England besides hundreds of thousands of other labourers in all departments will help to free immediately the corresponding number of men in England and France for the colours. China has any number of artizans who are all sound men and who could without much training do all the work of munition factories.

Thus as regards Man Power, the Chung-Hua Republic can afford to give vital assistance which if quickly and wisely rendered, would be effective in more directions than one. Even in matters of finance, the Chung-Hua republic may succeed in floating a substantial loan in America, Japan and England, for the proper carrying out of the help to the Allies. Though China is at present a poor country, she is potentially very rich, and when properly developed, she must rank among the first nations of the earth in virtue solely of the industrial, mineral and agricultural resources that cry for exploitation. Therefore to go to war when the whole world is being thrown into the melting pot, is a necessity—if the country is to uphold its position in the ranks of the great nations of the future. The whole world of business is going to be changed after the war. In consequence of what the Germans have done to the civilised nations of Europe, there must be a distinction made against the Germans in the markets of the world. There will be a trade war afterwards. There will be social barriers. Whatever diplomats may say or do, the Germans will be outcasts or pariahs after the war at least in our generation. The Republic of Chung-Hua must range herself amongst the great democratic nations since the only chance of her survival as an independent democracy will depend entirely upon the victory of the French and their Allies.

It has been loudly asked, even by those who should know better, what gain could China possibly derive from participation in the war. That China could benefit in many ways from the economic and diplomatic points of view could be easily demonstrated. But the question of material advantages is entirely beside the point. China must decide solely on the grounds of righteousness. Surely with the Confucian Canons in evidence, and the words of Mencius sounding as the tocsin of war, the first democracy of Asia must be prepared to fulfil the Confucian ideal of self-sacrifice and self-immolation for the completion of the moral ideal. Has not the sage of China declared—" self-sacrifice even entailing death is preferred by the man of virtue to any dereliction of duty which though insuring safety destroys honour." In view of the enormous crimes of the German government against mankind the Chung-Hua republic must make a definite pronouncement of her national protest against the terrible wrongs committed by Germany both on land and at sea, not only against belligerents but also against neutral nations. The Chung-Hua Republic should decide to go to war entirely upon the moral issue. Is it right for China to declare war against Germany ? What gains can be got, or what sacrifices must be made are purely secondary and must not be permitted to overcloud the real object of making the protest. In a moral cause unworthy motives must be put aside and placed entirely out of court. China must come forward ready to suffer the utmost for the cause of civilisation. This is the teaching of the ancient religion of China. It is the faith of the Great Allies in their titanic efforts to free the world from the incubus of despotism and tyranny. The opportunity is a sure one of showing the world that China has not been properly understood and that her people have been always actuated by moral consideration in all important matters. It is also very appropriate the Chinese should help to put down the Kaiser's militarism because the Chinese of the North have had bitter experience of its ruthlessness and its wanton disregard of human feelings and human rights.

Has not Confucius said : "All men are brethren?. The educated man makes no class distinctions. The world must be harmonised by moral suasion and not by legal enactments." The wicked must be punished. The enemies of mankind the Germans and their auxiliaries must be brought to reason, and China as the oldest civilisation in the world, must throw in the whole weight of her influence—whatever it may be—on the side of Great Britain, France, Russia and the United States. It were best if Chinese Statesmen could cast aside all material and economic issues when they would consider this tremendous international problem. But it is not difficult to indicate how a wise decision to take her stand definitely on the cause of justice and liberty will not only be right, but also advantageous from every point of view. Let there be no hesitation. The natural promptings of human nature, the echoes of the Voice of God, call upon the great democracies of Chung-hau to declare war upon the cruel, faithless and cunning Germans, who have trampled upon all laws and treaties, and who have disregarded all the amenities and charities, which religion, ethics and humanity have established in human society for two thousand years. The Chinese have suffered, after a fashion, all the horrors and the humiliations which the Germans have inflicted upon the unoffending and unhappy Belgians, who have heroically defended their homes against tremendous odds. The Chung-hua Republic has every obligation as a free and independent State to come forward to assist the Belgians and their Allies so that Peace may speedily be restored upon the secure foundation of righteousness and justice.

> [*Addendum* :—Since the above was printed off, China had again passed through another revolution but the German inspired attempt to restore the Empire was promptly nipped in the bud, and the new Republican Government has declared war against Austria-Hungary and Germany.]

WAR TIME LECTURES AND ESSAYS.

IX.

The Prospects of the Straits Chinese.

A Lecture before the Malacca Chinese Literary Association.

MR. PRESIDENT AND GENTLEMEN.

Your energetic Secretary has kept his argus eye upon me for so long that I am at last to-night the victim of his importunity. I have had so many things to attend to of late that I feel sure that nothing I can say deserves all the trouble you have taken to make arrangements for this lecture.

I hope the subject is one that will appeal to all of you though I find it is more troublesome to deal with than it looks at the first blush. However with your indulgence I shall venture to lay before you what the prospects of our promising community are in the future, and to indicate briefly in which directions our Society working as a living organism can use its influence for our good. Peradventure, you will pardon any plain speaking and any warning against possible dangers ahead.

SOCIAL WORK.

From the social standpoint, we recognise that the maintenance of health is a big and vexed problem—and that unless the body is sound and healthy, the possession of much wealth is only a source of misery and vexation, As a community, we must arouse the social conscience to the existence of evil tendencies that undermine the constitution not only of the present but also of future generations. There is the eternal problem of intoxication by opium or alcohol. There is the question of vice and the attendant evils of disgusting diseases that spread like plague, and are as deadly in their blighting effects both upon health and upon morals. The physique of the race is deteriorating. We are confronted with perplexing questions affecting marriage. We must solve the delicate but important problems connected with the freedom and education of our women-folk. Nor must we forget the value and influence of æsthetics upon the higher life. Art and music as well as athletics must in the future receive adequate attention.

The Religious Problem.

There is also the religious problem. There is a tendency to scoff at superstitions just as the half educated Romans used to do. But our imperfect English education, which most of us have received, is a very unreliable guide. There is much wisdom in the old practices and until we have really something better to offer in substitute, it is safer to let people believe in immortality and in the persistence of the spirit—beliefs that underlie the whole doctrine of filial piety. But after all it seems some of the best minds in Europe—men like Mr. Stead, Sir Oliver Lodge, Sir William Crooks, Dr. Saleeby M. Maeterlinck and many others propound views of the spiritual world, that confirm in a remarkable manner the so-called superstitions of the East.

For this reason, I believe that the Confucian religion that teaches moderation and reverence in all things, and that inculcates altruism as the basis of justice, righteousness and humanity should not be neglected during this period of transition. It teaches us duty to God and to man, as well as to ourselves. It points out a great ideal—the perfect man for all to follow and it provides a system of ethics that is rational and practical.

Education.

But above all things, Confucianism lays stress upon a proper education of the individual. It urges that we must distinguish mere instruction from education. "To stuff" a youth's head with facts is no education at all. True education must touch the whole individual. The conscience must be sensitised and the whole being must be transformed.

But culture alone does not suffice to-day. There must be sufficient training in some useful arts, and our young men must be made to realise that the old rule of thumb is no longer "good enough" but that modern requirements entail prolonged study of the exact sciences, and first hand knowledge of things and mechanical processes.

In these days of keen commercial rivalry—we are all becoming materialists and often forget that the old Chinese view of education is still of use—viz: that the chief value of education is the acquirement of the art of self-control. We are apt to demand so much of instruction or mere knowledge of facts that we overlook the true character of education. For years, experts have been telling us that we must learn from Germany how to run our education. We have seen already the bitter fruit of that one-sided materialistic education in the devastated regions of Belgium, France and Poland. The world is staggered at the colossal egotism and irrationality—not to speak of the barbarity of the German nation. This all comes from the divorce of ethics from education, and from the selfish application of scientific methods to barbarian schemes of conquests. From quite a different standpoint, we must watch with misgiving the effects of a similar line of education for our future generation. What ideals are we putting before our children? What means are we providing them for estimating the intrinsic values of things and of human actions?

EXISTING EVILS.

But education like medicine must be prescribed according to our needs—sufficient in quantity and appropriate in kind. It is next to useless as the Chinese proverb says "to scratch the wrong place when one suffers from itching." A suitable education must eradicate whatever is undesirable and implant something that uplifts and that enobles life.

Ignorance may inspire us with false hopes and a momentary bliss—but surely no sensible people could for ever build castles in the air. If existing evils are not remedied, and we shut our eyes to them, we may pass unscathed for a time but we shall be only enjoying a fool's paradise, as the Germans are doing, and before long, disillusionment will come. At any cost therefore a sound but simple education must be brought within the reach of all Straits Chinese males and females.

We hear frequently frantic appeals by parents and husbands to government to assist them in stopping women from gambling. We are told that gambling is rampant. Surely every one must know that no government can absolutely stop all gambling without resorting to very harsh and stringent measures. The chief harm of gambling is not so much the loss of money, for often the gambler recoups his losses, but is in the establishment of a bad habit of "killing" time, and in the development of a mental attitude so fatal to the highest interests of morality and civilization. Gambling, like all bad habits, makes slaves of its devotees. It engenders selfishness, "cuteness" and guile. The mental habitude is therefore subversive of all that is best in human culture.

It is very noticeable that the Straits Chinese are not capable of sustaining such a concord and co-operation among themselves as the Chinese generally can do. Perhaps there are often too many "cooks" for their leaders have conflicting ideals and regard one another with jealousy and suspicion.

People of experience say that we lack public spirit. This observation is a just one, and we must confess that it is a trait inherited from the social environment in which the rulers despoil the people as in China even to this day. But it is high time that every Straitsborn man realises it is a free citizen's duty to regard the interest of the State as his own, and therefore to accustom himself to bear cheerfully and willingly the responsibilities and the burdens of citizenship if he seeks to enjoy the privileges of peace and freedom.

How much of our failings are due to the tropical environment cannot be decided off-hand. We see the Malay people in their simple blissfulness around us. Have we inherited something from Malay progenitors that rebels against the arduous and continuous application to work—that so marvellously distinguish the Chinese as a race? The laws of heredity as demonstrated by Mendel indicate the re-appearance atavistically of individuals resembling one or other of the ancestors. This is a phenomenon which every Strait's family is confronted with. We can't shut our eyes to its existence. We must trust to an efficient system of training by which the personal attention of the teacher can be given to each individual child in special high class schools to save aberrant forms of child personality. For such children the ordinary schools are useless—and indeed they are often rather harmful. These boys play truant, rebel against all authority, and revert to Malay surroundings and habits with the greatest ease. They are children of nature. They dislike the restraints of civilization and its conventionalities. They have no ambition. They are spendthrifts and like the sparrows will neither work nor worry for unto them sufficient unto the day is more than plenty. It seems to me that under the older strict Confucian home-training, the social tendencies were more successfully repressed for by force of habit and by frequent repetition the child acquired the belief in the sanctity of old customs, and strove to maintain what survived of the ancient communism. But under present conditions, such persons show marked traits of a restlessness that is characteristic and that is encouraged by the individualism which permeates modern European thought and institutions.

There is a total lack of life as a social unit. The community is moved only by fits and starts. It is true in the Clubs we see some attempt at organization for social purposes, but we must confess the influence of many Clubs has not been altogether beneficial. The Straits British Chinese Association is endeavouring to fill a role that will greatly assist the advancement of the whole community.

Economically the bulk of our Straits Chinese have indeed a black prospect. But I fear in this matter many of the Straits Chinese may regard my humble opinions as the ravings of a modern Cassandra because an ugly truth is always resented. I am not referring only to a few wealthy families but to the great majority of those who work for their living as clerks or employees of merchants in the towns. In a certain locality I have watched with a heavy heart devolution of a once prosperous community. Twenty-five years ago there were vigorous business houses. Now they are in the last stages of decay—and many have already disappeared. The majority of the sons of those merchants are employed as clerks of lawyers, of great importing houses, or of the Municipality and the Government. Their great plantations were neglected. The squatters and the managers have started new concerns and have either turned out the Straits-born sons of the Towkays or reduced their shares to quite insignificant proportions. As traders we are nowhere. With a few exceptions, the Straits Chinese have shown no aptitude for "shop-keeping," though quite a number succeed as "Chetties" (money lenders) if usury can be properly called a trade. In Malacca and Penang, however, they are more successful as traders. But all over the country, we must try to stop the suicidal policy of fitting our young men only as machines of the merchants. It is of the highest importance to arouse them from the lethargy which has possessed them, and to stimulate the imagination of our youths to view with eagerness and enthusiasm the exertions and efforts which commerce, agriculture and mining necessitate. The School training which our youths receive no doubt incline them to the adoption of the seemingly ideal life of the mercantile clerk—regular work— regular hours—regular holidays as at School—and regular pay with no worries—no responsibilities after office hours, leaving the evenings free for jollification! What a life this is compared with the lot of the Chinese merchant—who is busy day and night, who has no holidays and who makes voyages and

expeditions that often involve hardships and risks. I am sure
in the special locality mentioned, it is a contrast such as this
that has driven nearly all the sons of those merchant agricultur-
ists of a generation back to the counting houses in the town
or to Government service, giving away often for nothing the
business, which they find it too strenuous to maintain.

A REVIEW OF THE PAST.

Although I am not by any means a pessimist nor am I
conscious of any excessive weakness as a *laudator temporis acti*,
yet stern facts are stubborn things, which it behoves the student
of social progress to understand, if he is anxious to find the
best solution for the difficulties and obstacles that stand in the
way of social advancement. A cursory survey of the monumental
achievements of the Chinese in the industrial and social
development of British Malaya—demonstrates that Chinese
settlers have been from the earliest days patient and persever-
ing workers, ready for the most strenuous exertions and willing
to take every risk that the climate, the occupation, or the
circumstances might demand. The majority of the great
merchants had acquired a firsthand knowledge of men and of
places and of the things which formed the articles of trade.
Many of them had travelled extensively and had intimate
knowledge of the requirements of each locality. They all had
acquired a high sense of honour and probity in trade transac-
tions and throughout Malaya till our own day, the word of a
Chinese was as good as his bond—indeed much better than the
verbose and often unintelligible documents to which now-a-days
every merchant attaches his signature. Then the men of the
past generations lived simple lives and were economical—
moreover they were very ready to assist one another in every
way. It has been always a remarkable feature of the Chinese
community to have constantly raised men from the poorest and
humblest positions to eminence and affluence through sheer
merit and ability. This fact gives great encouragement to the
new comers, and makes them contented and steady workers as
they feel their zeal and honesty will be rewarded in due time.

If we compare our position to-day with what was the
situation of our forefathers or with that of the Chinese
generally, we must find much to be dissatisfied with ourselves.
We seem to be worse off than those, whom many affect to

despise as "*Sin Khe*" (*i.e.* new guests) as they are called by the babas of Netherlands India.

With the prevailing ignorance, with our stubborn insular narrow-mindedness, and with our inborn tendency to swank and to shirk work, we fail to avail ourselves of the opportunities lying at our doors. It seems the strangers are rising to the top, and we are slowly but surely sinking!!

Fortunately these national failings are nearly all remediable, and we hope that a real effort will be made to purge our errors and to safeguard good positions all along the line.

The fact is I hope to have led you up to a sort of mental Nebo height from which the Straits Chinese may behold the promised land of future prosperity and happiness in these rich and flourishing regions. It seems we behold the way before us leading within a short distance to a bifurcation—the right one a narrow difficult path leading up to what is glorious in every respect; and the other a broad road with an easy descent to the depths of degeneration and decay.

To a very large extent, we resemble the Jews in political status in different countries in the Far East. Although we are racially Chinese, from the political point of view, the native-born Chinese of the Malay Archipelago and of the Indo-Malayan Peninsula belong as subjects to the Great European powers including Holland. There are immense and profound differences between the Straits-born Chinese, the Sino-Malayan peoples of Netherlands India and the Chinese proper. We may claim direct interest in the British Empire not only by virtue of the geographical accident of birth—which may mean little indeed as the attitude of Germans has shown since the commencement of hostilities, but also on account of the English ideals and of the British political aspirations—which unite us with the other peoples of the Empire through the bond of a common loyalty and of a common language, apart altogether from the far greater economic and commercial relationships that are certain to come after the great war. As a people, we are now indissolubly attached to the British Empire. Her interests are ours—her enemies are ours too and we should courageously and freely undertake to accept our fullest share of her stupendous burdens so gladly and so willingly borne by Great Britain and the Dominions overseas. Thus it seems to me we may achieve our full emancipation as a unit however small of the Empire—and as an element worthy of the liberty and the justice for which England has staked her all. Let us all show that at this crisis in the national history, we are men fit to be entrusted with the onerous duties of defending the Empire, and that we are ready to sacrifice our all like others in all parts of the King's vast dominions. The day must come when the native born people of this part of His Majesty's realm will enjoy the same privileges as Europeans. Let us claim little or nothing but let us rather live up to the grand Confucian maxim, to earn by meritorious deeds the right to recognition, and in the end truth and justice must prevail.

Personally, I am quite confident that good and great leaders will arise among our people, to guide them in the right way so that our children will flourish, and continue to be the same happy, loyal and prosperous community which the King and the British nations will be proud to number among the numerous units of our glorious Empire.

WAR TIME LECTURES AND ESSAYS.

X.

The Sounding for Peace.

Every body must concede that it is the Pope's duty to hold up the banner of the Church, and to attempt to make his feeble voice heard amidst the din of battles. But it is very difficult to conceal the suspicion that the Peace message of the Vatican was inspired by something more than the altruism of the Church. In fact the very phraseology seems to betray the raucous voice of the Huns. "Moral force" and "freedom of the Seas" are what the Allies are fighting for, and had the Vatican been really anxious "to stand up" for right, these observations that have been sent to all belligerents, should have been addressed to the Kaiser as the party responsible for all the bloodshed and horrors of the War. Had Christian principles or the ordinary ethical maxims of civilization had any weight with the Kaiser and his military henchmen, the war would not have created the intense loathing with which the Germans are now regarded by all nations beyond the sphere of influence of the enemy Powers. We can see quite clearly that what the Germans now dread is "the War after the War." Hence they are so desirous of humanity and lasting peace in order to obtain a return to the status quo, as the Pan-German schemes have all been found to be unworkable and unrealisable without a great Victory over the Allies, a thing now impossible of attainment except in the wildest German dreams. The Pope's intervention at a moment when the last straw is to be added to break the back of the proverbial Camel—in this instance the demon of Germanism, cannot be expected to be warmly received among the Allies. The Vatican must be fully aware of the serious causes that drove the reluctant American nation under Dr. Wilson to declare War against Germany. The most pacific peoples on earth—the Siamese and the Chinese so far away from the actual fighting area, have also felt constrained to throw in their lot with the Allies. Is it possible to imagine that these new and ancient nations would have wantonly declared War against Germany if they did not realise the futility of maintaining permanent peace with Germany as the supreme power in the world.

The painful history of the attempts of Dr. Wilson to save America from War illustrates to a nicety the hopelessness of mankind relying upon moral right without the strong arm to enforce the claims of justice and righteousness. China and Siam have also learned from bitter experience in the past that a nation unwilling to defend its honour has practically no right in the presence of Powers which recognise only material profits and the claims of superior arms. The hope of the Allies is that the Dragon of materialism and selfishness may be slain so that righteousness may have full sway in the council of nations, making it possible to ensure freedom and justice to small and unmilitary nations. The Pope's good wishes will not have the least effect in the world if the Germans, still unredeemed, continue in power.

History has repeatedly proved that human society reflects the character of the individuals of whom it is composed. So long as selfishness still plays a large part in the conduct of human affairs—private or public, it is vain to expect that a small or weak nation can depend solely upon the justness of its cause in any serious difference of opinion existing between itself and a stronger Power. To what extent will a powerful nation concede to a non-military state in a dispute concerning its commercial interests or political privileges? There is no adequate guarantee that the people of a strong country will voluntarily forego claims that can be forcibly established by arms against a weak or defenceless nation. The justice of a given case can be easily interpreted from the most favourable and patriotic point of view, so that the Government will be bound at its peril to adopt the views of the general population as reflected by the press and by the political agencies. Up to the outbreak of the present War, international law existed only in theory, and the Germans plainly cast the whole thing over-board, when they commenced their War against civilization. If by sufferance and mutual consent, cases had been adjucated —there was no practical machinery by which the judicial decisions of the Hague Court could have been enforced. The moral sanction derived from such a tribunal must remain a dead letter and was openly and shamelessly disregarded by the Germans.

It is therefore quite plain that if the objects of the allies are to be realised in the permanent peace, which is to be the result of the war, the victorious allies must constitute themselves into a League of nations to uphold the claims of freedom justice and righteousness. The most feasible scheme will be to continue the alliance for a period of twenty years or so, when the allies may consider whether the enemy nations may be permitted to join them on equal terms. The great point to be established is not disarmament but the destruction of the spirit of militarism, that is, the incarnation of the Devil. As a punishment for the dastardly outrages committed against civilization, the Central powers should be obliged to keep no troops except such as would be required for police purposes. Then the allied nations could, by arrangement, determine the forces which each power should maintain as an international police to enforce the decisions of a council of nations. The scheme naturally bristles with difficulties and contains innumerable pit-falls so that it is very questionable whether except as a pious opinion, it has any chance of seeing daylight in the realm of practical politics. On the other hand, without the direction and the authority of a superior power, backed by adequate force, there is no prospect of maintaining peace among the struggling nations of the earth with all their jealousies and idiosyncrasies, each eager to outwit the other and to seize the utmost profit possible. The churches have failed to make mankind regulate life according to the principles of ethics and religion. Man still retains too much of the character of the beast of the field to steer his course solely by the star of Heaven. Just as in each Community, the police is necessary to maintain peace and order, so it is obvious for generations to come, an international police is indispensable to prevent the colossal misfortunes such as those which the Germans have inflicted upon civilization.

The allies have joined in a holy war against infamy tyranny and savagery. They should continue the alliance in the name of right, freedom and law. If the representatives of all nations meet on terms of equality and understand thoroughly that they must be guided by considerations of justice and righteousness in the general interests of mankind as a whole, there is ground for hope that the experiment may prove eminently successful.

The great war has inaugurated a new era of peace for the world. Unless it does so, all the sacrifices of the nations will have been made in vain. But it will be necessary for the thinking part of mankind to thoroughly understand the issues at stake, and to utilise every possible means of propaganda to make the man in the street appreciate the moral questions involved. If the democracies are to make their power felt in the government of the world, the individual in every democratic country must be capable of understanding the nature of the spiritual and moral problems that call for solution in the progress of humanity.

Before it can be profitable to talk of the terms of peace, one must realise the nature of the problems calling for solution. Cessation of the present war is fraught with dire perils to the civilised world, unless the military power of Germany has been broken, and the German people have realised their errors and feel contrition for their crimes. The Germans have so consistently proclaimed their belief in the right of the stronger to take advantage of the weak, that nothing short of a crushing defeat will convince the victims of kultur that there is in reality a better and higher world than the arena of a fierce struggle for existence in which the weaker must go to the wall. More than a thousand years of Christian propaganda have failed to impress upon the Teutons that spiritual insight into the mysteries of civilization, that has so magnificiently distinguished the French and the British nations. Verily one is driven to ask "Can the leopard change its spots?"

If the civilised world is unable to make the Germans change their moral attitude towards society, there will be no peace without a strong backing of force. In dealing with children and savages, the ultimate appeal is always to the rod,—something which hurts and makes a coarse sensory impression upon some part susceptible of receiving it in a sufficiently strong degree. It would be quite impossible for the Allies to trust those German politicians who had been shown to be morally incapable of acting in good faith whenever the interests of themselves or their country were concerned. Chicanery, intrigue and treachery would be resorted to in every possible way. Men of honour could not work in such atmosphere. Justice demands that these men be punished for their crimes. It would be madness to negotiate with them the terms of any peace. On general principles therefore, there must be found the persons with whom the Allies could deal with any confidence. But then these men must be found by the Germans themselves. As long as they put their faith upon the Kaiser and the arch traitors to civilization, so long must the war continue, since it

would be folly to commit the future of the world once again to
the pledges of a faithless nation upon a mere " scrap of paper."

Then as to the terms which will be acceptable to the democracies of the world. The Allied Powers have clearly enun-
ciated their terms in unmistakable language, and every further
experience of German frightfulness, has served only to confirm
the necessity for demanding adequate reparation for criminal
acts of devastation and spoliation as well as efficient guarantees
for the future. The case of Belgium stands out pre-eminent
and admits of no discussion. Even the German in his sober
moments must agree with Herr Bethmann-Hollweg that Germany committed a grievous wrong to a great nation, whose only
crime was to stand in the way of Teutonic aggrandisement
which was absolutely contrary to the sanctions of International
Law and to the established rights of nations. The Great
Nations of the West, including America have pledged their
honour that Belgium must be resuscitated and as far as possible
rehabilitated and recompensed. The wanton destruction of
Northern France, contrary to the sanctions of civilized warfare
calls for substantial reparation. Among the safeguards against
future friction and misunderstanding, is the question of nationalities and races. The problems involved are of a far-reaching
character. Sincerity in all concerned is required in any attempt
to find a practical solution of the intricate tangle of perplexities
which surround this subject. The United States could point to
the Civil War as a precedent for risking all on behalf of a backward and servile population enslaved and treated as chattel but
yet capable under suitable conditions of responding to the environment of a progressive civilization. In Europe and Asia, the
small and weak nations are already homogeneous and highly
organised. Their independence can be easily secured by the
judicious guidance of the great Powers—once these are freed
from the tyranny of a soul-less commercialism and from the
intoxication of a selfish nationalism. The great Powers must
give up once for all the greed of Empire, and must be prepared
to assume the rôle of trustees in the general interests of mankind.

The horrors and the sufferings of the great war have
brought home to civilised men the true solidarity and the
essential unity of the human family. Political partition of
geographical areas, irrespective of the wishes of the peoples
concerned, has been a fruitful source of irritation and unrest,

WAR TIME LECTURES AND ESSAYS.

and the natural reaction of the human mind against restraint and oppression, has called forth cruel persecution and repressive measures which have served merely to embitter race against race, and to increase by progressive summation, the suspicion jealousy and hatred even between races otherwise closely akin to one another. But when the facts are courageously faced, it will be evident at once that the world is scarcely ready yet for that realisation of the democratic ideal of the freedom of man. Is Russia fully prepared to act liberally with regard to the wishes and aspirations of the Finns, the Mongols, the Cossacks and other sundry tribes who form the enormous population of the Russian Empire? How could Austria survive dissection and dismemberment? But perhaps the example of Switzerland, and the experience of the British Empire, and the Federation of American States might indicate the rough outlines of any possible rearrangement of states according to nationalities. It will not be an easy matter even without German intrigue. The Irish question should make the most optimistic wary of possible pitfalls under the best conditions. Yet the time seems to have arrived for the Great Powers to act fearlessly in putting into practice the grand ideals of justice and liberty about which so much has been said in the last two years.

China is now one of the belligerents but China is suffering from the effects of Treaties dictated by victors, who subordinated the claims of justice to the noisy demands of commercialism and self-interest. The Races of India are expecting constitutional reform, and are trusting to the pledges of the British Government. In Europe herself, the claims of races and nationalities are conflicting. Peace for the world cannot be assured, unless the delicate problems connected with racial antipathies and prejudices can find some sort of solution or compromise, and in any case, there will be the necessity of maintaining sufficient force behind the International Council, which is to arbitrate for civilization and, to enforce the mandate of civilised mankind. There will be no satisfactory peace till Education has become universal, and till the elements of Social Ethics and of Democratic politics are understood by the masses of the great nations of the Earth and are made the ordinary rule of their daily lives. Even then it will take many generations more to live down the existing prejudices of race, colour and religion.

WAR TIME LECTURES AND ESSAYS.

Some Problems of the Great War in the light of Chinese History.

XI.

A Lecture delivered before the Oldham Hall Literary Society.

The Great War like a giant Upas tree over-shadows the thoughts of small men and renders nugatory all attempts at thinking of something apart from the current topics connected with the momentous struggle. Day by day the insensate fury and the unreasoning despair of the Germans urge them to acts of desperation which involve the perpetration of uncalled-for tragedies and losses everywhere. Never before in the history of the world, has a nation which from external evidences at any rate, seemed to have reached the acme of material progress, suddenly lost its mental balance and revealed all the ferocity and the brutality which once characterised its pre-historic progenitors in the forests of Germany. The world is appalled at the universal spoliation and ruin with the accompanying calamity to millions of human beings of all classes, sexes and ages. A century of peace in Europe and the spread of education together with the advancement of science and the growth of commerce, have made it very difficult for many people to realise that it would be possible to plunge civilisation into chaos by a universal war involving nearly all the principal nations of the world. Yet that is what Germany has done in order that the idea of "world power" in German hands might be translated into terms of practical politics at the psychological moment on the appointed "Day."

All at once the nations are confronted with many difficult political, economic, legal, commercial and ethical questions and problems provoked by the unscrupulous and reckless conduct of German troops, and secret as well as official agents. History tells us that Frederick the Gross was infatuated with Machiavelli's politics and schemes of intrigues intended for the extremely corrupt and wicked courts of the petty principalities of the Renaissance Period. But he was cunning enough to write a

pamphlet against Machiavellism in order to allay the possible
suspicions of his neighbours upon whom he intended to lay
violent hands in order to rob them of territories he had long
coveted.   The German Kaiser to-day has permitted his government to repeat the intrigues of the 18th century without the
excuse which his ancestor might plead, and without the genius
which certainly inspired that great villain of a Hohenzollern.
The whole civilised world has been overwhelmed with grief and
suffering, often without knowing the reason for all the
economic cataclysms that have swept over the globe.   Those
who have suffered are not in a position to think impartially of
the vexed problems that demand a solution.

Fortunately most of the questions that have attracted
universal attention as a result of the war are not new but are
merely the old puzzles of natural existence in a world of conflicting interests with races in varying degrees of spiritual
development, contending for supremacy.   Chinese history
affords as a mirror a view of the continuous struggles of a
civilised democracy emerging from the gloom of primeval
times and passing through periodic epochs of chaos and
convulsion, till it has finally overthrown the representatives
of brute force and irresponsible autocracy by the establishment
of the Chunghua Republic.*   Incidentally the Chinese people
have in the past been confronted with the same difficulties and
perplexities that are now standing between the state of War and
the realization of a permanent peace among civilised nations.
The impartial verdict of history may be found to be a better
guide towards the discovery of a rational reconstitution of
international relations, than the perturbed and distorted views
of the contending partizans.   In this great and cruel conflict
of fundamental issues there are no neutrals, as continual reve-
lations of German intrigues are proving to the hilt.   The
experience of the Chinese nation may prove interesting and
helpful in the attempt to solve the riddles of national independence and of the surging tide of a rampant militarism.   China
like Belgium has been the cock-pit of the warring nations.
She has suffered from the contentions of every generation of
militarist adventurers.   The new War cries sound to Oriental
ears like echoes of similar voices that have come down all the
centuries.   Liberty—that is the right of a small or weak nation
to live its own life in its own way, and the right to hold ideals

---

* This is the Official Name of the Republic of China.

of justice, of religion and of philosophy according to the impulses of racial idiosyncrasy, has been a question that has agitated mankind since the first dawn of cvilization. Love of freedom is the first fruit of the incarnation of the Spirit. Just as the struggles for existence have given us organic evolution and the differentiation of organs in the individual and of races in the living world, so has the emancipation of the Spirit been the main-spring of the development and progress of humanity. It is true this ascent of the spiritual element in man has necessitated war but it is not true that wars alone are the indispensable conditions for the continued and further advancement of civilisation. So long, however, as the animal instincts and impulses survive in man, and tend to repress the human tendencies towards the realisation of more spiritual ideals, so long must the higher organisms be ready to combat the aggression thrown upon them. This is in short the meaning of the latest phase of the conflict of the nations. After long years of warring, the Chinese had come to hate war and to love peace but only after they had discovered a modus vivendi through which by mutual consent, peace could be maintained. The history of China affords a striking illustration of the vitality of democracy as well as the perils which follow in the wake of a peace which does not secure the essential conditions for the development of the spirit. The world does not want rest and peace at any price for, then, the price of peace is stagnation and death. A cursory review of Chinese history will show the pit-falls which may be avoided, as well as the directions in which the progress of democracy may be assured.

As far back as the time of Confucius the evils of militarism had attracted the attention of moralists. The Confucian system was the outcome of the deliberate attempt to base all political action by the state upon a definitely moral and humanitarian basis. Confucianism is the continuation of the ancient culture of China, as modified and interpreted by successive thinkers and statesmen. It has been the unalterable constitution and the best bulwark of the people throughout all the centuries, in spite of the civil wars and barbarian conquests. Though tyrants and despots have endeavoured to avail themselves fully of the so-called Divine rights of kings, they have been powerless to suppress the ethical and political principles which are grounded upon the communistic and democratic institutions of antiquity. The commonly accepted notion that Confucianism is opposed to a republican regime has no other basis in fact than the undoubted continuance of despotism for so many centuries. This has been due to causes beyond the control of Confucianists. Moreover the ruler whom Confucianism would invest with supreme authority would correspond in character and function more closely to the President of the United States than to the anæmic and ignorant tyrants on "the Dragon throne." "The Emperor would have to occupy his throne not only by virtue of might but also to a greater degree on account of his eminent virtues. He would rule his people for their own good and would not prejudice their welfare in pursuit of some vain ambition. He would consult the wishes of the wise and the good in the land. He would encourage learning, and industry, and would secure the protection of the country as well as provide measures for the production and distribution of food. Such would be the rôle of the ideal ruler according to Confucian ideas. Mencius denounces despotism in plain language, and eulogises rebellion against tyrants as a meritorious and virtuous action in the interests of mankind and civilization. The Mencian principle is that no tyrant deserves to rule. According to Mencius, the chief of a state must be guided by public opinion and must act solely in the interests of the people, in strict conformity with the requirements of humanity and righteousness. The Mencian state like Plato's Republic or Moore's Utopia has so far remained a pure ideal, but it stimulates thought and gives rise to aspirations of democratic freedom, that have made it possible for the Chinese to approve of a republican form of government.

The Chinese have derived their principal notions of government and politics from the Institutions established by the Chou Dynasty under the able and wise direction of the Duke of Chou. The happiness of the people was to be the sole object of government. The result it will be observed is identical with what modern democracy aspires to secure. If it was not " a government of the people by the people "—it was certainly a government devoted to the entire interests of the people. It was an aristocracy working for the good and the happiness of the people, but the aristocracy was to be recruited from the men of good character and sagely wisdom. The chief ruler, as already indicated, was to work as the chief servant of the State, and to make himself personally responsible for any misery or calamity befalling the nation. Such a paternal government was not created by the genius of the Duke, for the Historical Canon—certainly gives plain indications that the root-ideas had come down from a remoter age. But there is no doubt that the labours of the Duke of Chou systematised the political and ethical views of the ancients and welded them into a consistant and practical system, which has served as the skeleton for all subsequent modifications and accretions in all matters relating to politics and ethics in the Far East. It was obvious, however that the plan was too idealistic, and utopian.

Long before the age of Confucius, the Great Empire of the Chou dynasty was crumbling to pieces. The Feudal Chiefs were struggling for supremacy among themselves, and the rival factions were frequently engaged in civil war and intrigue, while the Suzerain Power was losing its influence and territory. It was a time of anarchy. Right and law were openly disregarded, and out of the constant wars, grew the various political makeshifts—balance of power—disarmament, neutrality, offensive and defensive alliances, peace conventions and so forth, which have in our own day been attracting public attention for a quarter of a century before the great war in Europe. History is repeating itself. "The warring states" of China were prolific in the suggestion of schemes for the regeneration of society and for the regulation of the inter-state relations with the view of securing permanent peace.

Wang Hsü was a recluse of the time. He retired to a mountain gorge which enjoyed the unenviable name of "the Devils' Valley." We do not know whether this title was given to the place on account of its weirdness and inaccessibility or through the perfidious and devilish doctrines of the political adventurer who elaborated diabolical plots in that remote solitude. Be that as it may, Wang is known to posterity as the philosopher of "the Devils' Valley," an opportunist of the first water, he seems to have anticipated the main doctrines of Machiavelli and to have boasted that his pupils would succeed in any political rôle either as the advocates of war or as the protagonists of peace! His adherents travelled from court to court, giving counsels and promoting intrigues, and were ready to join every faction, for they claimed that their sophistry would suit any one whether in the right or in the wrong. There were others again, who hawked about all sorts of political schemes, alleged to be perfect means for the alleviation of the social and economic distressess of the times.

Opposed to the materialism and opportunism of such a school, were the followers of the Confucianist teachers. Mencius stood out pre-eminent among the thinkers of that troublous period. He never tired of asking rulers and statesmen to look deeply into the principles of things and to base government not upon ephemeral advantages but upon the bed-rock of human nature. For example he pleaded with the Prince Hui of Liang for a better understanding of the basis of all political actions, alleging that happiness of the people and of the state, depended mainly upon a full understanding of the implications of a sincere belief in the justice of a righteous and benevolent government. He combatted the prevailing greed of power and influence, and he justly contended that unless the rulers of the rival states adjusted their deeds with the claims of humanity and right, they would encourage lawlessness and strife by their own example of unbridled ambition and reckless adventure to secure their own selfish ends. Mencius denied that man must struggle like the beasts, and annihilate the weaker brethren. The teaching that a higher destiny awaited mankind fell upon deaf ears. The prophecy that endless wars would result from the policy of selfishness and greed was fulfilled, and the ceaseless wars between the feudal chiefs brought the old state to the verge of chaos and ruin. Moral considerations were lightly put aside in view of the material advantages, which militarism could achieve. Thus the demagogues and the disciples of the sage of the "Devil's Valley" prospered exceedingly for a time and the great patrimony of the Chous was torn to pieces by continual wars and upheavals. During the long years of misery, and anarchy, the state of T'sin which had at first stood aloof, rose to great eminence through the wise policy of Duke Hsiao who welcomed refugees from the arenas of war, and thus made his country the centre of commerce, art and industry while his neighbours were languishing from the exhaustion and misery of long wars. For about two hundred years T'sin had been free from any political trouble, this made the state comparatively wealthy about the beginning of the fourth century before the Christian era. There lived then two extraordinary men. They were Chang I and Su T'sin, both of them disciples of the notorious recluse of the Devil's Valley. But true to their political cult, they became rivals. Chang I espoused the cause of T'sin. His whilom companion, travelled throughout the feudal states, preaching war against the rising power. In course of time, he succeeded in forming a league of six nations with the object of crushing the militarism which was seen approaching like an avalanche. Su T'sin was appointed generalissimo of the allies. Both in history and in romance, much has been made of the brilliant scene in which he figured as the hero of the day, when the representatives met in grand review to invest him with plenary powers on behalf of the six allied states. Up· to this day, a representation of this great event on the Chinese stage is one of the most picturesque sights in the Chinese theatrical world, reflecting in a realistic manner one of the stirring episodes in the long annals of China. T'sin was in many respects the prototype of Germany-to-day. Alarmed at the success of the preparations for war, which the foresight of Su T'sin had called forth, the ruler of T'sin employed every conceivable means of breaking up the union. One of the means adopted was to send emissaries to every state, and to sow dissensions among the allies. Chang I, however, succeeded in breaking up the alliance by causing civil war among the contracting powers, and the unfortunate adventurer abandoned by his treacherous supporters fled from state to state and was ultimately hunted down and assasinated. The allies first became suspicious of one another through the misrepresentations made by T'sin's propaganda, for like Germans to-day, Chang I's master stooped to every form of duplicity, misrepresentation and bribery to achieve his ambition. The Allies indulged in civil war among themselves and the state of T'sin had no insuperable task in defeating them in detail. Upon the ruins of the feudal system, was raised the First United Empire of China. The chief styled himself the First Emperor of the T'sins. Like the Kaiser William, he was a dreamer of dreams, but unlike the Kaiser, he was also a man of genius. He was more like Alexander the Great, or Napoleon than the mediocre German Kaiser who is leading his countrymen to perdition. The first Emperor was at once a stateman and a warrior. He destroyed feudalism, reformed the government, and built the great wall of China. He also resembled the Germans in his fondness for colossal structures. The O-fang palace built by him could seat 10,000 people, and was so spacious that it was one of the wonders of the age. The resemblance is almost complete, when one reads of the programme of frighfulness systematically taught. He was thoroughly detested by his people on account of his ruthlessness and tyranny, and his memory has been execrated to our

day. Curiously enough there was a pessimist at that time by the
name of Hsun K'uang, having doctrines of which the Niltzschian
philosophy seems to be the faint echoes. His disciple Li Ssu
was the Von Treitschke of T'sin. From his studio of historio-
graphy, he elaborated a form of "Kultur," which was to replace
the system of Confucius by means of persecution and dragoon-
ing. Hsun K'uang the prototype of Nietzsche propounded the
theory of frightfulness because in his view, the mailed fist was
required to break in the human beast. He believed in the
doctrine of ruthlessness and foolishly imagined that by means
of brutal hammerings, the brute could be beaten into proper
shape. Hating the conservatism of the Confucian School, he
advised the burning of all historical, philosophical and ethical
literature, so that the national annals might begin with the
achievements of the arch-tyrant. The dream of a universal
Empire distorted his view of life, and infected the opinions of
his pupil Li Ssu, and those of his master. Despotism became
the key note of the new Empire, and the patriots had to endure
persecution and tyranny until the general revolt destroyed
the oppressor and brought about the literary restorations of the
Han period.

Amidst the political turmoils, one stedfast patriot Ch'ü
Yuan—a scion of the ducal house of Ch'u, remained quite
unmoved by the sophistry and machiavellism of his contempo-
raries. "Peace talkers" and wily intriguers gained the ears
of the Duke of Ch'u. while his warnings were unheeded. His
prince sent him into exile, when he composed the pathetic
lament—the Li Sao one of the purest gems in Chinese literature. In this melancholy poem, the patriot traced the origin
of civilization, indicated the only path which a ruler could
pursue—righteousness, and proved the connection between
right and honour as the sole bond between the ruler and the
people. Prince Huai who fell a victim to the schemes of the
plotters was defeated in one of the battles made to establish
equilibrium and peace and died in captivity. His son likewise
disregarded Ch'ü Yuan's protests. The poet and statesman
retired to an obscure spot and ultimately threw himself into a
river, as he could not bear to see disaster coming to his country
without being able to render any help. This historical event
took place on the fifth of the fifth lunar month. A grateful
prosperity has celebrated this fateful day as a national holiday
and throughout China, the people now hold the dragon boat
festivities with the object of searching for the lost hero.

So far only the barest outline of the internecine struggles has been mentioned. While the civilized states were bent upon self destruction, the savage tribes of the north had been continually pressing southwards from the frigid Siberian snows. The First Emperor did great service by the building of the great wall, which enabled the agricultural populations to withstand the impetuosity of the wild horsemen. The merit for this colossal achievement has not been duly recognised on account of the universal reprobation of the militarism and its consequent despotism. But to-day especially in the light of the present War, people will realize that universal service was the only adequate measure to meet the terrible danger of barbarian invasion, and posterity will doubtless revise its estimate of the greatness of the work finished by the First Emperor of T'sin, by his enforcement of compulsory sacrifice by the nation in defence of civilization against the ruthless ferocity of the barbarians. Since that age till the fall of the Manchu dynasty, the Chinese had continually struggled in defence of culture and civilization. The tide of barbarism ebbed and flowed as the successive waves of Huns, Tartars, Mongols and Manchus descended upon the flourishing cities and the cultivated plains of the Flowery land. Time and again the Chinese yielded to the military prowess of barbarian invaders, after the vain holocausts of their patriotic heroes. But in every case, the forces of civilization have proved victorious in the end, for the barbarians began to decay and degenerate, whilst the interaction of reason, intellect and imagination had always brought triumph to civilization, as the fitting close to the struggle between force and right. As soon as individuals in a civilized state realise that in a national struggle, all petty thoughts of selves must be subordinated to the interests of the nation, the resources of a civilized state will always suffice to repel invasion or to establish a certain degree of freedom at least, since those who can appreciate the value of liberty, prefer extinction to serfdom. Tyranny and oppression have never yet crushed the spirit of any nation. Extermination of body and soul, extirpation of all sources of national inspiration, may perhaps ultimately succeed. But the history of nations does not lend any authority for such a view. The Chinese, and the Jews have survived for thousands of years in spite of persecution and disasters. Thus the preservation of national existence has been the perpetual problem of philosophy and politics. The barbarians have always yielded to the superior powers of civilization and have become fused with the general population in course of time. Yet in spite of the fact, that in all such contests between races, submission was the result of exhaustion after the death of the patriots and fighters, the conquered if more civilized would never cease to make attempts to throw off the foreign yoke, and if they should happen to be in a lower stage of civilization, they would continue from time to time, to break out in mutiny and revolt. The spirit of liberty is thus never utterly extinguished. In the darkest days of the Sung epoch, when the Mongols were pouring into North and Mid China, Wen T'ien Siang persistently advocated national unity, and demanded from all the utmost sacrifices in order to stem the barbarian incursion. In 1260, he fearlessly impeached those in high positions, especially the favourites of the court, who were allowed to continue in high command in spite of their incapacity and cowardice. Unfortunately for China, destiny was cruel to her. The great patriot met with one misfortune after another, in his courageous attempt to rally the national forces. After many encounters, and escapades he ultimately fell into the hands of the Mongols. He spurned all the kindness shown him by the chief Bayan, who desired him to pursuade the Emperor to submit to the Mongols. But Wen T'ien Siang was unmoved. After a confinement of three years, he was summoned before the presence of Kublai Khan, and was commanded to express his own desire as to the treatment to be accorded to himself. His characteristic reply was :—"I cannot serve two masters. I only ask to die." Alas, his unshakable loyalty was unavailing since the nation was quite enervated through long years of disunion and misrule, and above all through the annihilation of all patriotic men by the enemy's forces, and by the political intrigues of traitors at home.

The fate of another celebrated statesman of this period is worth recalling. Wang An Shih had foreseen the danger of the Mongol invasion. His learning, his influence at court and his enthusiasm contributed largely to the initial successes of his vast democratic schemes by which national resources were to be husbanded by public organizations, national defence was to be ensued by universal service and national wealth was to be secured by state monopoly and control. Unfortunately he was opposed by all the great men of his day, and the people did not appreciate the sacrifices of self interest because they did not visualize the peril that was to enslave the whole nation. Thwarted in every direction, he found his grand schemes going wrong and he failed to realize the wonderful results which his perfervid earnestness had led him to promise to his patron—the Emperor, who gave him every possible encouragement. But when he did not succeed in his great economic innovations, the Emperor was almost reluctantly compelled to yield to the demands of the politicians and the masses, who regarded him as an ambitious schemer and a heterodox expounder of the Confucian Canons. The favour of the Emperor did not save Wang Ah Shih from disgrace and exile. Posterity, however, must regard him as a genius and a patriot for had his economic and military reforms been fairly tested, the Mongol Invasion would probably have failed to cause the utter disruption of the once powerful house of Sung. The history of the British Empire in the decade before the War, contains a strange parallel to this melancholy narrative. But for the preparedness of the Navy, and the hands of fate, the German Invasion would in all probability have eventuated in appalling losses to Great Britain. In any case, the Great War has fully justified the aims of the great Sung statesman, who was in fact endeavouring to fulfil the economic theory of antiquity. The maintenance of industries, the exploitation of mineral and agricultural resources, and the universal training of the manhood of the nation for War, are all intimately correlated in the vast machinery for national defence.

The prototype of Wan An Shih was the famous Kuancius— who flourished in the 7th century before the Christian Era. This statesman and philosopher anticipated the principles and politics of Bismarck, and created an immense industrial development, which brought wealth and power to the country. He earned a great reputation for the enormous wealth which he created. But Confucious while admitting his great services in achieving so much material progress and in contributing to national defence, could not regard his wholy materialistic scheme as the ideal for human society. The ultimate ruin of the state of of Ch'i to which he belonged was laid at his door, just as to-day, we could with certainty trace German megalomania to Bismarck, and also hold him responsible for the present consequences of his iniquitous and treacherous diplomacy.

Turning now from the scenes of battles, and from the mephitic atmosphere of intrigues one hears of military honours, and of complaints against the distribution of the awards of merit. Angry feelings are freely expressed when due recognition is not forth coming of some fighters' valour or of the civil workers' special efforts. The grumblers may perhaps be edified by the example of Chieh Chih T'ui who in the seventh century before Christ, was too proud to ask for reward. In 635 B. C. he accompanied his prince in the latter's flight. On one occasion, they were on the verge of starvation. The faithful minister fed his master with a slice of his own flesh. When the prince was able to return to his state in triumph, the services of the faithful Chieh were overlooked and forgotten. Instead of clamouring for recognition, he quietly retired to live in obscurity, while lesser lights came into prominence. His friends, however, urged him to remind the prince of his services, for the bustle and the splendour of the Court had, for the moment, made the prince forget his faithful friend. Chieh regarded the political world with scorn, as he saw therein everything topsy-tursy for "rulers rewarded the crafty and the classes mutually deceived themselves and one another." One day, however, some one placarded the palace gate with a reference to Chieh. The Prince was instantly struck with remorse, and began to search for the companion of his exile, and his great benefactor. But Chieh was not to be found. The prince endowed his native place with a piece of land with the object of holding memorial services in honour of his loyalty and modesty. In the present war, there must be many persons in all countries, too proud to ask for recognition or reward, but it behoves those in authority not to be forgetful of the labourer when the work is done, for remorse and regret avail nothing, when the man deserving of merit shakes off the dust of his feet and bids farewell to a forgetful people and to an ungrateful country.

This lecture is already too long. But in conclusion I must just make a passing reference to the tragedy of modern China. The long series of misunderstandings between the Chinese and the "foreign" residents in China ended in "the Boxer revolt." The truth is that up to that extraordinary event in the world's history, the white nations had been trying to carve out Empires out of the Manchu possessions. The "open door" favoured for China was denied to the Chinese in "the white man's countries." In fact, the Chinese discovered that the white Christians in their commercial and political dealings had no faith at all in the ethics and altruism of the sermon on the Mount. Now has come the nemesis of the neglect of justice and righteousness in international relations and just as Mencius prophesied two thousand years ago, nations have risen against nations because they have made "profit" or material advantage the criterion of national prosperity. China's sages have declared that humanity and righteousness are the only secure foundation for the happy state and for the civilised world. The Great War has awakened Europe from the moral apathy which has been sapping the bulwarks of society. The horrors of a brutal War, in which the Germans have seriously put into practice the doctrines of materialism, have resulted in the formulation of ethical principles for the guidance of rulers and diplomats. These are in essential agreement with the well established maxims of the Confucian School. The Great War will have proved itself a blessing in disguise if it succeed in arresting "man's unhumanity to man" and in establishing righteousness in the world.

WAR TIME LECTURES AND ESSAYS.

XII.

Race and Empire with special reference to British Malaya.

Historically the problems of Race and Empire have ever been closely intertwined. From time immemorial every Empire has always had subject races owing allegiance to the ruler of the nation, which has established its supremacy by means of war or by peaceful negotiation. There have always been moreover as in the case of the United States of America, alien peoples who have immigrated to new centres of trade and industry.

The old Roman controversy over the distinctions between the Patricians and the Plebians is only another form of the same question. The bitter struggles of the masses for equality and freedom have been continued, with many interruptions through many epochs of political upheavals, and in every age the conquerors have attempted though often with little or no success to impose an impassable barrier between themselves and the peoples whom they have overthrown and whom they therefore rule as subjects. In British history, the Norman conquest resulted, for a time in the establishment of a French Aristocracy totally out of sympathy with the Saxon *villains*. It is one of the strange ironies of history that the language of the despised subjects has survived, and that the conquerors were ultimately absorbed by the conquered. The same thing also happened in China where the Chinese completely absorbed the war-like Manchus.

As the Romans continued to extend their military adventures, it seemed likely at one time that the Roman civilization would swallow up all the tribes and races of Europe ; Asia and Africa which had succumbed to the might of Rome. Circumstances, however, set alien Germanic barbarians on the throne of the Cæsars, and brought about the disruption of the Empire before the assimilation of the European races was far enough advanced. But the modern Romanic nations and the British peoples are the representatives of the Roman culture in more ways than one. Thus the British can trace their origin to divergent sources. The influence of the Roman culture however is still evident in the laws, language and institutions of the British Empire. Though the English language is now the language of the whole country, "the nations" of the main stocks are as proud to-day of their individual characteristics as in the days of old. The Scotch, the Gælic, the Welsh and the Irish are not in any way anxious to become merged in the name of Britishers. Observe how the proud and victorious Normans had been completely absorbed. From time to time, efforts have been made to revive the ancient tongues of Wales, of Ireland and of the Scottish Highlands. Thus so far as the British peoples are concerned, the distinct racial elements are as clearly defined to-day as when they severally fought against the Romans—their common and deadly enemy.

When finally through its own internal corruption, and the external pressure of barbarians from the North and from the East, the Empire of the Cæsars fell to pieces, the most important stocks of the pre-historic races emerged once more from the obscurity which was cast over them by the shadow of Roman civilization. The Iberian nations, the descendants of the Gauls, the Belgians and the Germans not to mention the others have displayed in modern times the same characteristics as those of their ancestors that had been so faithfully pourtrayed by the Roman historians. If the modern Italians are not in all respects the equal of the ancient Romans, they are perhaps no longer of the same Latin race or stock as the modern Italians must be a very mixed race, in consequence of the many invasions, and of the complex mixture of races, which had been drawn to Italian soil.

The Spanish Empire in America failed to destroy the native character of the many tribes although it has imposed upon all the Spanish language and the Catholic religion. In the Philippines, the Spanish language did not entirely supersede the barbarian dialects of the Archipelago.

Within the British Empire, the French Canadians have preserved intact their French characteristics and their language. The Boers will always remain Dutch in dialect and sentiment. Throughout India, the races will remain distinct. They will develope their own languages and literature.

This brief and incomplete resumé is enough to prove that whatever may be the politics of an Empire the racial elements will tend to persist. Austro-Hungary is a veritable Babel, and has not succeeded in inducing the non-German races to allow themselves to become denationalized in the interests of the Pan-German movement. The Great War is the direct outcome of the race intrigues by means of which Austria had hoped to delude the Serbian elements into acquiescence in Austro-Hungarian rule. The Hungarians, the Czecs and other nationalities continue to be as jealous of their own race ideals and their ancient languages as they have ever been.

Although the Poles are now without a country, they have never ceased to agitate for freedom. The Germans have tried every conceivable plan of inducing the Poles to become German, but they have met with very poor success. On the whole, the British policy of educating the alien elements in the English language, and of familiarising the natives with English ways and thoughts without any attempt to interfere with the use of native tongues is in the long run the safest course. It certainly brings together the different races to understand one another, and to recognise the value of the Empire. By the law of the survival of the fittest, English is displacing less adequate languages in a natural and peaceful way.

The question arises whether it is feasible to extend the principles of British democracy to all parts of the Empire.

Before the War, a strong movement was set on foot to maintain a distinctive position for the white races to the disadvantage of the coloured races. It was evident also that the discrimination was based entirely on the question of the colour of the skin, irrespective of the social status, education or culture of the individuals concerned. The Dominions wanted to exclude all coloured races and went so far as to subject Indians to harsh and humiliating conditions that rendered residence in those British territories both irksome and intolerable. In South Africa, the Indians deliberately disobeyed the laws which discriminated against them and preferred going to prison rather than submit to the ignominious treatment. But neither the Raj nor the Imperial Government could do anything to alter Colonial opinion. There is not the slightest doubt that the failure of the Imperial Government to afford to its real protegés its full protection within the Empire was the cause of great dissatisfaction throughout India. Beyond India in the Crown Colonies a tacit understanding was established between officials and the influential European merchants that the so-called "colour bar" was to be vigorously enforced.

It is idle to consider these racial antipathies as of no importance. For they are at the root of much of the current disaffection. The Imperial Government has generally taken up a correct attitude but the question is complicated by the confirmed opinions of Colonials and Anglo-Indians as to the proper relation that should exist between the ruling race and the coloured subjects of the Crown. In times gone by, the white man was wont to receive the utmost deference and the native humbled himself and cringed before "the master" in a manner which Asiatic etiquette enjoined. The native servant, for example, fell down prostrate and kissed the feet of the enraged master. The lower classes would fall upon their knees on the slightest provocation. In Java, the native servants even now crouch down on the ground or squat on their haunches when addressing their master or when awaiting any message. A few years ago, it was a common and humiliating sight to see a native squat on the ground and remove his topi when a European passed by on the country roads of Java. Travel and education have brought about changes throughout the East. The old world ideas as to what is becoming are fast disappearing. The newer generations are giving up old Asiatic superstitions and are imbibing European notions and copying European habits. They learn at school that many Oriental notions are obsolete or objectionable, and in course of time naturally apply the general principles of modern civilization to all things. But many Eurasians or Asiatics discover that when they leave school, and attempt to behave to white men according to European etiquette, their conduct is sometimes resented. It seems at first preposterous that "a native" should expect to be treated as a gentleman. Then comes the temptation "to put him down" and "to show him his proper place." The white man if he himself be "an upstart" shows his displeasure by rudeness and brusqueness, and if he does not actually kick "the upstart" out of his office, he seldom fails to give the unfortunate native a good impression of his social superiority to the infinite chagrin and discomfiture of the coloured man. Europeans in India have often wondered why Eurasians of the lower classes tend to lapse into native dress and habits. Such treatment as is here referred to, rankles in the mind, and drives the coloured man to desperation. Necessity obliges him to perform "the kowtow" but he has lost all respect for the white man, who has shown by such a behaviour that he is no better in up-bringing and behaviour than the darkest despot whose conduct is at least justified by his ignorance. Much of the ill-feeling engendered by the colour question has arisen from such little incidents in the intercourse between natives and Europeans. If the European often draws wrong and unjustifiable conclusions from insufficient data, the native as often makes perhaps a more sweeping deduction from his own unfortunate experience, to the white man's discredit. It is impossible to generalise safely with regard to conduct, in respect of a whole tribe or nation, from the behaviour of a few individuals. No community consists entirely of rogues or fools. There is a black sheep in every fold; but the herd consists of average units, which are pretty much the same all the world over. There may be peculiar views, tenets and superstitions that seem to determine conduct variously among different communities. But as a rule, owing to the mimetic instincts, man readily copies from his fellow man and is to a large extent a creature of circumstances. To this extent, men even as the ancients recognised, have always betrayed the failings, weaknesses and mistakes of the class to which they belong. At the same time, good social qualities and moral attributes are no monopoly of white races. An impartial enquiry into the ethical conduct of mankind, must reveal the rather appalling fact that in their sins, their follies and their crimes, all races, whatever the colour of their skin, show an amazing likeness which goes far not only to prove their real affinity from the point of view of physical organization but also to confirm the belief in their common origin and in their spiritual and moral destiny.

Any such discrimination against the natives of a Crown Colony is an entirely retrograde step and is at variance with the promises contained in the Royal Letters Patent transferring the Straits Settlements from the East India Company's rule to that of the Crown. British statesmen have always spurned with contempt the suggestion that England would use her might to exploit the natives of the Colonies. Even the enemies of England must admit that the great success of the British Empire lies in the just and liberal treatment of subjects belonging to alien races. The Great War has conclusively proved that the British Colonies with their various races and tribes have manifested gratifying proofs of loyalty and devotion to the mother land.

If we consider the immense variety of the indigenous races within the British Empire, we must at once recognise that there are vast differences in their social, ethnic and intellectual conditions, and that common sense alone should teach us the utter impossibility of reducing the principles of governing these to one common rule. The Basutos and the American Indians, the Pacific Islanders and Papuans and the Dyaks and Sakais not to mention others are mere infants as regards the stage of civilization which they have attained, but even among them, there are degrees of development of intelligence, and social instincts so that what might prove suitable for the savage Papuans, might be highly unreasonable for the much more advanced Basutos. It would be rank folly and gross injustice to compel the dark skin races of India for example to submit to regulations framed for the administration of a dark skin African Colony. This point is so obvious that it seems unnecessary to have to point it out but there is too prevalent a belief among some Europeans that one colour line and one common rule may suffice for all practical purposes. Though in no British Colony is this colour differentiation as here hinted at known in law, yet in reality, the natives notice the distinctions made, so that the general impression is that there is a rule of exclusiveness. Asiatics in the Straits Setlements demand equal opportunities and equal treatment. Ostensibly no difference is made, but in fact, there are patent discriminations. Fortunately our superior authorities have always been careful to observe strict impartiality. With one or two exceptions, the Colony has been fortunate in having Governors, who have been able to sustain the high ideals of the British Nation, and who have gained for the Empire the loyalty and devotion of the coloured subjects of the Crown. In the interests of peace, and good government, and of the solidarity of the Empire, all petty and needless distinctions should be done away with. British rule is based on justice, and moral suasion. The white man must earn respect by intrinsic intellectual and moral qualities and not by despotic orders to be enforced by the police! Further the word Asiatic has come to be used in the Colonies as an epithet of contempt. But there is no valid justification for the implied suggestion that an Asiatic is by nature an inferior being. There is on the contrary ample evidence to prove that

Asiatics are highly endowed with brain capacity and consequently with intelligence and mental adaptability equal to those of any white race. The very fact that the Jews are Asiatic and the white races themselves are of Asiatic Origin, show the absurdity of basing Imperial state craft upon differences of race, and upon mere geographical accidents of origin. "The Asiatic" has no need to be ashamed of the name, and can at least predict his future from the brilliant past records of his ancestors.

There are three possible methods that may be adopted towards alien races within any Empire :—(1) extermination or expulsion, (2) assimilation or adoption, or (3) serfdom in some form. These means are also employed between nations and states in the course of their competition for political supremacy or for territorial expansion. All aggressive empires have employed these devices to establish the powers of an absolute monarchy. The Roman state, for example, found that after long experience, all it could do to maintain the supremacy of the Latin race was to destroy the power of Carthage. The Germans of to-day aims at crippling France before delivering their blow at England. This is the real cause of the great world catastrophe. The Colonials in Tasmania used to kill off the aborigines. But the stupidity of the proceeding apart from its wickedness was not realized till too late. On the same principle the Germans in West Africa have practically decimated the Hereros. The Russians and the Turks have time and again resorted to this inhuman and barbarous practice. We are not now referring to the acts of a frantic mob but to the well considered policy of a government. During this Great War, the Turks have nearly exterminated the Armenians ; and but for the help of the Allies, the Germans would have destroyed the Belgians, Serbians and Roumanians, and absorbed their respective countries. The Dutch in the East Indies, and the Japanese in Formosa have been confronted with irreconcilable tribes, the pacification of whose districts often involved a veritable massacre. As a cold-blooded extermination of human beings is too ghastly an affair to be entertained by a civilized nation, white men in recent years have resorted to exclusion or expulsion, in various ways, of races whose presence is not desired. This was the old barbarous policy of the ancient Asiatic countries which have been severely punished by European powers for wishing to exclude their nationals. China and Japan were originally exclusionists but the West thundered at their gates, which had to be opened to all comers. These countries are now open to Europeans but Asiatics from these countries have now to claim the same rights of residence and work in America, Australia and Canada, as have been acquired by white men in the East. The Jews in Russia have suffered cruel wrongs and throughout Europe till quite recently have met with much persecution. Even now anti-semitism is a force to be seriously reckoned with in all European states. The terrible injustice committed in the notorious Dreyfus affair caused a sensation throughout the civilized world, and succeeded at last in arousing public feeling in France which is after all the pioneer land of liberty and freedom.

Assimilation or adoption is the means favoured in England and France and America in their colonies where coloured races prevail. Small groups of individuals are easily assimilated. But in the case of large communities, experience has proved that it is almost impossible to attempt assimilation without the use of coercion. Forcible assimilation of races who are akin to the ruling race has caused the greatest wrongs in all political history. The Germans, Austrians, Russians, and Turks have been most guilty of this offence. The English had failed long ago to assimilate the Irish. The French Canadians and the Boers will remain racially intact, and yet are thoroughly loyal Britishers. So it will be in India and the Crown Colonies, where the races and tribes will continue to cultivate their own languages and to maintain their social and religious institutions under the ægis of the Union Jack. This toleration of an alien race within the Empire may be conveniently termed adoption. The French are equally successful in pursuing the policy of adoption, and in winning the trust and loyalty of many different races of mankind. The great support of French Colonies given during this war, proves that our gallant French Ally has solved the problem of Empire for a great democracy. The Americans in the Philippines have carried out momentous experiments in inter-racial politics, and have succeeded beyond all expecta-tions. By firmness tempered with justice and benevolence, the great white Republic of the West has reduced chaos to order, and has lifted up semi-barbarous races to the very threshold of civilization. The United States are making a nation of the Filipinos, though the work must be continued for a century at least before the fruits of these laborious efforts can be fairly expected. The Spaniards failed, and the Dutch have not succeeded because they had ingrained prejudice that the natives were not fit to be the equals of the whites in any-thing. The Spaniards learnt their lesson too late. The Dutch are beginning to appreciate the real teaching of history, and it is only just to state that of late years, they are striving to make up for lost ground, and that in due time, they will afford to the Malayan and other races under Dutch rule, all the bless-ings of modern training and education.

In the Straits Settlements, the British Government has allowed the traditional *laissez faire* administration to tolerate adoption, but we are drifting along without any definite policy though the inhabitants are beginning to experience the opera-tion of the colour bar policy, which is giving rise to consider-able irritation in all directions among all classes. Throughout British Malaya before the advent of large numbers of European planters and merchants, drawn from all parts of the world, the white man came to stay here and to remain during the best part of his life, and therefore he made friends with the natives and endeavoured to understand them. In the end, he came to appreciate them. The natives learned to love and respect " the ourang puteh," (white man). There was therefore no room for any colour prejudice. But as education and travel have made a change in the ways of the natives, and as new comers from Europe increase in number, the gulf separating the groups has become wider every year. The natives find that the Young, Hamilton, Reid, Scott, Currie and such like type of Englishmen is replaced by another which is not at all so friendly. They find men who do not live in the country and move among them long enough to know them sufficiently well. These newer men are jealous of power and position. Some have come from India, Africa and China, and like to introduce the discriminations enforced against the coloured man in these countries. In the Straits and F. M. S., such discriminations have never been tolerated, and consequently the behaviour of such European snobs cause great annoyance, for these Europeans would like to be exclusive ; but the free natives, accustomed to the freedom for which we are indebted to the genius of Stamford Raffles and his distinguished successors, do not want to be serfs in their own country.

The Indian Empire is a colossal example of the success of the British policy of adoption by means of an enlightened bureaucracy which whatever faults it may have, has never forgotten the duty of governing the great country entrusted to its care in the interests of its teeming millions. Despite the so-called grievances of extremists of the Indian National Congress, and of fanatics outside that, the Raj has no doubt marvellously succeeded in creating the embryo of a nation out of the jumble of races, who not very long ago, would engage in ceaseless conflicts, and who could only have peace enforced by the sword of a conquering despot. Great Britain has solved many problems for the Indian races. She has given the races and tribes a great gift in the shape of the Lingua Britannica which is to be the universal language of civilization as it has become the language of India and of the Empire. She has conferred upon India a wonderful code of laws, which though reminiscent of the remarkable institutions of ancient Rome, has also incorporated in its all embracing meshes, mediæval and modern European experience as well as every thing best in Indian legal lore. She has given peace and justice and prosperity to all classes. She has caused a universal toleration of religious differences and has lifted the low and depressed castes out of the bondage of ancient customs. She has successfully translated into practical politics a considerable portion of British democratic principles, among alien races hitherto unaccustomed to anything but tyranny and despotism. With all, she has been a true foster mother to the tribes and races of India, and a great benefactress of mankind in her vast social, commercial, industrial, educational and philanthropic efforts for the uplifting and succour of the victims of centuries of misrule. In order to carry into effect these gigantic purposes, white men have made great sacrifices for the sake of the Empire. Wars had to be waged, but in every case the warrior races have become the staunchest supporters of the Imperial regime. The proud Rajputs, the warlike Sikhs, the pugnacious Gurkhas, the irritable Pathans and many others are to-day loyally fighting for the Emperor and the flag. The non-combatant races are also doing their share of war work in a thousand and one ways. The Great War has proved to the world the tremendous success of British rule in India, for Great Britain has won not only the gratitude but the love of India's millions. The existence of sedition merely shows that the Government of India has sown broadly the seeds of freedom. The parable of the wheat and the tares has its meaning both for the fanatics and the Raj. Nothing bad comes out of good. When therefore here and there, sedition crops up, the authorities must ascertain its cause, and remove it, without resorting to ill-advised general measures based on colour distinctions. As a matter of fact, the Raj in India has recently adopted wise and conciliatory measures. The suggested reforms will add another corner stone to the great structure, and the new age after the war will see the inauguration of a further understanding between the Europeans and the natives so that all will learn to sink racial differences in the greater interests of the Empire and of civilization.

The other way of dealing with alien races is to leave them to grope in their own darkness, and to keep them down by various prohibitions and restrictions backed up by brute force. They may be left to do mechanical and other work as mere tools under the direction of their masters. The Spaniards in the early days of their colonization in America used to employ the natives as if they were animals especially in working the silver and other mines. The Chinese coolies in the Rand mines were recruited on terms, which denied them rights of free men. These are extreme examples. But in insidious ways, attempts have been made to limit the natives to positions of dependence in all Government and Municipal Departments. The common plea is that the natives are not fit and not trustworthy. But if the authorities do not attempt to fit the people for the best positions that may be available, but on the contrary discourage them by refusing to use them in responsible situations, it is scarcely the fault of the native races that they do not become fitted for positions of great responsibility. No one among the natives asks for the appointment of a person who is not fully equal to the demands upon his capacity and character. The grievance is that the law is laid down that no matter what may be the capacity of a native, he must for ever remain a mere machine and must not aspire to the highest which his attainments might justify him in so doing. Let us take the professions. Under this " colour bar " ruling, no native would be given "the plums" that might be his, if only his colour had been favourable. Even if it is admitted that Asiatics have shortcomings, is it possible that they will be contented to remain always in this degraded position ? Will they love the Government that condemns them as inferior things and yet will do nothing to improve their condition, as obviously otherwise the only way to dilute the colour is by a process of miscegenation, which is more objectionable than mere toleration of coloured men as equals ?

What has happened everywhere is that through sheer prejudice, the Eurasian is treated as a native, and is sometimes driven to find in native circles the satisfaction of his social wants. Occasionally there is unreasonable antipathy against the Eurasians in élite circles which condescend to humour better class natives with a patronising recognition. Indifferent pay, and social ostracism have practically confined the opportunities of the Eurasians, who have found it an almost Herculean task to surmount the obstacles raised against their path to bar them from proceeding in an upward direction. There is no written law specially directed against them. But they find that in effect, they are neither liked nor trusted. Having denied them opportunities of employing their undoubted talents, the same class of white men turn round and declare that the Eurasian and native are not trustworthy. Sweeping statements are freely made reflecting upon the whole class, creating ill-feeling and discontent. Two courses are open. Either the Eurasians and coloured races are to be educated and adopted in due time as citizens. This has always been the professed attitude of the British Imperial Government towards Indians since the days of Macauley. Or they must be kept down to serve as a sort of modern villains to remain always as clerks or to hold the subsidiary routine appointments under white chiefs. If the latter be the policy, where then is the vaunted freedom? A slave may be bound by his chains and the coloured races understand only too well that such chains need not be of iron. The social and political embargo is far worse than a prison wall. When the coloured subjects of the Empire realise that these obstacles have been raised mainly by ignorant prejudice abetted by fear of loss of prestige, they cannot help feeling highly dissatisfied. It is the established habit of the East to honour a good man and to respect a man in a superior position, but it is always recognised that politeness is a mutual understanding of good manners, between two parties. Between high and low, rich and poor, the scholar and the rustic, the master and the servant, there is a clearly defined code of etiquette known to all civilised nations. So long as this code of honour is duly observed there can be no occasion for the complaints of "the presumption" of natives. The white man must not expect civility when he himself is prepared to show none. The time is past when the coloured man, like the unfortunate subjects of Montezuma, is likely to believe that "the pale face" individual is a god in the flesh. If he treats a native roughly without cause, and behaves himself like a fool puffed up with pride and self-importance, he need not be surprised to find that the humble Asiatic suddenly forgets himself and asserts his manhood. Some Europeans have found it dangerous to travel in the interior of China, but those who are prepared to treat Asiatics as reasonable human beings have never found it necessary to provide weapons and to use force in moving about anywhere in China. There is therefore no valid reason for all the colour discriminations in Eastern Colonies, where the Europeans have perforce to be only birds of passage.

The pioneers of British colonization in the Malayan region were men of broad spirit and sympathetic nature. We have the evidence of Munshi Abdullah who knew Sir Stamford Raffles and others intimately that every courtesy was always shown to natives, who returned the civility with interest.

There is no doubt that the attitude of the average European individuals sooner or later permeates the club, and then the general society. Then influence is exerted on the Government. Thus the so-called Higher or Queen Scholarships founded by the late Sir C. Clementi Smith for bringing the Colony and the mother country closer together, thus anticipating Cecil Rhodes in a broader spirit, was some years ago abolished because certain influential Europeans disliked the idea of sending Asiatics to England. The ostensible reasons published in the report of the Committee on Education are mere euphemisms, but the real reason is as stated. The same antipathy has brought about the rule that His Majesty's Civil Service in the Colony is only open to Europeans of "pure white descent." The fiction is circulated that coloured races have no confidence in coloured men holding official positions. There is no vestige of foundation for such an assertion. On the contrary the native community has strongly resented the petty indignities to which coloured gentlemen in Government service have sometimes been unjustly subjected. One coloured magistrate had to put up with a good deal of annoyance caused by "the cold shoulder" of his colleagues. Another coloured gentleman had to stir up the powers-that-be before he could obtain admission to a certain club, which it was necessary for him to join. Every one believes that the agitation for rights by these gentlemen, set on foot indirectly that movement which has resulted in excluding the natives of the Colony from the privilege of joining the local Civil

Service. Though natives of India have the right under certain conditions of competing for the Civil Service, the Secretary of State has by his autocratic fiat debarred the sons of the soil from entrance into the Civil Service of their country upon no terms whatever so long as they are not of pure European descent. The War has necessitated the employment of Malays in high positions in the Federated Malay States, and the High Commissioner in his recent speech in the Federal Council in November this year, has given his opinion that these Malay gentlemen have acquitted their duty with satisfaction. If this is so in the Malay States there is no reason why the native British subjects of the Colony may not turn out equally successful.

In the interests of the Colony and the Empire, we must desire to make the native population entirely loyal and patriotic. The people must be proud of their country and must feel respect for the Government. We cannot now refuse to educate the masses. For missionaries, in spite of the Government, will bring to them the light. The natives themselves are making exertions to educate their children. Therefore the Government will have to provide adequate educational facilities. Education is always a process of awakening. Why then awaken the political and social consciousness of freedom and then offuscate the environment like a cuttle fish, when the young men approach the foster parent for further help and guidance by drawing the colour line across their advancement in legitimate directions ?

It was quite patent that it would be impossible to keep down the Indians in their own country by such subtle colour distinctions, which might prove to be detrimental to their social, political and moral interests except by means of force. Lord Morley and Lord Hardinge truly grasped the real meaning of Indian sedition. The old trick of setting one Indian race against another is only possible now among the ignorant and illiterate masses. Yet white political agitators in India are always reminding the Raj and the Imperial Government, that the fighting men would not submit to the laws made by talking *Baboos* who used to be held in contempt by the warrior classes. But who are these fighting men ? Is it not a fact that the majority in the ranks are illiterate mercenaries ? The demand for political and social justice for the natives of the Empire is based on moral grounds. The obsolete views of illiterate rustics must give way to the deeply thought-out and well-reasoned claims for equality according to status, education and other qualities. The real grievance is that the Government has really made the tint of the skin the index by which it will class a human being.

One hears much about the necessity of European supervision. No doubt generally this must be, as long as white men create and maintain the conditions that render such supervision indispensable. You provide no proper educational facilities, hedge the natives and Eurasians within social and political walls, and circumscribe their position in Government services, then you wonder why these people are so helpless and so wanting in backbone. Vertebræ, it must be remembered, have been evolved as a result of keen competition. The mole and the eyeless mud fish of South America are the results of prolonged living in darkness. The conditions in which the natives have to live are responsible for much of their failings. If the Government will endeavour to remedy the evils which sap the character of the community they will help to remove the causes that produce the undesirable features in native character, and that prevent the full adoption of the native elements as citizens of the Empire.

There seems to be no halfway house between freedom and serfdom. The British Empire has embarked for weal or for woe for democracy, and has at infinite sacrifice, rooted out slavery once for all. In theory therefore British statesmen have adopted everywhere the generous policy of educating the natives. Probably natives have clamoured for the fruit of this process of assimilation, before the fruit is ripe. On the other hand, many of the Europeans not unnaturally regard the agitators as dangerous and too self-confident. Between these two conflicting views, truth may lie hidden. The Great War, however, has afforded an opportunity for surveying the whole question afresh.

In semi-barbarous and savage colonies, autocratic rule in some form is indispensable. But even here in justice to the democratic ideal, the Imperial Government must adopt the policy best suited to bring out the best in the native population and to prepare the people for a higher form of social life. There must be an honest endeavour to civilise these backward children of nature. Otherwise these human beings must degenerate within the environment of modern civilization. The great force that operates in nature will cease to exist. The fit and the unfit will survive. Then the backward races will find it hard put to resist the temptations of food and drink—let alone other things. Improvident, ignorant and poor, the "inferior races" without the paternal care of Government must sooner or later be driven to the slums, and disappear through poverty, vice and disease. Slavery is preferable to this form of social degradation, which is one of the conditions imposed by a heartless Commercialism upon the working masses throughout the world.

In the case of Asiatics, who have inherited the ancient customs and ideals of the East, the idea that no matter what their position, education, or character may be now or in the future, they must be totally excluded from positions of trust and responsibility in the Government of their own countries, is at once repugnant and intolerable. The coloured races do not grumble at a stage of preparation, but they do demand that an honest effort be made to initiate such preliminary training, and to give a fair chance to their children, as soon as there is a decent opportunity. This is the burden of the coloured man's appeal. If democracy is going to be a reality and a living force within the Empire, then this voice of the races must find a responsive echo in the hearts of our white rulers—especially to the men on the spot, whose duty it is to bridge the gulf between the Sovereign and the people. This war has brought home to everyone that community of interests and ideals can effectually bind the most diverse races in making the greatest sacrifices. Therefore it is no longer reasonable to differentiate against the people of the Empire merely on account of their colours. Further, this war has also demonstrated that all are in the same boat. Military expenditure will have to be borne by all. Man power will have to be found by the whole community. The State must rely fully upon the people. If India and the Colonies are to be integral parts of the Empire, their coloured populations must not only be contented serfs, but must be raised to the status of free citizens. There is much talk of "the open door" policy in China, what is badly wanted is "an open door" policy within the British Empire for the coloured British subjects.

It is impossible to do justice to this big and controversial problem within the space of a single article, and only hints are possible; but the time has arrived for all concerned to think seriously of the facts, and to realise what their moral and spiritual implications are with reference to the Empire.

The coloured races, on their part, will have to choose for themselves the path which they will follow. If the Government wisely opens a way for emancipation and conditionally removes unfair and undesirable or glaring disabilities and inequalities, the alien races will no doubt acquire those habits and ideals which will fit them for the places to be filled. They will have the aspirations of free men. They will learn to put into practice the lessons of a free democracy. They will prove by deeds and by sacrifices that they are worthy to be citizens of the British Empire.

But if the Government deny them all opportunities of advancement, and keep them from all positions of danger or responsibility, how are they to prove their sincerity or their fitness? Self-respect is essential to a democratic population. This we must teach or we must fail to bring out the native from the traditional commune.

"We are not wanted"—is the refrain one hears among coloured circles in the Straits. There is a deep if silent despondency which chills all enthusiasm. What is "safety" to a community with great aspirations and lofty ideals, if that "safety" is only purchased by the denial of freedom to share in the heroic deeds that alone will win salvation? Enforced safety is to free men as intolerable and galling as enforced rest in prison.

There is now a true desire throughout the world for a durable peace based on justice and righteousness. It is also universally recognised that this is not attainable without the destruction of militarism. As a corollary to the main proposition, there is added the independence of races and nationalities, as one of the questions that must be settled. Therefore, it seems opportune to call attention to the race problem within the Empire, and to demand from all alike, careful consideration of the intricate issues involved, so that our British Empire, which has done so much for the coloured races of the Earth, may begin after the war to elaborate a just and righteous solution of the difficulties and perplexities which confront the practical statesman in carrying out in actual administration the principles of the British Constitution for all races and tribes owing allegiance to the Sovereign of the British Empire. Destiny has favoured the British Empire. The genius of the British races has already adumbrated the paths that will lead to success. The Empire to-day is the monument of the greatest human enterprise in the world's history. It is no longer ruled by despotism. In spite of mistakes and imperfections, our Mighty Empire stands as the most magnificent democracy in the world. Justice and righteousness are the basis of our professed principles of administration. Only sympathy and knowledge are needed to complete that stupendous edifice of Empire raised by the union, the co-operation, and the love of the multitudinous races, owning one allegiance and recognising the one mother, whose noble example may well be the prelude to the federation of the world.